The Creation of Modern Georgia

# NUMAN V. BARTLEY

# The Creation

# of Modern

# Georgia

## SECOND EDITION

The University of Georgia Press
Athens and London

© 1983, 1990 by the University of Georgia Press
Athens, Georgia 30602
All rights reserved
Designed by Francisca Vassy
Set in 10 on 12 point Caledonia

The paper in this book meets the guidelines for
permanence and durability of the Committee on
Production Guidelines for Book Longevity of the
Council on Library Resources.

Printed in the United States of America

03   02   01            P   6   5   4   3

Library of Congress Cataloging in Publication Data

Bartley, Numan V.
The creation of modern Georgia /
Numan V. Bartley. —2nd ed.
p.   cm.
Includes bibliographical references.
ISBN 0–8203–1183–9 (alk paper).
—ISBN 0–8203–1178–2 (pbk. : alk. paper)
1. Georgia—Politics and government.
2. Georgia—Social conditions.
I. Title.
F291.B26   1990
975.8′04—dc20            90-30699
CIP

British Library Cataloging in Publication Data available

# Contents

# Preface

This book is an interpretive essay on the evolution of modern Georgia. It might be called a sociopolitical history because it examines social groups that have influenced Georgia's development and explores how their interrelationships have been expressed in politics. The first edition of *The Creation of Modern Georgia*, published in 1983, was an attempt to understand southern history through the study of one southern state. That goal remains intact in the second edition, which places greater emphasis on recent Georgia history.

Several people who were colleagues at the University of Georgia were kind enough to read and comment on a draft of the first edition of this manuscript. Michael Cassity, Kenneth Coleman, Thomas G. Dyer, Gilbert C. Fite, William F. Holmes, and David Potenziani offered criticisms and raised questions about the way I dealt with Georgia's history. I do not accuse them of sharing my interpretations, but I do hold them responsible for forcing me to make more lavish revisions than I had intended to do. I am grateful to them and to Randall L. Patton, who offered valuable suggestions in his critique of the second edition.

It was my good fortune during the course of this study to be assigned on occasion a graduate assistant. Jimmy Kilgore, Todd L. Butler, and Stanley K. Deaton compiled much of the statistical data, little of which appear in the text, that served as the basis for a great many generalizations about the course of Georgia's development.

A number of interpretations probed in the following pages were first tested on University of Georgia undergraduates in classes on the history of Georgia and of the South. I remember how badly some of my most provocative insights fared when subjected to the glare of questions and comments in the classroom. I must also confess that on occasion an undergraduate research paper on Georgia history helped me to comprehend some point about which I had been particularly baffled. To such students as David Anderegg, Ginger Clifton, Glenn Exum, Butch Frye, Eric Schmidt, and Arthur Thomas—the list could go on—I am appreciative.

For important reasons that need not be elaborated I am indebted to Paul C. Nagel, who was formerly a colleague at the University of Georgia,

Lester D. Stephens of the University of Georgia, Jack T. Kirby of Miami University, Robert C. McMath of the Georgia Institute of Technology, James C. Cobb of the University of Tennessee, Hugh D. Graham of the University of Maryland–Baltimore County, and Charles East, formerly of the University of Georgia Press. Finally, my wife, Morraine Matthews Bartley, made more contributions to this work that I can adequately acknowledge.

In the broad sense *The Creation of Modern Georgia* grew from teaching, researching, and writing Georgia and southern history over a lengthy period. During these years I have borrowed ideas from many scholars and have incorporated them into my lectures and my thinking to the point that I now regard them as original. For this reason among others, I have not included a bibliography. I have endeavored to acknowledge some of my more outrageous thievery in notes at the end of the volume. A competent bibliographical guide to the literature on Georgia history can be found in the second edition of Kenneth Coleman and others, *A History of Georgia*.[1]

N.V.B.

1990

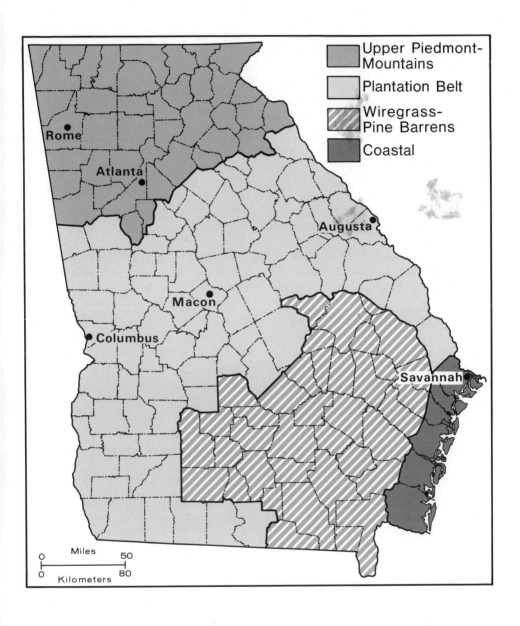

| | Upper Piedmont-Mountains |
| | Plantation Belt |
| | Wiregrass-Pine Barrens |
| | Coastal |

Rome

Atlanta

Augusta

Macon

Columbus

Savannah

Miles
0                    50
0                    80
Kilometers

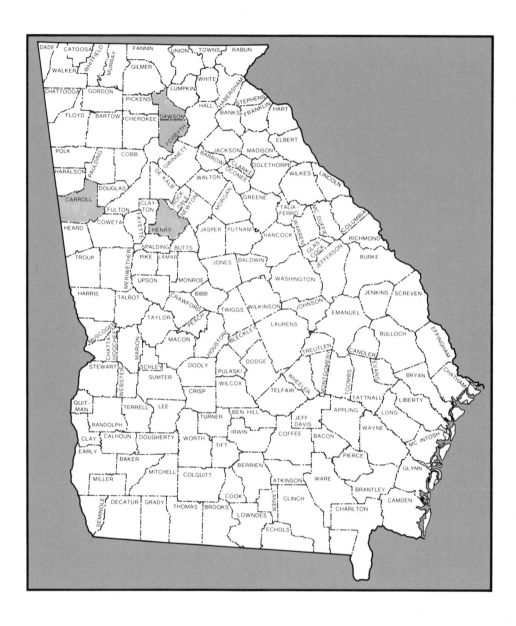

The Creation of Modern Georgia

# Chapter One

## *"That Paradise with All Her Virgin Beauties"*

Georgia began as a noble experiment. James E. Oglethorpe and the twenty other Trustees for Establishing the Colony of Georgia in America envisioned a virtuous yeoman's commonweal that would serve as a haven for the "worthy poor." Oglethorpe—aristocrat, soldier, politician—had fought in the name of Christianity against the Turks in eastern Europe and had been appalled by the condition of imprisoned debtors when he had chaired a parliamentary committee investigating the "State of the Gaols" in England. In varying degrees all of the original trustees were idealists and reformers who were involved in such benevolent groups as the Society for Promoting Christian Knowledge and the Society for Propagating the Gospel in Foreign Parts. With London abounding in poverty-stricken citizens, the philanthropic trustees set as their goal the creation in an unspoiled wilderness of a utopian sanctuary for England's downtrodden poor. Georgia possessed "fertile Lands sufficient to subsist all the useless poor in England, and distressed Protestants in Europe," wrote the trust secretary, "yet Thousands starve for want of mere Sustenance."[1]

In June 1732 the trustees received a royal charter to settle the land west of Carolina. To emphasize the benevolent nature of the enterprise, the charter prohibited any trustee from owning land, holding office, or profiting directly from the colony. The trustees, Oglethorpe stated, "will use their utmost endeavors to prevent luxury and oppression in the officers, and idleness and vice in the people."[2] Wealthy Britishers, including Lord Joseph Jekyll, whose donation was sufficiently large to be recognized in the naming of an offshore island, contributed to the worthy enterprise. Most important, the British government allotted generous subsidies.

Georgia was one of the few mainland colonies (and the only one of the thirteen that were later to rebel) to receive direct governmental support, and the king's ministers expected commercial and strategic advantages for the empire. After all, Georgia occupied approximately the same latitude as China, Persia, and the Madeira Islands. Thus, according to a trustee publication, "England may be supplied from thence with raw Silk, Wine, Oil, Dies, Drugs, and many other Materials for Manufactures, which she is obliged to purchase from Southern Countries."[3] As Oglethorpe explained, Georgia was "always serene, pleasant and temperate, never subject to excessive Heat or Cold, nor to sudden changes; the Winter is regular and short, and the Summer cool'd with refreshing breezes." It was a land that would "produce almost every Thing in wonderful Quantities with very little Culture."[4] Georgia would also provide a military buffer zone between the profitable rice-growing Carolina colony and the Spanish in Florida.

The settlement's defense role coincided with the trustees' vision of a town-oriented society of tradesmen and small farmers who would also be conveniently available for military duty. But the trustees had no desire to emulate the single-crop, slave-labor economies of the sugar colonies of the British West Indies, the rice-growing areas of southern Carolina, or the tobacco-producing regions of Virginia. Instead the trustees promised "a more equal Distribution of Lands, the Want of which has been so prejudicial to the well-settling of Jamaica."[5] Consequently, Oglethorpe and the trustees placed economic emphasis on the small-scale production of silk, wine, and olive oil, none of which was very successful. The mulberry trees that grew wild in Georgia were the wrong kind for the support of silkworms, and in any case silk culture was too labor-intensive to be viable in a frontier society. Georgia wine, needless to add, graced few dinner tables.

The trustees labored enthusiastically to recruit the "worthy poor" to people their Georgia colony. Indigent settlers who survived the trustees' screening process were eligible for free passage to Georgia, fifty acres of free land, and a year's rations. The land allotment included a town lot, a nearby five-acre garden plot, and, further out, a forty-five acre farm. Trust stores provided rations which, as a result of Georgia's slow development, usually continued for longer than the promised one year. In return, settlers agreed not to sell the land, to pay quitrents to the trustees, and to plant mulberry trees. By 1741, almost twelve hundred people "on the charity" had arrived in Georgia. More than one thousand additional settlers paid their own way to the colony. Those not "on the charity" could claim up to five hundred acres of land, depending on the number of indentured servants they brought with them.

Following the establishment of the first settlement at Savannah in February 1733, the trustees formulated the basic laws for the governance of the colony. The laws banned from Georgia slavery and hard alcohol, as well as blacks, Roman Catholics, liquor dealers, and lawyers. Wine, which was to be fermented locally, and beer, which was Oglethorpe's favorite drink, were permitted. Combined with earlier regulations prohibiting ownership of more than five hundred acres of land, the trustees' laws provided formidable support for a colony of virtuous yeomen. Slavery promoted large landholdings, encouraged idleness, and through the specter of slave revolt undermined the effectiveness of a citizen's army. Alcohol, at least according to Oglethorpe, contributed to poor health, encouraged idleness, and had disastrous consequences when employed in the Indian trade. Lawyers, incidentally, were unnecessary in a righteous society where each man pleaded his own case. During the early 1740s, the restrictions on landholding and rum were relaxed, the latter because it was almost impossible to enforce, the former at least in part because the arbitrary assignment of farms often created genuine hardships. Nevertheless, the essential legal structure of the trustees' vision remained in place until the mid-eighteenth century.

Under the trustees' antislavery, antiplantation policies Georgia made greater progress than critics sometimes conceded; yet the colony remained the poorest and the smallest of the king's American possessions. Georgia continually faced economic hardships, and its people drifted away to other colonies to seek their fortunes. By 1741, more than twenty-eight hundred settlers had migrated to the colony, yet its population was less than half that number. The root of the problem was Georgia's failure to produce items for export with which to pay for sorely needed goods from abroad. With parliamentary subsidies declining during the late 1740s, Georgia faced long-term economic difficulties.

The trustees' vision of a virtuous yeoman society came under increasing attack from those who looked to neighboring South Carolina as a model for colonial development. The solution to Georgia's economic problems, malcontented settlers claimed, was to establish a slave-labor, staple-crop economy. In South Carolina, planters grew wealthy from the cultivation of rice, and planter affluence and the existence of a commodity for export opened opportunities for limited numbers of merchants and land speculators. Never mind that the majority of South Carolina's population—the slaves who provided the labor—lived a miserable existence on the malaria-infested rice plantations and had probably the highest death rate in the mainland colonies nor even that a great many South Carolina whites failed to share in the colony's prosperity. Compared to Georgia's lackluster performance, the opportunities in South Carolina appeared glittering.

It was ironic—though perhaps inevitable—that Georgia malcontents would choose as their model precisely the kind of society that Georgia's founders had sought to avoid. Sir Robert Montgomery, the first of His Majesty's subjects to attempt the establishment of a colony in Georgia, had warned against a commitment "to some single Product," which would "take up all the Labours of their People, overstock the Markets, stifle the Demand, and make their Industry their Ruin, merely through a Want of due Reflection on Diversity of other Products, equally adapted to their Soil, and Climate."[6] This was the view adopted by the trustees. Yet plantation agriculture offered the quickest route to riches for those in a position to take advantage of the opportunity.

Ambitious Georgia settlers launched a campaign to abolish the trustees' laws and emulate the South Carolina success story. For a decade the debate over slavery rocked the Georgia colony. In general, the opponents of the trustees' vision were the more affluent members of the Savannah community. Opposition to slavery came from the Scottish Highlanders around Darien and the German Salzburgers in Ebenezer as well as from Savannah artisans who feared slave-labor competition. To these settlers, "those Folk who wanted to bring in Negroes, . . . would put an End to all White Men's Work."[7]

Gradually the trustees retreated, modifying their land and rum policies and ultimately capitulating on the crucial issue of slavery. Pressures from James Habersham, the colony's most successful merchant and a spokesman for the Savannah business community; George Whitefield, the colony's best-known minister; and others proved too formidable to resist. The trustees' twenty-one-year charter was nearing its end, and the British government was discontented with Georgia's feeble commercial contributions to the empire. In 1750 the declining trustees lifted the prohibition on slavery. Two years later they surrendered their charter to the crown. The great utopian experiment had come to an end.

Perhaps the outcome was destined because Georgia stood in the path of the westward expansion from coastal slaveholding areas. Certainly it is not surprising that ambitious Georgians looked enviously at the alluring model of South Carolina. Yet as Oglethorpe's most recent biographer has argued, Georgia was not preordained to be a staple-crop, slave-labor, plantation colony. To the North, other colonies survived quite nicely with town-oriented settlement patterns and small-scale agriculture, although, to be sure, Georgia faced special problems that it did not succeed in overcoming. Committed to an "almost naive faith that the environment can make or remake a man," Oglethorpe and his associates promoted a utopia in the wilderness that failed to survive. [8]

The future belonged to people with a different vision. By 1760 more than one-third of Georgia's people were property; by the time of the American Revolution slaves comprised almost half the population. Trading centers—Ebenezer, Frederica, Sunbury, Hardwick—disappeared as the trustees' township settlement pattern collapsed under the weight of plantation agriculture. The retreat from the trustees' vision became a rout during the era of royal government.

Georgia's royal governors and especially James Wright, who was chief executive from 1760 until his expulsion during the American Revolution, viewed Georgia's economic problems from an imperial perspective. Unlike Oglethorpe, who concluded that South Carolina was what Georgia should not be, Wright had served in a number of governmental positions in South Carolina and regarded it as a model colony that produced rice and raw materials while providing a market for slaves and finished products. The royal governors, the first of whom arrived in 1754, promptly set about reforming Georgia into a colony more compatible with the needs of Great Britain.

The new government's accomplishments were substantial. By 1773 Georgia contained an estimated thirty-three thousand people (approximately 45 percent of whom were slaves), almost ten times the population of two decades earlier. Increased production of rice, indigo, and other products provided the colony with foreign exchange and generated among some elements a burgeoning prosperity. Georgia's growing population and expanding plantations needed land, and Governor Wright aggressively pursued "treaties" with surrounding Indian tribes. Wright's successful "diplomacy" more than quintupled the size of the colony.

The establishment of a Commons House of Assembly provided Georgia with experience in representative government. The trustees, hoping to carry out their utopian experiment with as little interference from the subjects as possible, avoided creating a colonial assembly until 1751. Even then the assembly was only an advisory body. The Commons House of Assembly, composed of members who owned at least five hundred acres of land and elected by voters who owned not less than fifty acres, had greater authority than its predecessor, but the real power in government lay with the appointed governor's council.

The royal governor in council defined law, made appointments, and granted land. Unlike the trustees, council members were not noticeably squeamish about profiting from the colony they governed. Governor Wright soon owned eleven plantations and 523 slaves; Lieutenant Governor John Graham held twenty-five thousand acres and at least 240 slaves; Council President James Habersham possessed ten thousand acres and 198 slaves; and others in the king's service demonstrated little evidence of want. By 1773 some sixty people owned twenty-five hundred or more acres with twenty holding in excess of five thousand acres. These sixty men, who comprised fewer than 5 percent of landowners, held more than 50 percent of Georgia's slave population.

To promote slavery and to make it convenient for masters to encourage their black laborers in the performance of the backbreaking chores required for the cultivation of rice and indigo, the new government promptly rewrote the slave code. After accepting slavery in 1750, the trustees had promulgated a benign code that protected blacks from physical abuse and required that slaves be provided religious instruction. The trustees even hired a teacher to instruct slaves in writing and religion. The royal slave code, modeled on that of South Carolina, made teaching a slave to write a criminal offense, and it placed few restrictions on a landowner's control of his human property. Again reversing trustee policy, the king's government permitted slaves to be artisans, thereby undermining urban development by depriving skilled townsmen of markets in the countryside. As a leading student of colonial Georgia society has observed, "white artisans were devalued by slave competition."[9]

So, too, were smaller farmers. Government land policy during the royal period encouraged planters and speculators to acquire large acreages, while the high cost of initiating a profitable rice or indigo operation made it difficult for small farmers to establish a cash income. As Milton Sydney Heath has concluded, "The great body of small proprietors benefited in no such positive way from these policies; in fact, the aggrandizement of landed estates pushed them back onto the poorer and less advantageously located soils and thereby increased the degree of economic inequality."[10] Subsistence farming was nothing new to Georgia's yeomanry, but the success of plantation agriculture created a widening class chasm. It was hardly surprising that royal government was not notably popular among upland farmers, the people, as Habersham expressed it to Governor Wright, who "are really what you and I understand by Crackers."[11]

Georgia played little role in the coming of the American Revolution. It produced no Patrick Henry or Samuel Adams; indeed, it is probably best known as the only one of the thirteen colonies that complied with the Stamp Act, that was not represented at the first Continental Congress, and that initially sent no official delegation to the Second Continental Congress. In the war for independence, Georgia was a minor theater, noted mostly as the launching place for three unsuccessful invasions of British Florida, for a somnolent defense that permitted a British army to march into Savannah undetected, and for the failure to recapture Savannah after it had fallen. But if Georgia contributed little to the American Revolution, the American Revolution had enormous consequences for Georgia.

From the beginning, the Revolution in Georgia concerned considerably more than independence from Britain. The question involved not only home rule, but, perhaps more fundamental, which Georgians would rule at home. Unlike Virginia, where a mature and self-confident aristocracy led a war for independence from Great Britain, Georgia possessed a newer and less secure leadership that divided on the question of independence and in the tumult of war lost much of its power to spokesmen for the "crackers" and other outgroups who had found little place in royal Georgia.

Before the Revolution the colony had developed three loosely organized political factions. One supported Governor Wright and royal rule. It included much of the emerging aristocracy and drew support from ordinary subjects, especially from those of English ethnic background and Anglican church affiliation. The center of royal authority was the governor's council. There James Habersham, a schoolteacher who had become the colony's leading merchant and one of its largest planters, was president, and its membership included such men as Noble Jones, a medical doctor who had served the colony in various civil and military positions and who was a large plantation owner. They joined Governor Wright, Lieutenant Governor Graham, and other officials to uphold royal prerogative in Georgia.

The earliest of the opposition groups found its forum in the Commons House of Assembly. Soon after the formation of royal government, the Christ Church faction established control of the lower house. Centered in Savannah and the adjoining parishes that constituted "Old Georgia," the Christ Church faction represented those planters, merchants, and other social elites who were not part of the royal establishment. Among the coalition's leaders were the Habersham brothers, sons of James Habersham, and Noble W. Jones, son of Noble Jones. As this generational continuity suggests, the royal and Christ Church factions were socioeconomically similar. Both groups were conservative, and, like the royal regime, the Christ Church group was "a political coalition based on family ties, economic connections, and social compatibility, which those who were not included had little hope of overcoming."[12] The coalition represented the growing spirit of home rule in America, and its leaders demanded greater powers for the elected lower house of Georgia government, which also meant greater power for themselves. Since Wright and the council refused to share governmental authority, the Christ Church coalition became the early defenders of liberty and home rule and thereby reaped the political benefits of being on the popular side of the colony's most pressing controversy.

Joining in the opposition to royal authority was the country faction, which appeared in the early 1770s. The country faction emerged from the outlying parishes that had little voice in the older political coalitions. Planters who had achieved economic success but not political influence; Puritans, Scotch Presbyterians, and other dissenters from the established Anglican church; and, increasingly, smaller farmers of the uplands and town artisans formed the social base for the country faction. Its most prominent early leader was Button Gwinnett, who failed both as a merchant and a planter, blamed the frustration of his ambitions on the royal system, and turned to radical politics with a vengeance.

Royal government collapsed before the combined opposition of the Christ Church and country factions, known collectively as whigs. Georgia's second Provisional Congress and its Council of Safety took effective control of the government in July 1775. Early in the following year the Council of Safety arrested Governor Wright and several royal officials, who soon afterward broke bond and departed on a British warship. With the demise of royal government, the divided whigs established a new governmental structure. The country faction won the heated election campaign of 1776, which permitted its leaders to dominate the writing of Georgia's first constitution and made Button Gwinnett president of the Council of Safety. The whigs also attempted to prepare Georgia for war.

Factional strife consistently hampered the state's war effort. As council president, Gwinnett commanded the Georgia militia; Lachlan McIntosh, a conservative stalwart, led the Continental forces in the state. Personal animosities between the two men created serious problems and contributed to the failure of an ill-fated attempt to invade Florida in 1777. Each blamed the other for the fiasco, with McIntosh labeling Gwinnett "a Scoundrell & lying Rascal." The duel that promptly followed left Gwinnett mortally wounded. Such open hostilities within Georgia's wartime leadership were indicative of the widening split between Christ Church conservatives and country radicals.

The struggle again became three-sided after the British occupied Savannah virtually unopposed in December 1778. British officials revived the loyalist cause and organized a sizable tory militia. Governor Wright returned to take charge of the restored royal government, and the *Georgia Gazette*, the colony's newspaper, resumed publication under the title *Royal Georgia Gazette*. Driven into the uplands, the revolutionary government split apart. The lowland conservatives created the Supreme Executive Council as their government of Georgia; the country, upland radicals organized a competing Executive Council as their instrument for carrying on the struggle. Augusta, which changed hands four times during the war years, served as the occasional capital of the Georgia governments.

The fighting in Georgia became intensely bloody. An attempt to recapture Savannah following the arrival of strong French army and naval forces in September 1779 failed disastrously. Soon afterward most of the British and Continental forces in Georgia were shifted to more important theaters, leaving tories, patriots, and Indians to settle their scores in Georgia. Since the beginning of the war, Georgia tories, who had fled to Florida and organized themselves as the Florida Rangers, had battled patriot forces in the southern part of the state. By 1780 guerrilla war had spread throughout Georgia.

With Savannah and the older plantation areas—at times virtually all the plantation region—under loyalist control, the lowland conservatives lost influence. Their Supreme Executive Council enthusiastically supported the French-colonial effort to recapture Savannah; the defeat that followed further undermined conservative credibility. Because the war was waged in the fringe areas of Georgia settlement, upland farmers carried the burden of the resistance, and their spokesmen gained increasing prestige. In 1780 the creation of a state assembly reunited Georgia's revolutionary government under radical and upcountry leadership. The assembly declared all actions of the conservative faction's Supreme Executive Council illegal and selected a full slate of state officials. Hardly had the new government been established before the tories recaptured Augusta, forcing the newly elected government into hiding for more than a year. This period in exile, much of it apparently spent in the countryside, strengthened identification with the backcountry crackers.

The war came to an end in Georgia as a result of outside forces. In 1781 Continental troops recaptured Augusta, and in July 1782 British misfortunes elsewhere forced the evacuation of Savannah. Almost seven years of war in Georgia—with royal forces in control of the older and more developed areas of the state for about half that period—had redistributed political power in the state. Exemplifying the new and more diverse Georgia leadership were such men as Elijah Clarke, an illiterate frontiersman from North Carolina and a tough guerrilla fighter; William Few, who had participated in the North Carolina regulator revolt and continued his rebellion after moving to Georgia; George Walton, a Virginian orphaned as a child who had become a minor but ambitious Savannah attorney; and James Jackson, a recent migrant from England who promptly took up arms against his homeland. Whatever their contributions to American independence, their participation in the Revolution broadened opportunities for common folk in Georgia.

The leveling effects of the Revolution were in part a result of the economic convulsions suffered by planters and merchants, many of whom were tories. Governor George R. Gilmer exaggerated when he later recalled that "Tories had little chance for fair trials, if permitted to be tried at all,"[13] but state confiscation of tory property was substantial. Even for whig planters, the years of British occupation, fratricidal warfare, and social disruptions often made it impossible to market crops, offered opportunities for slaves to flee in search of freedom, and made the upkeep of the plantation more difficult than ever. Cultivation of indigo collapsed with the disappearance of the empire bounty, and rice production did not regain prewar levels for two decades. Lachlan McIntosh, whose duel with Button Gwinnett was only one episode in his almost seven years of campaigning, was a large and prosperous rice planter before the war but spent the remainder of his life desperately attempting to hold his creditors at bay. The large merchants suffered with the planters, and both lost status in relation to the victorious upland farmers. The latter, too, bore economic hardships, but for many of them, the bad times soon passed.

For ordinary whites the postrevolutionary war decades were boom times. A variety of governmental, social, and economic trends merged to promote democracy, individualism, and equality of opportunity. To be sure, black Georgians, upon whose labor white prosperity increasingly depended, and Indians, whose lands the growing white population seized, might well have found other adjectives to describe this hectic era. But for white Georgians the years that followed the revolutionary war offered abundant opportunities for the hardworking, the ambitious, the talented, and even, in fact, the lucky.

Nowhere was the new spirit better reflected than in public land policy. Georgia claimed not only the land within its present boundaries but also most of the states of Alabama and Mississippi. In possession of such a bountiful empire, Georgia's revolutionary government enacted a generous land policy. It permitted a head of household to claim for dirt-cheap fees up to two hundred acres in addition to other acreage for family members and up to ten slaves. This arrangement obviously benefited slaveowners, but compared to the plantation policies of the royal regime, it was a major step toward economic democracy. A leading scholar on the subject evaluated the new policy: "Thus the amount that a man of small means might obtain was greatly increased, while the rich planters' rights to public lands were drastically curtailed."[14] But this was only the beginning.

During the war the government offered a bewildering array of veterans' bonuses. Desperate for recruits—and growing more desperate as the war progressed—the revolutionary government offered land bounties to almost anyone who might aid the Georgia cause. Georgia veterans, soldiers from other states who served in Georgia, British soldiers who deserted to the patriots, and others were eligible for bounties, which were in addition to grants available under the revolutionary headright policy. It was difficult to be a white male in Georgia and not qualify for virtually free land.

Fortunately, Governor Wright had acquired a substantial amount of land just before the Revolution. This acreage was available for the government to pay off some of its promises, although the promises far exceeded the acreage. More "treaties" with neighboring Indians opened more land and fed the growing land fever. Speculation grew apace and so did corruption. By the late 1780s surveyors were authorizing and governors were endorsing grants substantially in excess of legal maximums. Two enterprising surveyors invented approximately three million acres of nonexistent land, acquired title to it, and presumably headed north to offer speculators unusually good prices. The disposal of imaginary land hardly affected Georgians, nor did anyone seem overly concerned about land speculation and corruption. After all, government policies permitted almost anyone—always provided he was white—to get in on the action.

What did sober most Georgians was the Yazoo land fraud. Four land companies purchased for $500,000 approximately thirty-five million acres of western land, which encompassed about three-fifths of Alabama and Mississippi. To encourage passage of the Yazoo bill that permitted the sale, land promoters bribed Georgia legislators and other government officials on an impressive scale. The transaction generated immediate controversy; as the scope of the sale and the extent of the corruption surfaced, the reaction became a storm of protest. Throughout the state, public meetings and grand juries condemned the legislation; newspapers and orators demanded the law be repealed; poets denounced "the hellish fraud of that infernal crew of speculators";[15] and James Jackson resigned his United States Senate seat to lead the attack on the Yazoo fraud and to fight four duels with people who disagreed.

A newly elected legislature, not content with merely repealing the Yazoo act, burned the law and all associated documents with divine fire by reflecting the sun's rays through a prism. Although the rescinding act levied a $1,000 fine on any state official who took future notice of the Yazoo affair, a dozen years after the event the Georgia legislature was still passing resolutions that viewed "with abhorrence the attempt made by a set of unprincipled men, commonly known by the appellation of Yazoo men, to corrupt the majority of the legislature of this state in the year 1795."[16]

The vociferous reaction to the Yazoo fraud suggested the popular outlook in Georgia near the end of the eighteenth century. The storm of protest centered not so much on corruption per se; that was nothing new in Georgia. It was the elitist nature of the corruption that was deemed to be aristocratic and not "democratical." Georgia's land policy assured property to virtually any white head of household; the Yazoo sale involved such a massive amount of territory that it threatened this policy; Georgia's increasingly democratized citizenry responded with outrage. The crackers had come to expect a great deal more from government than they once had.

The Yazoo scandal led to important changes. The legislature adopted a lottery system for distributing the public lands. Every free white male got a draw, two draws if he had a wife and minor child. Widows with minor children and revolutionary war veterans also merited two draws. There were a few other special dispensations, particularly for veterans, but in the main the law treated all white males alike. The land was virtually free, netting the state about seven cents per acre, and the lottery remained unmarred by scandal. Under this system

Georgia gave away about three-fourths of the state to more than one hundred thousand individuals and families.

The Yazoo fraud also contributed to sealing the fate of Georgia's Indian population. Much to the ire of many Georgians, the United States Supreme Court accepted the legality of the Yazoo transaction, despite repeal and arson on the part of the state legislature. With legal complications mounting, Georgia officials turned the task of settling with the Yazoo claimants over to the federal government in 1802. In exchange for the present states of Alabama and Mississippi, federal officials paid Georgia $1,250,000 and agreed to remove the remaining Indians from the state. General Andrew Jackson's victory over the Creeks during the War of 1812 hastened the end. In 1838 federal soldiers marched the last significant group of Georgia Cherokees down the "Trail of Tears" to Oklahoma.

Georgians wrote three constitutions during the late eighteenth century, and all expressed due regard for white common man democracy. The revolutionary Constitution of 1777 provided for virtual manhood suffrage by enfranchising adults who paid taxes on property of ten pounds value or who followed an artisan's trade. It even included punishments for eligible electors who failed to vote, although this provision was never enforced. The document assured such basic civil liberties as freedom of the press, religion, and trial by jury. The popularly elected House of Assembly held most of the power of the new government. The constitution accepted local control of local institutions by creating no judicial body above the county superior courts.

The Constitution of 1789 brought Georgia government into conformity with the newly adopted federal Constitution. This document enfranchised all adult citizens who paid any tax at all and, literally interpreted, would have permitted tax-paying women to vote. It established a popularly elected senate, thus forcing the lower house to share authority with another independent legislative body. The state's third constitution, written in 1798, introduced the federal ratio—that is, the counting of a slave as three-fifths of a person—in legislative apportionment. Political pressures from the resurgent plantation counties combined with the rapid growth of slavery in the upcountry to generate support for this provision, which continued to discriminate against predominantly white counties until the Civil War.

Constitutional amendments and legislative enactment soon provided for the popular election of county officials, justices of the peace, and inferior court judges, although Georgia's growth ultimately forced the creation of a supreme court. An 1824 amendment shifted the election of governor from the legislature to the electorate. Property qualifications for legislators disappeared during the 1830s, and later they were removed for governor. Other amendments transferred authority to grant divorces from the legislature to the judiciary and further broadened religious freedom by removing all penalties for denying the deity and the hereafter.

The state legislature even flirted with the creation of a publicly supported school system. The Constitution of 1777 required schools "supported at the general expense of the state," and, although this provision was dropped from later constitutions, the idea for a time seemed destined for fulfillment. In 1785 Georgia chartered a state university and adopted a general plan for a comprehensive system of free schools. The legislators failed to develop a method for financing such an ambitious program (in part because the state's common man land policy produced so little revenue that money was lacking to fund a common man school system), although the concept of public education remained a subject for discussion during the early nineteenth century. In 1817 the legislature appropriated funds to be invested as a step toward "the future establishment and support of Free schools throughout the state,"[17] and in 1822 a common schools bill narrowly failed in the state senate after being passed by the lower house. Having rejected a publicly supported general school system, the legislature enacted a considerably more modest plan that divided educational expenditures between the poor school fund for white children of indigent parents and public assistance for the elite-oriented private academies, the latter absorbing one-half the school fund while serving one-tenth of the white children. For the bulk of Georgia whites, education remained a private enterprise.

The expansion of the Georgia frontier opened rich new lands, and for the first time the upland farmers found profitable cash crops. By the 1790s settlers pouring into the state from Virginia and North Carolina had introduced tobacco culture, which quickly transformed Augusta into a thriving tobacco center and sharply increased Georgia's exports. But hardly had Georgia farmers mastered tobacco cultivation before it was virtually driven from the fields by the arrival of cotton. Short staple cotton had been around all along, but not until Eli Whitney perfected the cotton gin in 1793 did it become a profitable crop. In 1791 Georgia produced one thousand bales of cotton; in 1801 it marketed twenty thousand bales. Soon Georgia produced more cotton than anywhere else in the world. After 1840 Georgia fell behind the booming cotton states to the west, but absolute production continued to increase. In 1850 Georgians marketed approximately one-half million bales and in 1860 more than seven hundred thousand. Despite all of Oglethorpe's efforts, few people ever wore Georgia silk; millions were to wear Georgia cotton.

The coming of cotton revitalized slavery in Georgia. The peculiar institution had never been in danger, of course; the great accomplishment of royal rule had been to wed the state to chattel slavery. The disruptions of the revolutionary war and the success of Georgia's land policies in attracting new settlers had, however, increased the relative number of whites. In 1773 slaves comprised 45.4 percent of Georgia's population; by 1790 that figure had dropped to 35.4 percent. The cotton boom reversed this trend. In the odd logic of one proponent of slavery, "It is fortunate for the blacks as well as the whites, that the cotton business sprang up, for the sons of Africa do not flourish in a state of freedom, and without the cultivation of the leading staple of commerce there would not have been sufficient occupation for them."[18] Cotton more than solved that problem. In 1800, 36.5 percent of Georgians were slaves, and by 1820 the ratio of slaves to free population had climbed to 44 percent.

But beyond revitalizing slavery, cotton democratized it, at least for a time. Ordinary white farmers could, and did, acquire slaves and even plantations. The lottery system of land distribution did not prevent the formation of plantations, but it did broaden opportunities for acquiring them. Unlike rice and indigo, cotton did not require heavy initial investments. The white staple lent itself to slave labor while providing the profits for its purchase. A popular jingle expressed the common vision clearly:

> All I want in this creation
> Is a pretty little wife and a big plantation.[19]

Land, cotton, and slaves—the emerging Georgia version of the American dream—were all available to the deserving. After almost a century of frequent strife and social conflict, white Georgians seemed to have arrived at a consensus that rested on the production of the white staple with black labor on land that had been taken from red people.

# Chapter Two

## *The Cotton Kingdom*

Cotton and slavery brought great wealth to Georgia, and Georgians paid dearly for it. Plantation agriculture restored the social and economic trends of the royal period and dominated the state's development. Successful planters grew rich, and many cultivated a graceful and widely envied style of life. But shrewd observers who peered beneath the glitter of plantation prosperity recognized the weaknesses of the system. "When Southern statesmen count up the gains of slavery," a British traveler wrote, "let them not forget to count its cost. They may depend upon it, there is a heavy 'per contra' to the profits of niggerdom."[1]

For the slaveholders, slavery was profitable. In 1860 the per capita wealth held by Georgia's 592,000 whites was twice that possessed by an average Pennsylvanian or New Yorker. A typical Georgia slaveholder owned property worth five times as much as a normal citizen of the North. An average Georgia farm was double the size of a farm in the Midwest, and Georgia contained more agricultural operations of one thousand or more acres than all of the nonslave states combined. "In glancing over the civilized world, the eye rests upon not a single spot where all classes of society are so well content with their social system, or have greater reason to be so, than in the slaveholding states of the American Union," declaimed Senator Robert Toombs in 1853. "Stability, progress, order, peace, content and prosperity reign throughout our borders."[2] Little wonder so many Georgia whites considered cotton to be king.

Approximately thirty-five hundred Georgians held thirty or more slaves, and approximately thirty-five hundred farms contained five hundred or more improved acres. These thirty-five hundred or so families, comprising just over 3 percent of the free families in the state, set much of the social and political tone in antebellum Georgia. About half of them owned fifty or more slaves and qualified for the top rank of the planter aristocracy. Typically they possessed eighty slaves and more than a thousand acres of improved land, with another 1,650 acres for livestock and future cultivation. Cotton was the principal cash

crop on the majority of plantations, although Georgia's limited number of rice plantations were often extremely productive and highly
lucrative enterprises. Indeed, large planters generally were people of
enormous wealth. In large part because of the land lottery system,
Georgia planters on the average held less princely estates than did
their peers elsewhere in the Deep South; nevertheless, a considerable
number of them ranked among the few thousand richest families in
the United States.

Most planters devoted their full time to agriculture. A few, such as
David Dickson of Hancock County, ran model plantations that were
showplaces for scientific farming, soil conservation, and high productivity. Dickson was among the first in Georgia to make systematic use
of commercial fertilizer and developed his own "Dickson's Compound." Beginning his planting career on a modest scale in the mid-
1840s, Dickson in 1859 marketed 760 bales of cotton and a variety of
other products, enough to buy a second plantation complete with slaves,
equipment, and livestock. By the time of the Civil War, Dickson owned
more than eight thousand acres, 143 slaves, and a total estate with an
estimated value of half a million dollars. Although well known and
successful, Dickson was never fully accepted in the planter society of
Hancock County. He lived openly with one of his female slaves, siring
several children and leaving her a substantial fortune when he died
in 1885.

Some planters, such as Colonel Joseph Bond, operated on a truly
impressive scale. Possibly the state's most resourceful cotton grower,
Bond owned six plantations, approximately 385 slaves, and an estate
that was appraised at more than a million dollars. In 1858, the year
before his death, Bond produced twenty-two hundred bales of cotton
that sold for $100,000, hailed by area newspapers as "the largest cot-
ton crop in Georgia."[3] He died from a gunshot wound that occurred
during a quarrel with a dismissed overseer. Equally ambitious if hardly
as dedicated was John B. Lamar, who managed eight plantations, including those belonging to his brother-in-law, Congressman Howell
Cobb. "I am one half the year rattling over rough roads," Lamar wrote,
"stopping at farm houses in the country, scolding overseers in half a
dozen counties & two states . . . and the other half in the largest cities
of the Union, or those of Europe, living on dainties & riding on rail-
cars and steamboats."[4]

A minority of planters actively pursued other careers, as did Howell
Cobb. Senator Robert Toombs was a successful lawyer and politician
as well as the owner of two plantations in Stewart County in southwest

Georgia. With 170 slaves and two thousand acres of improved land, Toombs's plantations produced a cotton crop in 1859 worth approximately $28,000, which was about one hundred times the annual income of an employee in manufacturing in the North.

Not many planters were as innovative as Dickson or as productive as Bond. Many would have doubtless agreed with Lamar: "I have found that it is unprofitable to undertake anything on a plantation out of the regular routine."[5] Some might have accepted the strategy of a planter described by Ralph B. Flanders, the historian of Georgia slavery, as a man whose "idea of a good crop was: an increase of Negroes; enough of everything made on the plantation to feed everything abundantly; improvement in the productive quality of the land; the placing of all equipment, mules, horses, and fences in good condition by Christmas; then, as much cotton as could be made and gathered under those circumstances."[6] Such an approach was by no means irrational. Aside from whatever cotton might be marketed, the rising prices of slaves in the late antebellum period and their natural increase, as well as the augmented value of improved lands, would ensure the planter a handsome return in capital gains.

As these examples suggest, generalizations about Georgia planters are difficult. The transition from a rough and tumble frontier society to a more stable antebellum social order was a gradual and never fully completed process. Along the Georgia coast, the planters raising rice and sea island cotton had a century before the Civil War to develop aristocratic airs. Here, as described by a contemporary, massive lawns with magnolias and moss-draped live oaks fronted "generous homes, and the hospitality there extended was profuse and refined."[7] Here, too, the swampy, mosquito-infested rice plantations extracted a heavy tribute from those who tilled them. Not unusual was a planter's passing observation in a letter to his son that the sickness "which was so prevalent among the Negroes last year, and of which many died, still lingers. Mr. Barnard, our neighbor, has lost four lately; and Mr. King told me that one-third of his efficient force was laid up with it."[8]

The "old" cotton area north and west of Augusta had half a century to reach respectable maturity. Wasteful agricultural methods depleted the red-clay soil, and many of these counties lost population, especially white population, during much of the late antebellum period. The proselytizing work of David Dickson and others and the increasing availability of commercial fertilizers revitalized agricultural productivity during the years just before the Civil War. By that time men such as John B. Lamar and Robert Toombs had already purchased plantations in the newer southwestern part of the state although they continued to live in their old communities. "Lord, Lord, Howell," Lamar reported to Cobb, "you and I have been too used to poor land to know what crops people are making in the rich lands of the new counties. I am just getting my eyes open to the golden view."[9]

Lamar's enthusiasm was not misplaced. The big cotton crops of the 1840s and 1850s came primarily from the less devastated lands to the south and west of Macon, most of which had been held by the Creeks until the 1820s. Here Georgia's "Old South" civilization retained a raw frontier quality. An appalled rice planter whose son had purchased a plantation in the region wrote: "My objection to the country is its godlessness! The condition of society is wild; the rush is for accumulation; the game played at is speculation; and the weather becomes very foul to the poor craft that falls astern!"[10] Few travelers could resist a derogatory comment about Columbus, the largest city in the region. An English visitor in the 1840s found the streets "swarming with drunken Indians, and young prostitutes, both Indian and White, a sufficient indication of the manners of the place."[11] A decade later Frederick Law Olmsted was disgusted with "so much gambling, intoxication, and cruel treatment of servants in public, as in Columbus."[12]

Most Georgia towns fared better. The same English traveler who found the raucous manners of Columbus so disagreeable described Macon as "a very pretty town, . . . which like all the towns in this part of the United States, has a cheerful appearance, not being cramped up as they are in the Northern states."[13] Georgia towns contained factories, of course, but none could be appropriately compared with the emerging "cramped up" industrial cities of the North. Instead they functioned as marketing, transportation, and service centers for agricultural enterprise, and their small but prosperous class of merchants, businessmen, and professional people looked to the surrounding countryside for patients, clients, and customers.

Almost all of the really wealthy townsmen were planters. A sizable minority of planters—especially the richer ones—escaped the isolation of the countryside by leaving their plantations to the care of overseers and residing for at least part of the year in town. Affluent urbanites invested their excess funds in plantations. As James C. Bonner found in his intensive study of David Dickson's Hancock County, "there appears a decided tendency for lawyer, doctor, carpenter, merchant, and tailor to move into agriculture as fast as the accumulation of capital would permit."[14] Dickson made his stake in merchandizing before becoming a leading planter, and Robert Toombs, although the son of a planter, prospered in law before purchasing land and field hands. Robert Habersham, whose R. Habersham and Son factorage house was among the state's largest, was also one of Georgia's most productive planters. A few large slaveholders were railroad construction contractors and manufacturers, and two were Savannah businessmen. Although about one in ten Georgians lived in urban areas of more than twenty-five hundred population and another one in ten resided in smaller villages, the distance between town and countryside in antebellum Georgia was far less than what it was to become.

Beneath the thirty-five hundred large slaveholders were twenty thousand prosperous farmers ranging from small planters to successful yeomen. Some twenty thousand Georgians owned at least five but fewer than thirty slaves, and a similar number of farms ranged from one hundred to five hundred improved acres. Approximately three thousand small planters owned twenty to twenty-nine slaves; more than seven thousand would-be planters held ten to nineteen; and almost ten thousand families possessed five to nine chattel laborers.

These 23,500 people—representing 21 percent of free Georgia families and the equivalent of 12 percent of all Georgia families—owned probably 90 percent of the wealth in the state and accounted for virtually all of its surplus production. A study of the cotton-growing regions of the South found the top 10 percent of farmers held 59 percent of all real and personal property, 61 percent of all slaves, 62 percent of total farm value, and produced 68 percent of the cotton crop.[15] The 6 percent of white Georgia families who owned twenty or more slaves, another recent study suggests, possessed more than half of Georgia's total property value.[16] Cotton and rice made Georgia rich, but it was wealth that the bulk of the population viewed largely from a distance.

The majority of farmers ranged from yeomen to poor whites. More than thirty thousand Georgia farmers cultivated less than one hundred acres each. About half were slaveholders owning fewer than five slaves. Although able to afford few luxuries, these yeomen were by no means destitute; the ownership of two healthy slaves alone made a Georgia family almost as wealthy as the average northern household. Even "the slaveless yeomen," as Wilbur J. Cash phrased it, "might wax fat in the sort of primitive prosperity which consisted in having an abundance of what they themselves could produce."[17]

Many of these yeomen lived in the hills and mountains of northern Georgia. Cotton plantations existed in the uplands in those areas where the juxtaposition of fertile soils suitable for growing the staple and rivers or railroads for transporting it permitted, and most yeomen cultivated plots of cotton both for home use and as a cash crop. In the main, however, the rough terrain, short growing season, and inadequate transportation of northern Georgia encouraged subsistence farming. Many north Georgia families led isolated lives on hardscrabble dirt farms, but most owned their own land, raised the bulk of what they needed, and thus maintained a sturdy independence.

In an earlier era, the prospects for ambitious small farmers were relatively favorable, but by the late antebellum period both slaves and land were becoming increasingly difficult to acquire. Slave prices rose steadily during the decade and a half before the Civil War. A prime field hand who could have been purchased for $600 in the economically depressed mid-1840s cost $1,800 in 1860. Indeed, from a white common man perspective, the inflation of slave prices began much earlier than the growth in actual slave values because small-scale farmers usually had to grow cotton to make their purchases. Relative to the price of cotton, the cost of slaves climbed steadily throughout the antebellum period. In 1800 it required 1,500 pounds of lint cotton to purchase a prime field hand; in 1818 approximately 3,500 pounds; in 1837 some 10,000 pounds; and in 1860 about 16,500 pounds. As a consequence, the percentage of white families owning slaves declined throughout the lower South during the late antebellum period.

Land remained inexpensive in comparison to the cost of slaves, but good land available for purchase became increasingly scarce as the prospering plantations grew ever larger. Smaller operators found themselves pushed onto the less fertile areas of the plantation counties and into the hills and mountains and pine barrens. Not only was wealth maldistributed but for common folk even the opportunities for social mobility were withering. Indeed, only the division of land and slaves of deceased planters among heirs prevented social mobility from being considerably more closed than it was.

Approximately one-half of white families did not own land and well over 60 percent did not own slaves. Among the landless and slaveless were young doctors and lawyers launching promising careers and skilled artisans and tradesmen who lived comfortable lives. The twenty-five thousand or so farm laborers and overseers included sons of affluent farmers who could realistically anticipate better times. Although farm laborers in the South appear to have had higher annual incomes than those outside the region, most had limited prospects, hardly better than the twenty-five thousand people who worked at such subsistence callings as laborer, factory worker, and servant. From this mass of largely propertyless people came the poor whites, who, according to the discontented English bride of a Georgia rice planter, "squat and steal, and starve, on the outskirts of this lowest of all civilized societies." [18]

This social edifice rested on the labor of Georgia's 462,000 slaves. Blacks responded to their lot in life in a variety of ways. Virtually all would have agreed with the sentiments expressed by a black woman in Milledgeville when northern soldiers occupied the town during the Civil War: "Bless de Lord! Tanks be to Almighty God, the Yanks is come; de day ob jubilee hab arrived." [19]

Not many slaves were so doggedly determined to achieve freedom as Fed, who after making good his escape from slavery changed his name to John Brown. Born in Virginia, Brown was still a boy when his family and friends were divided among three heirs following the death of his master. Soon afterward Brown was sold to a slave trader and eventually became the property of a planter family living near Milledgeville. Brown's new owner was unusually cruel. To survive Brown adopted tactics that were not uncommon on many other plantations. On occasion he protested his treatment by slipping into the woods and "laying-out" for several days, even though such a work stoppage was sure to result in punishment. For a time Brown perfected a servile "Sambo" role in an effort to avoid maltreatment and gain favor. Because rations were none too generous, Brown pilfered corn to trade to a local poor white for meal and other food items (slaves could not have the corn ground into meal).

Above all, Brown yearned for liberty. Not only did Brown's early life leave him without personal attachments to those around him, but he absorbed a practical vision of freedom from John Glasgow, a fellow slave who had been free and who had been shanghaied into slavery. After several attempts and a variety of adventures, Brown made good his escape. Glasgow never became regimented to slave life and died a broken man.

Brown and Glasgow were exceptions. A plantation was much more than a prison camp. Most slaves grew up in or became adjusted to a paternal order that stabilized plantation social relations. From master to field hand, there were generally accepted obligations, responsibilities, and personal relationships that softened some of the harshness of slave life. Paternalism, in the words of Eugene D. Genovese, undermined "solidarity among the oppressed by linking them as individuals to their oppressors." "The confrontation of master and slave, white and black, on a plantation presided over by a resident planter for whom the plantation was a home and the entire population part of his extended family generated that [patriarchal and paternalistic] ethos" that profoundly influenced the behavior of both blacks and whites.[20] Slave life also sustained more viable social institutions than the view from the big house might have suggested. Like whites, blacks found in religion and in family relationships solace from worldly travails. Unlike whites, black social behavior fused elements of African, American, and indigenous slave culture.

Between the slave world and the white world were the thirty-five hundred free blacks who resided in Georgia. An Atlanta newspaper expressed the prevailing white viewpoint: "Their presence in slave communities is hurtful to the good order of society."[21] Most free blacks were laborers engaged in a constant struggle with poverty, and all were denied citizenship and were subject to discriminatory laws and ordinances. Yet, remarkably, dozens of free blacks achieved sufficient prosperity to become slaveholders. Sol Humphries, a blacksmith who was freed while a young adult, accumulated the capital to open a successful dry goods store in Macon. "He employed white clerks," a recent study has reported, "and was held in esteem by his white friends."[22] Humphries purchased and freed his wife and father, bought land and slaves, and generally led an affluent life. In dealing with free blacks, whites gained their first experience with Negroes who were not slaves, and blacks set social precedents that influenced the conduct of freedmen after emancipation.

With the value of a slave averaging around $900 in 1860, Georgians owned well over $400 million in slave property, which was at least half of the total wealth of the state. Ask a planter about his cotton profits, a critical northern visitor observed, "and he will point in reply, not to dwellings, libraries, churches, school-houses, mills, railroads, or anything of the kind; he will point to his negroes—to almost nothing else."[23] Comparing the capital invested in slavery with the $11 million invested in manufacturing accurately summarizes the central direction of Georgia's development.

The point is perhaps better illustrated by Table 1. The amount of money per capita invested in manufacturing and the per capita value of manufactured products are compared for the South, the United States, Georgia, and "Free Georgia" (which includes only Georgia's free population and treats the slave population as property rather than people). Additionally, the table contains the estimated per capita value of slave property in Georgia in 1860. As the figures indicate, Georgia lagged somewhat behind the rest of the South in industrial activity and fell far below national norms, even if the state's slave population is excluded from the per capita calculations.

## Table 1: Manufacturing and Slavery in Georgia (in $)

| | Capital Invested in Manufacturing Per Capita | | Value Products Manufactured Per Capita | | Estimated Value Slave Property Per Capita |
|---|---|---|---|---|---|
| | 1850 | 1860 | 1850 | 1860 | 1860 |
| South | 7.60 | 10.54 | 10.88 | 17.09 | – |
| Georgia | 6.02 | 10.30 | 7.82 | 16.01 | 396.42 |
| Free Georgia | 10.40 | 18.30 | 13.50 | 28.44 | 704.36 |
| United States | 22.73 | 32.12 | 43.69 | 59.98 | – |

Source: Data for the South and the United States from Gavin Wright, *The Political Economy of the Cotton South: Households, Markets, and Wealth in the Nineteenth Century* (New York: W. W. Norton, 1978), 110; Georgia data calculated from Donald B. Dodd and Wynelle S. Dodd, eds., *Historical Statistics of the South, 1790–1970* (University, Ala.: University of Alabama Press, 1973), 18–21.

The modest value of manufactured products reflects the primitive, first-stage nature of the state's industrial establishment. Much of Georgia's manufactures were an extension of agriculture rather than industry. The gristmills and sawmills that produced the state's most valuable manufactured products—flour, meal, and lumber—were often located on plantations. A few planters successfully integrated agriculture and industry. Joseph Tooke, a prominent Houston County planter, established a manufacturing company that, with slave labor, produced furniture, wagons, and buggies and a cotton mill staffed by hired white labor, presumably because slaves were too valuable to expose to the health hazards of cotton manufacturing. Some cotton mills did use slave labor. In any case, most of the few actual factories in Georgia were cotton mills. In 1860 Georgia had thirty-three mills employing a total of approximately twenty-eight hundred workers. But compared to the huge per capita value of slave property, manufacturing enterprise was a minor concern. Scarlett O'Hara revealed an elemental truth about Georgia when she mused in *Gone With the Wind* that "she'd never even seen a factory, or known anyone who had seen a factory."[24]

Slavery absorbed Georgia's capital, and the plantation economy it supported offered limited opportunities for nonagricultural business enterprise. The relatively self-sufficient plantations provided little market for urban businessmen. Robert Toombs surely exaggerated when he boasted that medical service and salt were the only things purchased on his Stewart County plantations, but, whether large or small operators, Georgia's farmers generally grew enough food for people and livestock. Self-sufficiency in food declined during the 1850s, as improved railroad transportation made low-priced midwestern food-stuffs available and thereby encouraged Georgia agriculturalists to place even greater effort on cotton cultivation and to make up any food shortages with imports.

A plantation work force normally contained its needed complement of artisans. A large coastal plantation was described as having "a gang (for that is the honorable term) of coopers, of blacksmiths, of bricklayers, of carpenters, all well acquainted with their peculiar trades."[25] Plantation artisans were usually slaves; sometimes they were hired white laborers. A respectable plantation contained a cotton gin for separating seed from lint and a press for baling the cotton for market (or, in the case of a rice plantation, one or more threshing mills) and sometimes a sawmill and gristmill. These services were usually available at bargain rates to smaller farmers in the local area.

This economic system left scant room for urban business enterprise. Conventions of Georgia merchants often observed "that we furnish nearly all the articles of export in the great staples of cotton, rice and tobacco. . . . Yet, with all of this in our favor by nature, we employ the merchants of the northern cities as our agents in this business."[26] The South provided the bulk of the nation's exports—enough to keep fleets of merchant ships busy hauling them to Europe—but the region imported very little, thereby providing no cargo for the return voyage. Revealingly, the South did not become the entrepôt for goods to be sold in the North and West; instead, Georgia products were collected in New York to exchange for European goods to be mostly marketed in the North. From New York to Liverpool and beyond, financing, transporting, insuring, and manufacturing the cotton and other goods produced in the South played a vital role in the economy of the northern Atlantic community.

The lack of markets that thwarted urban commercial activity was equally injurious to the laboring class. As Ulrich B. Phillips stated, "Free workingmen in general, whether farmers, artisans or unskilled wage earners, merely filled the interstices in and about the slave plantation."[27] Unneeded slave artisans were often hired out in the towns, thereby decreasing skilled wages and stifling the growth of craft industry. The state legislature occasionally enacted laws purporting to protect artisans from slave competition, but they were ineffective and do not appear to have been enforced.

The economic system stunted public services as well. The self-contained plantation had little need for governmental services. A planter's most valuable property was mobile, and, in fact, planters often did move their slaves to fresher lands to the west. Consequently, large property owners had less stake in community welfare projects than they might otherwise have had. The great majority of poor people were slaves dependent on a master's paternalism rather than on public assistance, and indigent whites normally turned to kinsmen in time of need. Even law enforcement relied heavily on private rather than state action.

The chief recipients of public aid were railroads and banks, the two institutions most helpful for marketing cotton. Of the approximately $26 million spent on railroad construction, about half came from public sources. The state purchased stock in private railroad companies and built its own line, the Western and Atlantic, between Chattanooga and Atlanta, and local governments, especially Savannah, invested heavily in railroad development. Georgia also created its own central bank to serve as the state's financial agent, to stabilize the public currency, and to make long-term loans more readily available to planters and other men of property. Although the state bank closed its doors in the 1850s, these expenditures—particularly railroad construction and the servicing of debts contracted for railroad construction—accounted for most of the state's budget during the antebellum era. Less than 20 percent of state disbursements went to public welfare projects.

Most notably, Georgia schools lagged far behind educational development in the North. The motives for public school progress outside the South—promotion of social stability, the "Americanization" of immigrants, the preparation of students for their differing roles in a diverse society—were of scant consequence in a stable, rural society that attracted relatively few nonsouthern immigrants and whose leadership evidenced little enthusiasm for mass education. Periodically the legislature debated the issue. In 1835 the United States government disposed of its surplus funds by dividing them among the states. Georgia received more than $1 million, and in 1837 the legislature chose to invest part of this largesse in the creation of a common school system. Hardly had the legislature acted before the panic of 1837 touched off a general depression that quickly cooled legislative ardor. The general assembly not only repealed the common school law but virtually eliminated expenditure for education. In 1858 the state increased educational appropriations, but this effort was swept away by the Civil War.

Georgia parents relied primarily on "old field schools" to provide their children with rudimentary elementary education. Often located on unused fields, these schools were private, community enterprises; local people "built the school house, hired the teacher, furnished the children [and] paid the bills."[28] White scholars "of indigent parents," at least those who lived in counties that recognized the existence of poor people and whose parents were not too proud to accept public charity, received meager allotments from the poor school fund. Those white boys and girls who enrolled in the old field schools put in five to ten months of desultory attendance for two to three years. Substantial numbers of white children apparently grew up with little or no acquaintance with a classroom, and, of course, almost one-half of Georgia youngsters received no schooling because Georgia law prohibited the education of blacks. The children of affluent parents normally continued their education at private academies, which offered three or four years of study beyond the elementary old field school level. The better academies were usually of high quality; they were also expensive, charging perhaps $100 for tuition and board. The paucity of public school facilities was indicative of the level of governmental services generally.

Public education was only one area in which Georgia and the South lagged behind the rest of the nation. Ulrich B. Phillips, whose *American Negro Slavery*, published in 1918, served for many years as the standard work on its subject, concluded that plantation slavery obstructed industrialization, urbanization, and immigration. Writing sixty years later, economist Gavin Wright agreed that "slavery retarded the mechanization of agriculture, the development of manufacturing, the emergence of cities, and immigration into the South."[29] These points seem well established.

Not so well established are the attitudes and values of southern society. Certainly Georgians generally were profit-conscious, and clearly they shared cultural values with other Americans. Yet, at the same time, there is truth in Eugene D. Genovese's observation: "The South had a market economy; it did not have an essentially market society."[30] If Jacksonian Democracy marked the coming of age of a laissez-faire society and an ideology of free labor individualism that appealed to independent artisans, farmers, and businessmen in the North, then quite obviously the social relations of a slave labor system and a social structure in large measure shaped by slavery were not likely to produce a laissez-faire society or a free labor ideology in the South. Instead the social order and accompanying ideology called forth by slavery stressed paternal relationships, patriarchal values, and a static society—that is, in basic ways, a "premodern" society led by a socially traditionalist planter elite.

Patriarchy, paternalism, and deference were crucial elements of Georgia social relations. To many Georgia planters, northern capitalism, with its pitiless exploitation of labor and its tendency to reduce human relations to money exchanges, was the system that deserved condemnation, not southern slavery. Place, defined by race, sex, consanguinity, and class, governed—or, more accurately, served as the ideal that ought to govern—personal associations, and an individual's place determined one's obligations and responsibilities. Gunnar Myrdal summarized the proslavery view: "Slavery was only part of a greater social order which established an ideal division of labor and of responsibility in society between the sexes, the age groups, the social classes and the two races."[31] In practice the system of necessity made room for talent, individualism, and nonconformity, but, in its ideology, Georgia differed fundamentally from the free-labor North. By 1861 a thoughtful Georgian could write to his planter father that "in this country have arisen two races which although claiming a common parentage, have been so entirely separated by climate, by morals, by religion, and by estimates so totally opposite of all that constitutes honor, truth, and manliness, that they cannot longer coexist under the same government."[32]

Georgia and its leadership had much in common with other "third world" plantation societies, and few indigenous barriers obstructed the paternalistic and hierarchical values that grew from master-slave relationships. The socioeconomic system stunted the development of an independent bourgeoisie as it did a self-conscious proletariat or even a thriving class of skilled artisans. The Athens textile mill owner turned congressman who opposed the tariff on the grounds that his mill profits were unreasonably high was hardly a typical Georgia businessman; yet, merchants, factors, businessmen, industrialists, and professional people were all clearly subservient to plantation agriculture. Working-class whites had little opportunity to develop a sense of class-consciousness in a society where labor exploitation normally meant whites profiting from the labor of blacks. Northern free-labor ideology received scant hearing, particularly after the coming of the antislavery movement encouraged Georgia leaders to oppose the dissemination of Yankee viewpoints.

The most obvious source of potential dissent from planter leadership was the small farmer. With declining opportunities for climbing into the planter class, many yeomen had little or no immediate stake in slavery, and north Georgia yeomen were often outside the direct influence of plantation agriculture. This situation troubled at least a few members of Georgia's established leadership and became an openly expressed concern during the secessionist crisis of 1860–61. Following the election of Abraham Lincoln, Governor Joseph E. Brown felt called upon to point out to slaveless whites that, should the Republicans abolish slavery, blacks would "come in competition with their labor, associate with them and their children as equals . . . —claim social equality with them—and ask the hands of their children in marriage."[33] Before this time such dire developments surely seemed remote, as did the prospects for small farmers to serve as the social base for a serious challenge to planter leadership.

Following the Yazoo land scandals of the late eighteenth century, white Georgians had arrived at a consensus on major issues. Land should be taken from Indians; cotton and rice should be championed; and, above all, slavery should be advanced and defended. The promotion and protection of Georgia interests came to mean the advancement of the interests of planters. Such a political environment gave rise to vigorous partisan rivalry, and for the first and only time in Georgia history two relatively evenly balanced political coalitions sustained two-party competition for more than a decade. The two parties—Democrat and Whig—were in complete agreement on vital issues, and their policy differences were more tactical than substantive, but personal and partisan rivalries generated heated electoral contests and considerable sound and fury.

At the same time the antebellum political system did signify fundamental political conflict. The southern planters and their politicians were a formidable counterweight to the growing power of northern industrial capitalism. Although Georgia Whigs, such as Robert Toombs, supported modestly protective tariffs, they expected in exchange northern Whig support for southern interests. Georgia Democrats, such as Howell Cobb, identified their own ambitions and those of their region with the state rights and proslavery views of the national Democratic party. Both groups opposed the emergence of a government devoted to the expansion of large-scale northern business and industry—a significant precursor to sectional warfare.

Georgia was the fifth state to secede from the union in 1861, and it ultimately became a major battleground. The state provided some

120,000 men to the Confederate armies and was a central source for the armaments and provisions needed to supply them. Four of the Confederacy's eight large arsenals were located in Atlanta, Augusta, Columbus, and Macon, and the Augusta powder works was for a time the world's largest powder mill. Georgia shops and factories spewed forth cannons and freight cars, bowie knives and boots, powder and pistols, armor plate and uniforms, and a variety of other military materiel. By the middle of the war the Confederacy was able with its own production to supply the southern armies, at least at a spartan level.

Such a performance was remarkable. An agrarian, essentially premodern society virtually overnight created a substantial war industry. Unlike the North, the South did not rely primarily on private enterprise to accomplish this feat. The Confederate government expanded its own arsenals, built its own factories and enterprises, and maintained control of the resulting productive capacity. The South, as Raimondo Luraghi has observed, effectively leaped "over the capitalist era into a completely new era, a sort of state socialism"; and it did so without creating a new entrepreneurial class, seriously altering the social order, nor abandoning its paternalistic ideology.[34]

The Civil War brought hard times to Georgia, and they did not dissipate with the termination of hostilities. Willard Range, the historian of Georgia agriculture, labeled the post–Civil War period "the long Depression of 1865 to 1900."[35] In 1860 an average free adult male Georgian owned property worth about $4,000, approximately twice the estate possessed by a typical nonsouthern male. Ten years later the wealth of an average Georgia white man was somewhat more than $1,400 in constant 1860 dollars, well under half what it had been a decade before and only 70 percent the nonsouthern average. The average wealth of all Georgia males—white and black—was approximately $1,000, less than half the nonsouthern average.

Even the elements turned hostile. Severe weather conditions contributed to poor harvests, particularly in 1866 and 1867 when only federal, state, and private relief measures prevented widespread starvation. "The distress among the poor," former Governor Joseph E. Brown reported in early 1867, "is now very great, owing to the ravages of war and the severity of the drought last summer."[36] Robert Toombs, returning to Georgia in the spring of 1867 after a brief period in exile, found "bankruptcy & ruin widespread throughout the land [and] the presence of physical want absorbing the time and thoughts of the people."[37] As if to compensate for the previous year's drought, the growing season during 1867, another observer lamented, was marked by an "extraordinary quantity of rain" that "to a great extent destroyed the crops and the conditions of our people have, therefore, not been improved since the war."[38]

But economic problems were far more fundamental than these observations suggest. It took Georgia farmers two decades to bring cotton production back to 1859–60 levels. By that time, of course, the rural population had increased, and per capita agricultural production continued to lag. Thirty-five years after the Civil War, two economic historians have calculated, Deep South agricultural production was still 25 percent less per person than it had been in 1859.[39] The standard of living of Georgia's people accurately reflected the state's dismal record in agriculture. In 1880 Georgia's per capita personal income was 49 percent of the national average; in 1900 it was 42 percent. As Robert Toombs observed in 1879, "Pecuniary affairs grow no better but rather worse if possible. In this county [Wilkes] more people have gone under, dead broke, this winter than in any previous one in its history. We have reached the point when nobody prospers and no business pays."[40]

Georgia's economic woes were in part the result of the virtually total lack of capital in the state. Slave emancipation accounted for most of this loss. Some observers argued that emancipation simply transferred ownership from masters to the blacks themselves and consequently "nothing valuable has been destroyed."[41] Though in a sense true, this statement ignored the fact that slavery had absorbed an enormous amount of the entire society's investments. On top of this was the collapse of Confederate currency, the disappearance of some $25 million that Georgians had invested in Confederate bonds, the debasement of land prices, and the extensive destruction caused by the northern invasion during the final year of the war. Such massive losses left Georgia devoid of the financial resources that economic reconstruction would have required.

While Georgians were in revolt, northern Republicans enacted a hard money banking system, a high tariff, and other "reforms" to promote the interests of bankers, industrialists, and merchants to the North at the expense of the less developed sections to the South and West. Antebellum plantation prosperity had obscured the southern economy's overwhelming reliance on foreign markets and had masked the extent to which it had developed a dependent colonial economy that produced raw materials and provided little home market for domestic manufacturing. The new system of currency and credit largely ensured that Georgia would remain a capital-poor state, and the new tariff policy undermined the South's foreign markets. Additionally, postwar railroad construction bound the debilitated Georgia economy to the flourishing North. These developments transformed the South into a colonial appendage of the North.

They also help to explain Georgia's failure to build upon and expand its wartime economic development. The Confederate war effort had provided an insatiable market, and the Georgia economy had responded. The collapse of the Confederacy had also meant the collapse of consumer demand, and the state's postwar poverty prevented the emergence of a domestic civilian market. Federal government policies ratified these arrangements. The more developed northern economy and its government contributed to "the long Depression of 1865 to 1900," but Georgia also had profound social and economic problems that were not directly related to outside forces.

Despite its impressive wartime performance, the Georgia economy remained primitive. Cotton and slavery had created a society in which the most successful members were overwhelmingly concentrated in staple crop agriculture, the vast bulk of the white and black population was not only propertyless but uneducated and unskilled, industrialists were few and merchants adept mainly in the collecting and marketing of cotton and rice, the skilled work force was not only small but possessed of a longstanding rivalry between those who were formerly slave and those who were not, consumers had never purchased much and after the Civil War could afford little, and the established leadership remained committed to coercive forms of labor control and to a stable, hierarchical, and paternal social order.

To be sure, some people benefited from the disruptions of the 1860s. Black Georgians made genuine if limited gains in the immediate postwar years. Even in the poverty-stricken countryside, blacks were materially better off as free workers than they had been as slaves. Making impressive use of their new-found freedom, black Georgians successfully resisted the reimposition of plantation routine. Planters, understandably, endeavored to restore accustomed procedure, substituting wages for ownership, these often to be paid in substantial part in the form of food from the plantation corncrib and smokehouse and a small share of the crop when harvested. Blacks opposed the continuation of gang labor and refused to work slave hours. Particularly, black families demanded that women and children have greater freedom from routine field labor.

Following the poor cotton crops in 1865, 1866, and 1867, planters increasingly accepted a tenancy system. A variety of arrangements existed, but a growing number of tenants farmed a portion of the landlord's acres in exchange for a share of the crops. Landlords initially endeavored to limit workers to slave-labor returns, offering only a tenth or a sixth of the crop. The former slaves insisted on a larger percentage, and the division soon came to be thirds—one-third for labor, one-third for land, and one-third for mule, equipment, and housing—and within a decade after the war became a fifty-fifty split with labor alone receiving half. These changes in plantation organization and produce allocation appear to have been in large measure a direct result of the enhanced bargaining power of black workers.

Blacks succeeded in escaping plantation routine and in achieving a measure of personal freedom. As tenants farming an allotted acreage, they enjoyed more leisure than slave practices had permitted, and this was partially true of women and older children. During Reconstruction, Georgia Republicans seem generally to have viewed these developments with optimism. In the opinion of a Yankee abolitionist whose missionary zeal and greed for cotton profits brought him to Georgia during Reconstruction, sharecropping would "gradually" lead to "the system of self-reliant labor, which has accomplished so much for the northern people."[42] The Radical Republicans, during their brief period of power in Georgia, made no effort to reform the emerging system. Yet, beyond the early years, black economic progress was severely limited. Some black families did acquire land, but the results were not impressive. In 1900 blacks comprised 47 percent of Georgia's population and owned less than 4 percent of the agricultural acreage.

The defeated and demoralized planters had difficulty dealing with their newly assertive black workers. Howell Cobb was "thoroughly disgusted with free negro labor," and his overseer agreed: "Accordin to promis I write you to inform you how the negrows or freedmen air getting on. tha dont doo as well as tha did."[43] Yet the planters had the land, the law, and, by 1868, the Ku Klux Klan, and they soon regained control of the labor force.

Land ownership remained highly concentrated, and the majority of Georgia planters appear to have come through the upheaval of war and Reconstruction with land titles intact. The coastal rice plantations, with their complex and centralized drainage systems, did not lend themselves to sharecropping, and they never recovered from the destruction of slavery. Many of the Sea Islands ultimately passed into the hands of wealthy northerners to serve as winter retreats.* Along the

---

*The transformation of Jekyll Island from a plantation to the world's richest hunting, fishing, and sporting club—its exclusive membership composed of northern capitalists—was a capsule history of Georgia's relations with the union during the post-

coast, the former slaves often benefited from the decay of the plantations. More blacks became landowners in coastal Georgia than anywhere else in the state. Elsewhere the plantations survived and the
planters adjusted to new conditions. They divided their plantations at
least in part among tenants, and many opened their own commissaries
to "furnish" the families who worked the land. Reacting to black independence and to the politics of Reconstruction, they led the counterrevolution that restored something akin to the old social order.

In the wake of disastrous crop harvests in 1865 and 1866, the state
legislature enacted laws to stabilize labor conditions in the countryside. One law permitted planters "a lien upon the crops of their tenants" for goods "furnished such tenants, for the purpose of making
their crops." Merchants might take liens "upon the growing crops of
farmers for provisions furnished," but tenants could assign crop liens
only to their landlords.[44] The crop lien law was a frankly reactionary
effort to restore the practices of the antebellum years when planters
allotted a weekly ration to slaves, and yeomen often purchased on
credit goods at country stores to be paid for in cotton at harvest time.

The legislature also turned its attention to blacks who sought their
future outside agriculture. Two laws related to vagrants, defined among
other ways as "persons wandering or strolling about in idleness." The
punishment for adult vagrants was a maximum of one year's imprisonment, to be served either on a public roads work gang or on the
property of a private employer appointed by the court. A second law
provided that underage vagrants be bound out to responsible private
individuals.[45]

To restrict free labor practices further, the legislature prohibited
"enticement." In Georgia, it became a crime to entice a laborer "in the
employment of another, for and during his term of service, either by
offering higher wages, or in any other way whatsoever."[46] Counties
were permitted "to hire out, or bind out" convicts "to contractors on
the public works, or to individuals," and arson, horse or mule theft,
"burglary in the night," and "insurrection" became capital crimes.[47]

After 1866 government officials offered such encouragement to social stability as was deemed useful. In 1869 Georgia began leasing
state convicts to private individuals and corporations, and later legis-

Civil War era. The blacks who had provided plantation labor became the servants,
cooks, and groundkeepers at the "millionaires' village." Here William McKinley plotted presidential reelection strategy in 1899, and northern bankers in 1910 wrote the
first draft of the Federal Reserve Act which "reformed" the nation's monetary system.

lation provided for misdemeanor convicts to be turned over to any private citizen who paid the prescribed fine. An emigrant agent law levied prohibitive fees on anyone who encouraged laborers to migrate in search of economic opportunity outside the state. In the early twentieth century, the legislature made violation of a lien contract "prima facie evidence" of fraudulent intent and thereby a criminal rather than a civil crime. Most of these laws remained intact—sometimes in modified form—at the beginning of World War II.

The organization of the Ku Klux Klan was a direct reaction to the politics of Reconstruction and, perhaps less directly, to the independent behavior of blacks. The Radical Republicans through their Union League endeavored to organize black voters and often supported black candidates, thereby threatening to create a power base from which the former slaves might resist white domination. The planters and their allies responded with the Ku Klux Klan. John B. Gordon, a Confederate war hero and the apparent Grand Dragon of the Realm of Georgia, accurately described the Klan as "a brotherhood of the property-holders." In some instances, according to Gordon, "overseers had been driven from plantations, and the negroes had asserted their right to hold the property for their own benefit."[48] Klan terror decimated the Union League and destroyed any lingering black hopes that emancipation meant freedom.

The new system based on share-tenancy and country store credit rapidly became almost as inflexible and sometimes as exploitive as the slavery regime it succeeded. The coercive elements upholding this pattern of social and economic dependence, in the words of historian Pete Daniel, "came from the law, which increasingly tightened its grip on workers; from the contract, which became a year sentence on a few acres; from violence, which gave object lessons to those who objected to the system; and from illiteracy, which placed the worker at the mercy of the literate and kept him from seeking jobs that required more skill than plowing, hoeing, and picking."[49]

In a well-known passage in *The Hamlet*, William Faulkner described Will Varner, who "was the chief man of the county."

> He was the largest landholder and . . . the fountainhead if not of law at least of advice and suggestion to a countryside. . . . Judge Benbow of Jefferson once said of him that a milder-mannered man never bled a mule or stuffed a ballot box. He owned most of the good land in the county and held mortgages on most of the rest. He owned the store and the cotton gin and the combined

grist mill and blacksmith shop in the village proper and it was considered, to put it mildly, bad luck for a man of the neighborhood to do his trading or gin his cotton or grind his meal or shoe his stock anywhere else.[50]

Such men lived in Georgia. James Monroe Smith, in fact, would have put Will Varner to shame. "Colonel" Smith's plantation meandered over thirty square miles of Oglethorpe and Madison counties. In addition to as many as ten thousand acres in cotton and other crops, a thousand head of cattle, and three hundred swine, the plantation contained a cotton gin, a dairy, a fertilizer factory, a cottonseed oil mill, a brickmaking factory, sawmills, a planing mill, separate gristmills for grinding corn and wheat, a blacksmith shop, a woodworking shop, and two stores selling $75,000 to $100,000 in products annually. Colonel Smith built his own railroad spur to connect his operation to a main line near Athens. He incorporated his own town, Smithonia, with post office, hotel, and other buildings. Vendors, drummers, and the like stayed at his hotel, although the town's other residents were mainly white foremen and other employees on the plantation.

The twelve hundred or more blacks lived in settlements scattered around the plantation, where several churches and six schools for black children provided services. Colonel Smith did not like his black families drinking, gambling, or leaving the plantation; he twice faced federal peonage charges for allegedly holding workers against their will. But, as the Oglethorpe County newspaper boasted in 1891, "what Colonel Smith doesn't know about the nigger is not worth learning."[51] In addition to his other tenants and hands, Colonel Smith worked convict labor. Like many large landowners, Smith "bought" hands convicted in area courts for misdemeanors, usually working forty or more. Unlike most other planters, Colonel Smith leased large numbers of state felony convicts, often employing one hundred or more at Smithonia.

Like other planters, Colonel Smith invested excess profits in a variety of enterprises. He owned stock in some twenty-five area banks and served on the board of directors of one. He held controlling interest and was president of an Athens newspaper. Shortly before his death in 1915, he became president of an Athens oil and fertilizer company and purchased a cotton mill. Colonel Smith served several terms in the state legislature, was chairman of the Oglethorpe County Democratic Executive Committee, and was a member of the state Democratic Party Executive Committee. As in William Faulkner's

Yoknapatawpha County, Mississippi, it was considered bad luck for any man in the area to aspire to political office or to almost anything else without first seeking Colonel Smith's advice.

No other Georgia planter could match the scale of Smith's operations, but many ran impressive enterprises. A study of seventy counties in the Georgia plantation belt in 1910 reported more than sixty-six hundred plantations, almost seventeen hundred of which had ten or more tenants. These seventeen hundred households owned nearly two and a half million acres, worked almost twenty-six thousand tenant families, and employed substantial numbers of hired hands.[52] Another turn-of-the-century survey located four thousand planters who possessed cotton gins.[53] Larger plantations usually had their own commissaries and often contained country stores, sawmills, and other enterprises.

A few planters, such as Colonel Smith, began farming in the post–Civil War period. Some, such as Thomas C. Drake, accumulated funds in other endeavors and returned to restore the old home place. The Drake plantation in Emanuel County in east-central Georgia, a thriving enterprise in the 1850s, had been divided among several heirs in the 1870s. After prospering in the timber and turpentine business, Thomas Drake restored and expanded the plantation in the early twentieth century. By 1910 Drake had established a seven-thousand-acre plantation complete with two sawmills, cotton gin, gristmill, turpentine still, blacksmith shop, country store, and plantation commissary. He invested in railroads and other enterprises, was the leading stockholder in the local bank, and served on the Emanuel County commission. Most successful planters, such as David Dickson, apparently weathered the Civil War and emancipation and reorganized their operations. In 1870 Dickson's plantation occupied eight thousand acres and produced nine-hundred-bale cotton crops.

These enterprises rested squarely upon the existence of cheap and abundant labor. After emancipation black croppers and hands moved too frequently from one employer to another in a fruitless search for greater opportunity to permit a complete restoration of the antebellum paternal order. To some extent, as a recent study has argued, "the paternalistic ideal turned from a practical guarantee that most blacks would eat reasonably well into an abstract, impersonal, and often conveniently meaningless measure of the 'best interests of the colored people.'"[54] Yet important elements of the old ideology and social structure were salvaged from the wreckage of war, emancipation, and Reconstruction. Dependent on landlords for land, plantation commissaries for credit, and the planter-oriented white man's government for justice, most blacks settled into dependency status. Planters again spoke with a ring of conviction of "my niggers," and a customary identification of blacks was that they were so-and-so's "niggers." General John B. Gordon's daughter recalled late nineteenth-century social practices on the Gordon plantation: "As much as possible my father kept up the customs of the old slavery days at Beechwood."[55] An early twentieth-century planter voiced the reigning landlord viewpoint when he described his sharecroppers to a visiting journalist: "You've just got to make up your mind that you are dealing with children, and handle them as firmly and kindly as you know how."[56]

Just beneath the kindness, however, was the ever-present threat of violence. In an Erskine Caldwell short story, Christy Tucker was a black Georgia sharecropper who "wanted to get ahead." He and his young wife built a picket fence around their cabin, constructed a henhouse for their chickens, and made a purchase at another store to avoid going into debt at the plantation commissary. To the plantation owner, Christy was "one of these biggity niggers," one of those who "act like you think you're as good as a white man, don't you?" When the owner attempted to whip Christy, the black man resisted, and the white shot him. "The End of Christy Tucker"[57] was fictional; yet it explained a great deal about plantation race relations. The system made room for talented blacks who "knew their place," but self-confident and ambitious laborers who acted as if they thought they were as good as whites threatened the stability of the plantation economy. A black former sharecropper explained: "One thing you was working for was so the white man would say, 'He's a good nigger.' Then the others would let you alone."[58]

Georgia's population more than tripled between 1850 and 1920. Yet the bulk of people continued to live in rural areas, and the majority of the work force still labored in agriculture. The pressure on the washed and worn land was relentless. By 1910 there was a farm dweller for every fifteen acres of land, and by 1920 the average size of a Georgia farm was less than one-fifth what it had been in 1860.

Tenants occupied an ever-increasing majority of these farms. In 1880 owners still tilled more than half of Georgia's almost 140,000 farms; in 1920 more than two-thirds of 311,000 farms were occupied by tenants. In the early post–Civil War years, the bulk of tenants were black. By 1900 almost half of all tenants were whites, and the paternalistic order designed for blacks applied to them. White tenants fared somewhat better than blacks, having greater opportunities to commandeer the more desirable acres and often holding a tenancy status slightly more elevated than sharecropping. At any rate, tenant farms operated by whites were modestly more productive than those operated by blacks. But the similarities were far greater than the differences.

Black or white, virtually all tenants, many small farmers, and some substantial landowners relied upon planters and merchants for credit. Only a small minority of Georgia farmers could pay cash for food, fertilizer, and other goods necessary to bring in a crop, and the limited number of banks in the state confined their business to the more affluent. "The crop lien system," as C. Vann Woodward aptly phrased it, "converted the Southern economy into a vast pawn shop."[59] In Georgia during the 1880s merchants charged an effective interest rate of 60 percent. When the crops were gathered, they were turned over to the landlord or to the furnishing merchant who handled the sale and then "settled up." Certainly it was true:

> An ought's an ought
> And a figger's a figger
> All for the white man
> And none for the nigger.[60]

But many whites fared little better than blacks at selling time. If the crops brought more than the debt, a farm family could look forward to a merry Christmas; if not, the debt was carried over to the next year. Often the results were those described in a backcountry ballad:

> George Penny's renters they'll come into town.
> With their hands in their pockets and their head ahanging
>    down.
> Go in the store and a merchant will say,
> Your mortgage is due and I'm looking for my pay.
> It's a hard times in the country out on Penny's farm.[61]

The crop-lien system made merchandizing often more remunerative than farming and led to political conflict between merchants and planters. The 1866 lien law permitted only planters to "furnish" their tenants; country store owners were limited to dealing with independent farmers. In 1873 merchants lobbied successfully for a revised law allowing merchants to take crop liens from tenants. The planters struck back the following year, forcing repeal of the revision. Finally in 1875 planters and merchants compromised on a law allowing planters to assign their tenant liens to merchants. All three of these laws assigned to planters a special first lien on the tenants' crops for rent of the land, thus ensuring substantial protection for planters no matter who furnished the tenants.[62] Most planters apparently continued to supply their tenants as well as surrounding small farmers. Some landlords no doubt found it a convenience to turn the matter over to the merchants. For the ordinary Georgia farmer, however, it was only a debate over where—not whether—one owed one's soul to the country store.

Georgia law favored planters and encouraged them to become merchants. But in the north Georgia upcountry, planters and tenants were relatively few and merchants could compete on more equal terms. Railroad construction during the postwar years gave once isolated upper piedmont and mountain districts access to markets and made available the products of northern manufacturers. The increasing use of commercial fertilizer encouraged cotton production by causing the crop to mature more rapidly and thereby countering the areas's short growing season. As a result of these developments self-sufficient farming gave way to staple crop agriculture.

Storekeepers, cotton fields, and tenant farms proliferated through the uplands. Carroll County on the western edge of the upper piedmont had thirteen mercantile concerns in 1870 and seventy such firms in 1885. Cotton production in Carroll County increased from 4,000 bales in 1860 to more than 23,000 in 1900, but the number of farmers owning their own acres declined to 61 percent in 1880 and to 39 percent by 1900. The villages of Buford and Norcross in Gwinnett County near the center of the upper piedmont contained no general stores in 1870, but by 1885 Buford boasted thirteen and Norcross twelve. Gwinnett County's 2,400-bale cotton crop of 1860 expanded to almost 12,000 bales in 1880 and reached almost 31,000 in 1920. By that time only 36 percent of a once largely self-sustaining yeomanry still worked their own land. Jackson County in the eastern part of the state increased its cotton production from 1,600 bales in 1860 to 9,500 in 1880, 18,700 in 1900, and 37,500 in 1920. The number of landowning farmers fell from 77 percent in 1880 to 31 percent in 1900 and to 24 percent in 1920. The county's ten merchandizing firms in 1870 had grown to sixty-seven in 1885.

Such statistics charted the decline of independent small farmers into debt and dependence. As in the plantation counties, local private banks limited their loans to planters and merchants, leaving small farmers to find credit with the furnishing merchants. Rarely would a storekeeper extend credit to a farmer so improvident as to sacrifice good cotton acreage to corn, peas, and sweet potatoes. With continuing low cotton prices, many yeomen sank into an endless cycle of debt and often found themselves working the family acres that now belonged to someone else. As a hill country poet lamented:

> We worked through spring and summer,
>     through winter and through fall;
> but the mortgage worked the hardest and
>     the steadiest of them all . . . [63]

Particularly hard-pressed were young people attempting to get their start in farming; they were fortunate to have any other choice but to become tenants. Even the storied mountain craftsmen found the factory-made items that lined general store shelves to be formidable and sometimes crushing competition.

The principal beneficiaries of the economic transformation in the uplands were the successful merchants. To be sure, many of the country stores in northern Georgia, as elsewhere in the state, were small, poorly financed enterprises that normally operated on the edge of bankruptcy. One study of six counties found that of thirty-eight stores opening in 1870, only twenty-one still operated at the end of the decade.[64] But the more fortunate merchants discovered ample opportunities. Through foreclosures and investments, merchants often became substantial landowners, although unlike the lowland planters whose acres were normally adjoining, the landlords of the uplands usually possessed parcels of land scattered through the countryside. Like planters to the south, north Georgia merchants also expanded into ownership of sawmills, gristmills, cotton gins, and other, often town-centered, enterprises.

Social and political practices encouraged cotton culture, but individual Georgia farmers were not illogical in devoting their main effort to cotton. Agricultural economists have recently pointed out that cotton was probably the most profitable crop available,[65] and farmers at the time generally agreed. Given the soil and climatic conditions, cotton was the most reliable cash crop, and it promised—even if sometimes falsely—a money income that meant access to the shelves of the country and town stores as well as the social advantages of joining other countrymen on Saturday afternoon shopping excursions at the village or town. Diversified farms existed in Georgia, but it is yet to be demonstrated that they produced a higher return than did cotton.

The overall result of the ever-increasing acreage devoted to cotton was, however, to bind farmers to a static and impoverishing system. Once largely self-sufficient, farmers now imported from outside the state the bulk of work animals and a significant proportion of food products. Improved transportation contributed to Georgia's dependence on midwestern foodstuffs, a trend observable before the war, and so did the crop-lien system. Merchants obviously benefited by insisting that those who received credit devote their efforts to cotton rather than to livestock, poultry, corn, and sweet potatoes, because food products could be sold to the hapless debtor at a profit plus 60 percent interest. It seems apparent that dietary standards declined in the late nineteenth century. The small "one-mule" farms commanded limited credit, and malnutrition and protein deficiency became common. Pellagra and rickets thrived on a diet of corn meal, molasses, and salt pork.

For sharecroppers and farm laborers, housing was little different from that occupied by slaves during the antebellum era. "The one-room cabin is painfully frequent—now standing in the shadow of the Big House, now staring at the dusty road, now rising dark and sombre amid the green of the cotton-fields," W. E. B. DuBois reported following a tour through Dougherty County in southwestern Georgia in the early twentieth century. "Rough-boarded, old and bare, it is neither plastered nor ceiled, and light and ventilation come from the single door and perhaps a square hole in the wall."[66] Many yeomen farmers and more successful renters lived in "dog-trot" open-hall houses that, if modest, were roomier and considerably more livable than the one-room cabins described by DuBois.

It is easy, of course, to exaggerate the extent of rural deprivation. "The one-horse farmer of the past cannot be himself as we see him with modern eyes," wrote a north Georgia father and son in an effort to describe hill country rural life. "A brick house with a bath and a half is also a state of mind."[67] Many yeomen farm families lived comfortable and no doubt psychologically fulfilling lives despite the shortage of cash money and conveniences. Tenants learned to cope with their station in life, and for huge numbers of blacks and some poor whites tenancy represented material improvement when compared with antebellum life. A landless black in the early twentieth century pointed out: "On shares if you're a good farmer you try to be through laying by corn, cotton, and peanuts by July fourth. Then you set around and eat out the garden and go to church. In the summertime you fish a heap."[68] Planters, whether out of a sense of paternalistic responsibility or simply a desire to attract and retain a better class of tenants, not infrequently evidenced genuine concern for the welfare of their wards. Planters who failed to maintain some standing in the community and some personal relationship with their tenants might themselves become vulnerable. A recent study has reported that arson, especially the burning of gins, storehouses, and the like, was most common around "settling up" time in the fall and early winter.[69]

Despite the handicaps, a few blacks fared well in agriculture. In 1907 the Augusta *Chronicle* pronounced Cody Bryant of Newton County to be the "richest negro in Georgia." Bryant owned 1,650 acres of land, a cotton gin, and a sawmill and engaged twenty renters, thirteen wage hands, and eleven sharecroppers. He was, the *Chronicle* affirmed, "an excellent type of the antebellum negro."[70] In Dougherty County—the same county where DuBois found so many one-room cabins—Deal Jackson owned two thousand acres of land and ginned the first bale of cotton in the Southeast for more than a dozen consecutive years. But there was always a risk to being black and obviously successful. Bartow Powell, a planter, furnishing merchant, and cotton gin operator, died violently while driving through the town of Albany in his carriage. According to rumor, the unidentified murderer was "an envious white man."[71]

The first two decades of the twentieth century brought higher prices and comparative prosperity. Following the terrible years of the depression-wracked 1890s, cotton prices fluctuated upward, reaching the fabulous level of more than thirty-five cents a pound in 1919. Georgia even gained on the rest of the nation as per capita income increased from 42 percent of the national average in 1900 to 53 percent by 1920. The relative prosperity eased some of the burden of liens and tenancy. With more valuable crops, farmers were less likely to face the choice between debt and starvation or at least to have greater bargaining power with landlords and furnishing merchants. The inability of merchants and planters to dictate the terms of the lien probably accounts for the increase in the number of farms with gardens from less than half in 1900 to more than three-fourths in 1920. Similarly, the vaulting growth of tenancy leveled off after 1910. Yet the system, while becoming somewhat more bearable, remained firmly in place. The cotton rows consumed ever more of the state: about two and a half million acres in 1880, almost three and a half million in 1900, four and a half million in 1910, and more than five million in 1914. In that year Georgia produced 2,718,000 bales of cotton.

Long before, the original promoters of Georgia settlement had warned against a commitment "to some single crop" that would "take up all the Labours of their People, overstock the Markets, stifle the Demand, and make their Industry their Ruin." The admonition was ignored, and it came to pass.

# Chapter Three

## *Reconstruction: A Revolution*
## *That Failed*

The Civil War and Reconstruction disrupted the ideological unity that had lain at the base of Georgia politics and unleashed social convulsion and political conflict on a scale unknown since the revolutionary war era. Georgia whites divided sharply over the wisdom of immediate secession from the Union. Indeed, in the frantic political battles of 1860–61, a majority of rural voters apparently favored other alternatives. Only the heavy support for secession in the towns tilted the balance, and even then the fire-eaters might well have lost but for the effective leadership of Toombs, Cobb, Governor Joseph E. Brown, and most—though by no means all—of the Georgia political establishment.

At the end of the war in the spring of 1865, the state government was bankrupt, Atlanta was in ashes, transportation was in ruin, and famine stalked much of the area through which the Union army had passed. Bitter unionist whites blamed the Democratic party for the disastrous results of secession. The Yankee victories gave force to the Emancipation Proclamation, which was soon to be reinforced by the Thirteenth Amendment, and former slaves tested their new-found freedom and demanded further rights. The defeated ex-Confederates looked to the national capital to learn the additional consequences of rebellion and blacks the meaning of freedom.

Washington had no ready answers. The causes of the Civil War were complex, and northern war aims—beyond restoration of the Union— were often ambiguous. In part the war grew out of a struggle between northern capitalist elites and southern slaveholders for control of the national government. In part it was a conflict between northern free-labor ideology and southern paternalism that increasingly centered on the question of slavery in the western territories. In addition to such fundamental sectional conflicts, ethnocultural rivalries, differing concepts of local versus centralized governmental authority, the emotional hysteria of a long and costly war, and a variety of other tensions complicated decision making in the North. The war and the Thirteenth Amendment broke the national power of the southern planter class, and Yankee victories on the battlefields largely assured the ascendance of northern-oriented banking and tariff policies and a free-labor West open to homesteaders, speculators, and developers. The central issues of Reconstruction revolved around establishing barriers to the revival of planter power and ensuring that the reconstituted southern leadership accepted the Union victory.

President Andrew Johnson took a benign view of the matter. Johnson's presidential plan for reconstruction required Georgia and the other southern states to draw up new constitutions that abolished slavery, repudiated the Confederate state debt, recognized the supremacy of the Constitution, laws, and treaties of the United States, and rejected secession. Such a program left black southerners outside the pale, lacking civil, political, or economic rights, subject to whatever place in society whites chose to assign them. Johnson and his followers, including the northern Democrats, had little interest in expanding the authority of the national government in order to "reform" the South and were content for blacks to occupy a social status somewhere between slavery and freedom. Johnson's plan had the added virtue of permitting the rapid reentry of the South into the Union and thereby providing much needed white southern congressional reinforcements to counter the rising power of the Radical Republicans. For two years after Appomattox, President Johnson directed Reconstruction.

The motives of the congressional radicals have been much debated, and their peculiar blend of millennial idealism, bloody-shirt animosity, and spoils-politics partisanship creates interpretive problems. Yet just as Johnson represented the conservative version of northern war aims, the radicals epitomized a more extreme position. Fearing that Johnson's program would permit southern planters to reestablish dominance by imposing a modified form of slavery, the radicals demanded nationally protected political and civil rights for blacks. In the short term black enfranchisement would produce Republican congressmen and dam the flood of southern Democrats to Congress; in the long term it promised to encourage a free-labor capitalism that would make the South more like the North and promote a Republican version of national harmony. In the spring of 1867 the congressional radicals gained control of policy and launched their program.

While acrimonious conflict between the president and Congress raged in the national capital, Georgians attempted to restore economic and social order at home. In May 1865 Union General James H. Wilson issued a proclamation removing "the rebel state authorities" and thereby relieving Georgians "from the bondage of rebel tyranny."[1] Shortly afterward President Andrew Johnson appointed James Johnson provisional governor. A Columbus lawyer and a unionist, Johnson proved to be an able if not particularly aggressive or inspiring governor. Under Johnson's guidance, Georgia whites elected a constitutional convention that recognized the abolition of slavery, repealed the state secession ordinance, acknowledged the supremacy of the national Constitution, and, after considerable debate, repudiated a war debt of more than $18 million that Georgia could not have afforded to pay anyway. Otherwise, the statement of fundamental law was generally a copy of the 1861 Confederate state constitution, and it limited the franchise to "free white male citizens of this State."

The convention issued a call for state elections, and in the absence of organized political parties the delegates nominated their own candidate for governor. Charles J. Jenkins, a prominent prewar unionist Whig who had served on the state supreme court during the war years, was an influential participant at the convention and ran unopposed in the election. In December 1865 the newly elected legislature convened, ratified the Thirteenth Amendment, and attended the inauguration of Governor Jenkins. Just afterward President Johnson recognized the now reconstructed government of Georgia.

During 1866 Governor Jenkins and the Georgia legislature endeavored to cope with the disruptions brought by war and emancipation. A series of laws relating to the crop-lien system, vagrancy, enticement, the leasing of convicts, criminal surety, and similar matters sought to restore order to labor relations. Other legislation aimed toward the reestablishment of social services for whites while generally ignoring blacks. One law authorized common schools for whites but made no mention of schools for blacks. The Georgia legislature did not enact comprehensive "black codes," but laws excluding blacks from juries and curtailing the testimony of blacks made clear that the legislature had no patience with equality before the law. To emphasize the point, both houses rejected the Fourteenth Amendment, which extended citizenship, due process, and equality before the law to black men. Earlier in the year the legislators had chosen Alexander H. Stephens, former vice-president of the Confederacy, and Herschel V. Johnson, a former Confederate senator, as Georgia's new United States senators. These developments, along with the more extreme action of some other southern state governments, provoked opposition in the North and strengthened the position of the Radical Republicans.

In the spring of 1867 the congressional Republicans seized control of policy by enacting over President Johnson's vetoes a series of Reconstruction laws. These measures restored martial law in ten southern states and extended to black southerners in those states the right to vote. In Georgia federally appointed registrars entered on the voting lists the names of 102,411 whites and 98,507 blacks. Although the registration seems to have been conducted fairly, the number of white males was surprisingly high, given Georgia's large wartime losses and the fact that several thousand former Confederates were disqualified from voting. The Reconstruction Acts required Georgia to hold a convention to write black suffrage into its state constitution, elect a state government on the basis of the new constitution, and ratify the Fourteenth Amendment. After accomplishing all of this, the state would once again be eligible for readmission to the Union.

The Republican goals were lofty, but so were the barriers blocking their fulfillment. Congress enacted its laws; President Johnson executed them; and in the South they were administered by Union army officers. Certainly the United States Army–Freedmen's Bureau apparatus served constructive functions, providing food to blacks as well as significant numbers of whites, building schools and hospitals for the former slaves, overseeing labor contracts signed by freedmen, and performing other services. Yet many of the military officers hardly qualified as social reformers, and, during the first year of congressional Reconstruction, President Johnson labored doggedly to undermine the radical program.

But however lax their enforcement, these belated Reconstruction requirements could only be regarded by many white Georgians as outrageous. Almost yesterday blacks had been slaves; suddenly they were freedmen; and now Congress demanded they be citizens of Georgia and the United States who would enjoy equality before the law and the right to vote. As a perceptive white Georgian informed an English visitor, "the people are mad at the niggers because they're free."[2] "I think most of the gentlemen felt as I did," a Georgia planter wrote, "that the negroes voting at all was such a wicked farce that it only deserved our contempt."[3] After all, Georgia had already been reconstructed. Governor Jenkins recommended "a firm but temperate refusal" to accept the new policy and "a patient, manly endurance of military government."[4] Not all Georgia whites shared these views, of course, but the majority of them and the overwhelming preponderance of their leaders did.

Against this background, Georgia Republicans launched a vigorous drive to organize the vastly enlarged Georgia electorate. The emerging Republican coalition—the notorious alliance of scalawags, Negroes, and carpetbaggers—was diverse and, as events soon demonstrated, deeply divided. For a time the Republicans achieved sufficient unity to dominate state politics and to initiate a reform program so wide-ranging that it threatened the state's tottering social and political foundations.

White unionists provided one source of Republican recruits. Almost half of the Georgia electorate had opposed immediate secession, and many continued to dissent after the state cast its lot with the Confederacy. As a Georgia private stated in a letter to his family in 1863, "I am this day as strong a Union man as ever walked the soil of Va. I would hate to desert but if I ever get a good chance I will be sure to do it."[5] During the height of the war, Georgia's most outspoken unionist, former Congressman Joshua Y. Hill, opposed Governor Joseph E. Brown and another secessionist candidate in the gubernatorial election of 1863. Hill received more than eighteen thousand votes, almost 30 percent of the total, and his strongest support emanated from the small farmer counties of the hills and mountains of north Georgia.

Wartime developments intensified unionism, particularly among the less affluent. Confederate law exempted from the draft anyone who purchased a substitute or who managed a plantation containing twenty or more slaves. In addition, Governor Brown excused from the draft state militia officers and civil government officials, encompassing thousands of able-bodied men unaffectionately known as "Joe Brown's pets." The rich, established, or well-connected could avoid the war, and even the many planters and their sons who chose to go off to fight left behind them a slave work force to provide for wives and children. But poor people had no such recourse, and their wives struggled desperately and often unsuccessfully to keep up the farms alone. Many were soon writing their husbands about hungry children and desolate conditions, a factor that helps to explain the Confederacy's high desertion rate. To these people it was "a rich man's war and a poor man's fight."

The rank-and-file scalawags were common people, especially mountain and hill country farmers, who had never been enthusiastic about the slaveholders' war and who as a result of it faced debt, foreclosure, and economic ruin. Although the precise number of unionist Republicans is unknown, veteran Georgia politicians consistently estimated their number at twenty-five to thirty thousand voters. Former Governor Joe Brown stated that Georgia contained thirty thousand "original Union men" who were "white Republicans" and ninety thousand "colored Republicans," who together formed a solid majority of the state's electorate.[6] The problem, of course, was to hold such an alliance together. George P. Burnett, a north Georgia unionist Republican, was a vigorous advocate of debt relief, homestead exemptions, and other economically radical measures; he also insisted that Georgia was a state "over whose destinies the white man shall preside."[7] A great many ordinary scalawags apparently shared similar views.

White Republican leadership came from a variety of sources. Joe Brown, an ardent secessionist and turncoat Democrat, shifted to the Republican party as the most realistic strategy for expediting Georgia's reentry into the Union and promoting economic recovery. Purblind southern resistance to Reconstruction, Brown argued, would strengthen the position of the northern radical extremists who favored permanent disfranchisement of southern rebels and confiscation of their property. As a leading rebel and a large property owner with further political ambition, Brown argued that it was wise to "agree with thine adversary quickly."[8] Only by coming to terms with the northern conquerors could the South achieve the political stability that would encourage the flow of capital and labor into the region.

Brown occupied something of a centrist position among "moderate" Republicans. He recognized the practical necessity of at least nominally accepting the Reconstruction measures, including black citizenship and suffrage although not "social equality." He also recognized the political necessity of appealing to common whites with a program of economic reform. Brown's position as a lobbyist for several bankers who favored relief presumably did not dampen his ardor. But numerous other white "moderates" were unwilling to accept even these concessions. Burnett endorsed the economic reform but not the political rights of blacks. Amos T. Akerman, an influential north Georgia unionist who like a number of other prominent Republicans migrated to Georgia during the antebellum era after being born and educated in the North, identified the Republican party with broadened opportunities for merchants and businessmen. Although acquiescing on the issue of black voting, he favored profoundly conservative policies on almost all economic or social issues and had no sympathy with permitting debtors to escape their responsibilities. Georgia scalawags were a vital part of the Republican coalition, but their leadership was deeply divided and often conservative.

For a time the Union League was the organization of loyalist whites. Spreading from the North into Georgia just after the war, the league was strongest in north Georgia and established Union clubs in the major Georgia cities. The secretary and then head of the league was Henry P. Farrow, a small-town north Georgia lawyer and a Republican moderate. Born and reared in South Carolina, Farrow absorbed his Union sentiments from his father and older brother, both of whom actively opposed the nullifiers and secessionists in that state. After the league began an aggressive drive to recruit black members (in segregated clubs), white membership waned. Leadership of the league remained oriented toward Atlanta and north Georgia.

The Equal Rights Association cooperated with the Union League, but it also served as a vehicle for transferring Republican party leadership to the downstate area and particularly to Augusta. Almost entirely a black organization, the association devoted much of its effort to developing black schools and educational opportunities, but it was also intensely political. Its leadership was more black-oriented and more radical than that provided by the unionist moderates. During 1867 the association and the Union League combined to form the organizational structure for the Republican party. Among the association's promoters were John Emory Bryant, who was white, and Henry M. Turner, a black minister. Bryant served as president of the organization and as editor of its newspaper.

In many ways John Emory Bryant was the quintessential Yankee carpetbagger. A native of Maine and the son of a Methodist minister, Bryant was personally ambitious, believed firmly in temperance, antislavery, and the Republican party, and distrusted Catholics. At the outbreak of war, Bryant was a schoolteacher in Maine, and he promptly enlisted. As a junior officer Bryant participated in the Union occupation of the Sea Islands along the southern coast of South Carolina and northern coast of Georgia in the fall of 1861. The planters fled inland, leaving the islands in the possession of the Union army and the blacks. For the remainder of the war, blacks farmed what was for a time their own land, attended northern-sponsored schools, and many served in the Union army. Bryant commanded a troop of black soldiers who raided the South Carolina countryside recruiting soldiers from among the slaves on inland plantations, tapping Confederate telegraph wires, and evading or clashing with Confederate patrols. The raids were extremely successful, and Bryant and his guerrilla band were legitimate minor theater war heroes.

Bryant's commanding officer on the Sea Islands was General Rufus Saxton. When Saxton was appointed head of the Freedmen's Bureau in Georgia after the war, he called Bryant back to the South to become a

Freedmen's Bureau agent in Augusta. Both men were advocates of black rights, and, as a result, both lost their jobs. General Davis Tillson replaced Saxton and fired Bryant in January 1866, the same month that the Equal Rights Association held its first convention. Freed from bureau duties, Bryant devoted his considerable energy to editing the *Loyal Georgian* and heading the association. Through the pages of the *Loyal Georgian*, Bryant's views received wide circulation, not because most Georgia blacks received the paper or were sufficiently literate to read it but because black ministers often read from it and other freedom publications following worship services.

On policy matters Bryant was a reluctant radical, espousing equal rights for blacks but also advising gradualism, cooperation with whites, and pursuance of education as preparation for citizenship. Like most other white Republicans, Bryant assumed that whites should provide leadership and guidance for blacks during the transition to freedom. Like most other carpetbaggers, Bryant never really understood Georgia. "The civilization, society and religion of the South," he later wrote, "were entirely unlike the civilization, society and religion of the North."[9] To him, Reconstruction "reform" meant making Georgia more like New England.

Henry M. Turner was, in his own words, "a minister of the gospel and a kind of politician."[10] Born the son of free black parents in South Carolina, Turner learned to read and write as a youth (despite a South Carolina law prohibiting it) and, after entering the ministry, attended school in Baltimore, where he excelled as a student. By the time of the Civil War, Turner was a highly successful pastor of a large African Methodist Episcopal church in Baltimore. Turner helped to organize the first black regiment to participate in the war and served as its chaplain. Like Bryant, he was an employee in the Freedmen's Bureau for a brief period after the war.

Ambitious and talented, Turner had long been frustrated by the limited opportunities that white society allowed black men. Reconstruction promised new vistas for blacks, and Turner threw himself into organizational work with enthusiastic determination. An able orator, he promoted Union League clubs and Equal Rights Association chapters while doing occasional duty as a lobbyist in Washington. He also was a leading organizer of the African Methodist church in the state. Politically, Turner was careful to espouse views that would not appear threatening to his white allies. Later events were to move Turner toward a more radical position.

The heart of black militancy lay in the coastal counties. General

William T. Sherman, while in occupation of Savannah, had issued a special field order that "reserved and set apart for the settlement of the negroes" the Sea Islands and the coastal area for thirty miles inland.[11] Thus for good reason the blacks considered the land they worked as their own and resisted when President Johnson ordered it restored to the planters. On three islands just below Savannah, blacks established their own government to maintain order and defend the land from whites. In addition to farming, they sold wood to passing steamers and marketed wild game and other food products in Savannah. When northern lessees rented the two largest of the three islands, the black residents refused to be dispossessed. The managers took possession only after the arrival of federal troops made further black resistance futile. The leader of this unsuccessful effort for autonomy was Tunis G. Campbell.

Born in New Jersey and educated in New York, Campbell worked as a hotel steward and became a minister in the Zion Methodist Episcopal church. Like Bryant, he served under General Saxton in South Carolina and became a Freedmen's Bureau agent. Assigned to the Georgia Sea Islands, Campbell proved to be an able organizer, and his wife and two sons taught freedmen's schools. Appropriately perhaps, Campbell and his family lived in a house that had once belonged to Button Gwinnett, the radical firebrand of revolutionary Georgia. After the black population lost most of its land and Campbell his job, the family moved to Darien in mainland McIntosh County, and Campbell turned his attention to radical politics. He soon became one of Georgia's three black state senators and a justice of the peace, and his willingness in the latter capacity to convict or to jail whites contributed to the confrontation politics that marked much of the coastal region.

Joining Campbell in the senate was Aaron A. Bradley from nearby Chatham County (Savannah). Whereas Campbell was reserved, almost professorial in manner, Bradley was bombastic, incautious, and sometimes a bit erratic; he possessed, in the language of a Macon newspaper editor, more "self importance and insolence than are to be found in any other little nigger extant."[12] An effective agitator, Bradley was, in the words of Savannah's mayor, "a notorious disturber of the public peace," and his "insurrectionary language" led to his arrest by Union military authorities and a short prison sentence.[13] Like Campbell, Bradley urged blacks to defend their land from the returning planters. As head of the Chatham County Union League, Bradley championed a program of land, citizenship, and suffrage, and the refusal of his militant followers to accept less than equal treatment led to occasional civil strife and the frequent presence of federal troops in the streets of Savannah. Born of a slave mother and a white father, Bradley had escaped to the North while a teenager. In New York, he worked as a shoemaker, received an education and apparently studied law, gained some local political experience, and served a two-year prison term for "seduction." Bradley, Campbell, and other militants were spokesmen for black equality, and they often offended their unionist allies.

Given the vast array of viewpoints represented by the Republican leadership, it is tempting to dismiss the entire movement as an aberration. Certainly the Republicans attracted perhaps more than their share of patronage seekers, railroad promoters, and political adventurers. They also enlisted a considerable number of reasonably well-known public figures. A former governor, several former congressmen, two past mayors of Atlanta, two past mayors of Rome, a former mayor of Augusta, and a number of prominent businessmen embraced the cause. And despite the chasm between a conservative unionist such as Amos Akerman and a black militant such as Tunis Campbell, it would be a mistake to regard Republicans as an undisciplined band hungry only for office. In addition to its internal differences, the party represented a fundamentally important political movement.

In the broadest sense Republicanism was a revolt from planter leadership. Angry unionists, militant blacks, conservative promoters of economic development, and even passed-over politicians shared a rejection of the old regime. Republicanism was a nationalizing movement that thrust often clumsily toward rapid development of the state's material resources and that sought to bring Georgia into closer conformity with northern free-labor practices. With planter dominance already under attack from the federal government, discontented elements in Georgia presented a further challenge at home. But how broad Republican goals were to be translated into policies toward newly freed blacks, hard-pressed yeomen, and disoriented businessmen raised vexing questions.

The Reconstruction Acts required Georgia to hold yet another constitutional convention, and it met in December 1867. Although the state capital was Milledgeville, the convention assembled in Atlanta because Milledgeville hotels and boarding houses refused to accommodate black delegates. The convention got its revenge by moving the capital to Atlanta. Most Democrats boycotted the election for delegates, so the convention was heavily Republican. Among the 165 delegates were Bradley,* Campbell, Turner, and 34 other blacks and Bryant and several other white carpetbaggers. Missing was most of Georgia's established leadership.

A New York journalist reported that "a more seedy looking body of men never assembled together in Georgia."[14] Governor Jenkins regarded it was a "mongrel convention."[15] After J. R. Parrott of Atlanta was elected president of the convention, a Rome newspaper wrote:

> Parrott in the Chair, Monkey on the floor,
> Scattered round the hall, five and twenty more,
> Hundred odd of white skunks, mean as they can be
> That's the *tout ensemble* of this menagerie.[16]

Yet because both blacks and ordinary whites were represented, it was the most democratic convention that had ever assembled in Georgia.

The constitution that emerged from the convention's deliberations was strikingly different from those of 1861 and 1865, and it fairly accurately reflected the emerging political strategy and the balance of interest groups within the Republican party. The "Augusta Ring" composed of Rufus B. Bullock, Bryant, Benjamin F. Conley, and Foster Blodgett led the dominant radical faction. Amos Akerman and the moderate Republicans opposed many of the radical measures, as did a band of conservative Democrats. The radicals controlled the convention, however, and wrote into the constitution their program of capitalist liberalism. The resulting constitution offered inducements to lower-income whites, blacks, and growth-oriented businessmen. In so doing it presented a formidable threat to traditional Georgia labor relations and social structure.

The relief clause in the constitution prohibited the state courts from recognizing virtually all debts contracted before June 1, 1865. During the war borrowers incurred debts in depreciated Confederate currency that creditors later demanded be repaid on the basis of vastly more valuable United States legal tender. With the repudiation of the Confederate state debt, there was perhaps some justification for forgiving all public and private debts. The homestead exemption pro-

---

*Bradley attended only part of the convention. When conservative delegates demanded that he be expelled from the convention because of his conviction and imprisonment while living in New York, Bradley struck back by questioning the moral and family integrity of two of his detractors. So injudicious were Bradley's remarks that even the other black delegates voted in favor of his expulsion for "gross insults."

vided further protection for debtors and small property holders by placing $2,000 in real property and $1,000 in personal property beyond the reach of court foreclosure. While enjoying some degree of general popular support, these measures primarily benefited yeomen and other ordinary whites.

Virtually no blacks had debts before June 1865, and few owned homesteads, but other constitutional provisions did recognize black demands. The document assured blacks citizenship, equal protection of the law, and suffrage, features that Rufus Bullock optimistically predicted would settle "a question which might have been a source of serious trouble for our children."[17] The constitution prohibited whipping as punishment for crime, a ban that had virtually exclusive relevance to blacks. A guarantee of property rights for married women broadened opportunities for another sorely neglected group. Other measures applied to the less privileged generally. Convention delegates provided protection for the rights of mechanics and laborers and promised "a thorough system of general education to be forever free to all children of the State." The latter provision was Georgia's first recognition of an obligation to provide educational opportunities for black youngsters.

The convention authorized vigorous public support for economic development. The constitution permitted loans to private corporations to promote construction of railroads and other "public improvements" and allowed towns and cities to invest in or contribute to similar projects. These provisions revived practices that had been common in the antebellum era but had fallen into disfavor as state debts mounted and had been banned in the constitutions of 1861 and 1865. "The foundation of all prosperity," Rufus Bullock proclaimed, "is the successful development of our internal resources."[18] State support for economic progress and mass education were "modernizing" reforms that promised expanded governmental activity, and convention delegates endeavored to create a more efficient and more centralized governmental structure. The constitution increased the terms in office for governor, state senator, and some judges and sharply limited the number of elected officials while broadening the appointive power of the governor.

This same tendency to favor efficiency over democracy was evident in the convention's decision to retain a poll tax as a prerequisite for voting. Henry M. Turner cast his ballot in favor of the poll tax, although he later confessed that "I made a great blunder in doing so."[19] Perhaps other radical delegates accepted the poll tax because of oversight or "inexperience," but the decision to omit any specific statement that blacks had a right to hold public office was deliberate. When Democratic delegates threatened to bolt the convention if such a guarantee was approved, the Republicans agreed not to press the matter. It was a compromise the radicals were to have future occasion to regret.

After drafting the constitution, Republican delegates met separately and nominated Rufus Bullock as their candidate for governor. Declaring the constitution to be their platform, the Republicans launched a rousing campaign designed to unite blacks and poorer whites. Republican campaign literature demanded: "Be a man! Let the slave-holding aristocracy no longer rule you. Vote for a constitution which educates your children free of charge; relieves the poor debtor from his rich creditor; allows a liberal homestead for your families; and more than all, places you on a level with those who used to boast that for every slave they were entitled to three-fifths of a vote in congressional representation."[20] In north Georgia Joe Brown and other Republican orators assured voters that the constitution did not authorize blacks to hold office; in south Georgia, some fifty black candidates campaigned for legislative seats with full Republican support. But this simplistic Republican chicanery appeared touchingly innocent when compared to the fury of the Democratic counterattack.

The Democratic candidate for governor was John B. Gordon. The son of an enterprising Missionary Baptist minister who was also a planter, a coal mine developer, and the owner of a fashionable mountain spa, Gordon experienced difficulty in finding his niche in life. He attended the University of Georgia but failed to graduate. He began law practice in Atlanta but failed to attract clients. He became a journalist at the state capitol but failed to prosper. By the time of the Civil War, he had returned home to manage his father's coal-mining operation and to build a modest local reputation as a fire-eating secessionist orator.

Gordon served in northern Virginia throughout the war and quickly made a reputation as a bold and competent officer. At Antietam in 1862, he was hit five times by rifle fire and for weeks lay near death; he recovered to gain recognition as one of the most capable of Lee's lieutenants. Gordon's troops occupied Gettysburg several days before the fateful Confederate attack on Cemetery Ridge, and Gordon commanded the rear guard on the long retreat out of Pennsylvania. He fought with competence and often with unusual valor at the Wilderness, Spotsylvania, and a dozen other battlefields. It was Gordon who led the last desperate Confederate effort to break the siege at Petersburg, and Gordon who again commanded the rear guard as Lee's defeated army staggered toward Appomattox. An able speaker, the state's best-known war hero, the scar made by a Yankee minié ball gracing his cheek, Gordon became the Democratic nominee for governor and the generally recognized leader of the state's Ku Klux Klan.

Gordon was head of the Democratic party, but its heart was Robert Toombs. After serving undiplomatically as Confederate secretary of state and near disastrously as another of the South's rather too numerous corps of political generals, Toombs returned to Georgia to vent his rage toward Jefferson Davis and to be arrested and almost court-martialed for treason because of a rabidly anti-Davis tirade that he delivered before a unit of the state guard. Just after the war, Toombs dashed out the back door of his house as a Yankee patrol with orders for his arrest arrived at the front. With a young traveling companion, he made his way through the north Georgia mountains into Alabama and ultimately to New Orleans, where he took a boat into exile.

Toombs returned to Georgia in the spring of 1867 just as radical Reconstruction was getting under way, and he returned unreconstructed. Although unmolested by the government, he refused to take an oath of allegiance. "I am not loyal to the existing government of the United States & do not wish to be suspected of loyalty," he stated.[21] As he later explained to an Atlanta journalist, the federal government "is a temporary concern at best."[22] While remaining a staunch Georgia Democrat, Toombs became increasingly hostile to both national parties. Writing to his friend Alexander Stephens about the national Democrats in the election of 1876, Toombs observed: "They want Tilden elected for the same reason that Falstaff rejoiced at Prince Hal's reconciliation with the old King—'Hal, rob me the exchecker.'"[23] Always a believer in government frugality, he grew suspicious of government activity generally. While Toombs was on his deathbed, a visitor remarked that the state legislature was in session. "Lord, send for Cromwell," Toombs replied.[24]

Back from exile, Toombs became increasingly active and influential in the state Democratic party. "General Toombs may be put down at the head of the party," Joe Brown was soon to observe. "He furnishes the brains to it, and it follows his bidding."[25] Toombs returned the compliment: "In this state governor Brown is the leader of the Radicals aided by all the political buccaneers whom the radicals can buy, the rank file are the great body of the negroes, Yankees, refugees & such other warps & floats as can be alarmed by the cry of confiscation, or bribed by the expectation of place or plunder."[26] Toomb's law partner and son-in-law Dudley M. DuBose was the organizer and apparent district leader of the most powerful Ku Klux Klan chapters in the state.

The Democrats were slow to react to the Republican challenge. During the summer of 1867 former Confederate Senator Benjamin H. Hill rallied the resistance in a series of speeches and public letters. In December 1867 the Democrats held a convention in Macon. Hill served as chairman of the convention, to which only about half of the state's counties sent delegates. Participants spent much of their time arguing about whether all Reconstruction collaborators were "criminals" or whether it would suffice merely to brand Reconstruction "a crime." Some Democrats opposed labeling all who did not oppose Reconstruction as "criminals" on the grounds that such action would needlessly affront white unionists. Ultimately, the delegates announced that Reconstruction was "a crime."

During the campaign Democrats and their newspapers fervently assailed the "nigger–New England" convention and its constitution, and Ben Hill insisted that any white man who voted the Republican ticket "should be driven from the white race, as Lucifer was driven from Heaven into a social Hell."[27] The Democratic strategy was to elect Gordon governor but to defeat ratification of the constitution, which would prevent the formation of a government for Gordon to head.

But if Democratic political strategy sometimes seemed less than farsighted, party leaders demonstrated impressive organizational inventiveness. Anticipating twentieth-century leftist movements in other underdeveloped areas, the Democrats created a public political organization—the Democratic party—and a clandestine terrorist organization—the Ku Klux Klan—both directed by the same people.[28] Although the Democrats appeared to be gaining in the closing days of the campaign, they had launched their campaign too late to destroy the organizational network the Union League and Equal Rights Association had provided the Republicans.

In April 1868 Georgia voters ratified the constitution, chose Bullock governor, and elected Republican majorities in both houses of the legislature. Bullock received 83,527 votes; Gordon won 76,356. The election returns indicated that Republican efforts to woo black and white common men were essentially successful. For the first time in history, black Georgians cast ballots, and they did so in impressive numbers. Lewis N. Wynne's study of the returns found that 75 percent of the votes for Bullock came from plantation counties, where virtually all

Republicans were blacks. North Georgia counties supplied more than 20 percent, and of necessity a major portion of these votes must have been cast by whites. Indeed Bullock fared best in north Georgia in the poorer counties that had the fewest black residents. As Bullock later observed, his victory resulted in significant part from "the steadfastness of the white Union men of the Mountain counties."[29] The remainder of the Bullock vote, less than 5 percent of the total, came from the south Georgia wiregrass counties.

In the wake of victory, leading Republicans exuded optimism. Even Joe Brown, who preferred a moderate political strategy that deemphasized class conflict and made a stronger appeal to merchants, businessmen, and progressive planters, expressed contentment with the Republican position. The party, Brown explained, had a "safe working majority" in the legislature, and the inauguration of the new administration "will secure the patronage and power of the State government," now substantially enhanced by the greater number of appointive offices provided by the new constitution. Additionally, the governor controlled the state-owned Western and Atlantic Railroad, which "when properly handled . . . is worth 1,000 to 1,500 votes in an election."[30]

The Bullock administration assumed office in July 1868. Over the next several weeks it compiled a creditable record. The legislature ratified the Fourteenth Amendment, approved bond issues for the support of railroad construction, and enacted a law putting into effect the homestead provision contained in the new constitution. Because the Radical Republican Congress had expunged the debtor relief section from the Georgia constitution, the legislature approved a new, though less encompassing, relief law.

Governor Bullock demonstrated a political boldness that by past Georgia standards was astonishing. He dismissed white supremacy with the observation that "it is too late now to argue that a native American has no rights because his complexion is not that of the majority." "All civilized men are citizens," he stated. Not for a hundred years would Georgia have another governor who denounced white supremacy. Bullock condemned slavery as "the old system of labor, which was a continual oppression to the owner as well as the owned," and he lauded free labor as more "efficient and reliable." He called for state-supported internal improvements and economic development. "With the increased quality of the staple which may be expected from our improved agriculture," Bullock informed the legislature, "we shall be able to develop our internal resources, build railroads, maintain our educational institutions and take rapid strides along the path of peace and plenty."[31] The notion of draining capital from plantation agriculture to finance capitalist development may or may not have been wise, but in Georgia it was certainly different.

It was little wonder that strife rather than legislative accomplishment soon directed the course of Georgia politics. The Republicans enjoyed solid majorities in both houses of the legislature, but neither party was able to enforce partisan discipline, and the Republicans were rent with internal divisions. The membership of the lower house included sixty-seven Radical Republicans, twenty-six moderate Republicans, and eighty Democrats; the senate contained twenty-seven Republicans and seventeen Democrats, with Republican members divided about equally between radicals and moderates. These alignments provided Republican party leaders with, at best, a bare working majority. The Republicans elected their candidate speaker of the house by a vote of 76–75, and Governor Bullock's choices for Georgia's two United States Senate seats failed to be elected when Republican moderates backed their own candidates and the Democrats supported the moderates. For one of the Senate seats, Joshua Hill, the unionist candidate for governor in 1863, defeated his old nemesis Joe Brown, who had Bullock's support, leading Toombs to observe that "there was political justice in making the earliest traitor defeat the worst one and break down the party."[32] Both Bullock's radicals and the Democrats maneuvered to improve their legislative positions.

While the legislature was being organized, Bullock insisted—correctly as it turned out—that a number of the newly elected Democrats were ineligible for office. The Fourteenth Amendment contained a section denying the right to hold office to those prewar officials who had taken an oath to defend the United States Constitution and then had betrayed the oath by supporting the rebellion. The purpose of this measure was to bar the return of the South's established planter leadership, thereby encouraging the emergence of "loyal" leaders. The Reconstruction Acts applied this provision to Georgia before the ratification of the Fourteenth Amendment. Bullock pointed out that some of the Democrats failed to meet these standards. Neither house of the legislature was anxious to purge the delinquent members, however, and General George G. Meade, who was military commander in the state, refused to intervene.

The Democrats focused their attack on the blacks in the legislature. There were three Negro senators and twenty-nine representatives. Arguing that the state constitution did not recognize the right of black citizens to hold office, Democratic legislators introduced resolutions questioning the eligibility of all black members. For the Democrats, this strategy had the dual advantage of focusing public attention on the issue of white supremacy and at the same time forcing the Republican moderates to confront the question. In September 1868, first the lower house and then the senate voted to cast out the Negroes (except for four mulatto house members who were effectively granted the status of honorary whites and permitted to remain). The legislature then voted to fill the newly created vacancies not by special elections but by awarding the seats to the candidates who had finished second in the April elections. In all cases the runners-up were conservative Democrats. The purge gave the Democrats control of the lower house. In these maneuvers most of the moderate Republicans supported the Democrats by either voting with them or abstaining (as did a group of north Georgia legislators who were radical on economic but not on social issues).

Hard upon the coup d'état in the legislature came the November 1868 general election. The presidential race took on major importance in Georgia when the national Democrats in their party platform branded the Reconstruction Acts as "usurpation, and unconstitutional, revolutionary, and void."[33] Georgia Democrats could now visualize the destruction of the radical program not only in the state but in the nation. Inspired by this vision, the Democrats launched their campaign to crush radical Republicanism. Meeting in Atlanta during the summer to nominate presidential electors, the party attracted the largest political audience that had ever gathered in the state.

The campaign tactics tested in the spring were perfected in the fall. The Democrats called for white solidarity on a platform of home rule and white supremacy; they appealed for black votes with noblesse oblige and barbecue. Georgia did not, of course, have a secret ballot, and, in the words of one harassed black belt Republican, "The white people . . . surrounded the polls and watched every man to see what kind of ticket he had."[34] The Ku Klux Klan encouraged loyalty to the Democratic ticket and vigorously discouraged Republicanism. The Freedmen's Bureau reported that during August, September, and October 1868, there were 142 "outrages" against blacks—31 murders, 48 attempted murders, and 63 beatings. These figures in all probability represented only a fraction of the actual violence committed during the campaign and they do not take into account the even more common economic and social intimidation. The Klan was not only of crucial importance in its own right, but it also served as a model and inspiration for local independent terrorist groups and for acts of violence by individuals.

Blacks and unionist whites fought back, but they were rarely successful. The Democrats had economic power, organization, and, when dealing with blacks, the enormous psychological advantage that grew out of paternalistic social relationships. The Klan, according to John B. Gordon, "was mainly confined to the soldiers of the army, men who had shown themselves plucky and ready to meet any emergency, and who were accustomed to command."[35] Even those who successfully resisted the terrorist teams often suffered. J. R. Holliday, a unionist planter and businessman, single-handedly with shotgun, pistol, and pocket knife drove away a band of twenty or more Klansmen carrying their dead and wounded as they fled. Soon afterward arsonists burned Holliday's mill house, cotton mill, gin house, and stored cotton.

Aaron Bradley and the militant Chatham County Union League confronted the Ku Klux Klan directly. A public "notice" to the "K.K.K. and all BADMEN" threatened: "If You Strike a Blow, the Man or Men will be followed, and the house in which he or they takes shelter, will be burned to the ground."[36] Election day in strife-torn Savannah bordered on civil war. Early in the morning a group of white workers attempted to move ahead of a group of blacks already waiting in line to vote. The blacks refused to be displaced, but election officials and police supported the whites. In the ensuing battle two blacks and one policeman died and several people were seriously wounded before the blacks were driven from the polling place. During the day the irrepressible Bradley scoured the Chatham County countryside encouraging blacks to cast their votes. When Bradley and an armed group of potential voters approached Savannah that afternoon, a white mob barred their path. That shoot-out resulted in the death of a prominent Savannah white and several injuries.

By this time, being an active Republican required great personal courage. During the constitutional convention of 1868, a Republican delegate from Maine was murdered, and just after the convention, a leading radical delegate was assassinated. Over the next years, three Republican legislators were murdered from ambush. Terrorist squads gunned down three Republican sheriffs, one of whom was maimed but survived. A number of Republican officeholders, including at least a dozen legislators, "refugeed" in Atlanta because they were afraid to return to their home counties. Threats were common and beatings frequent. Henry Turner was often threatened but apparently never physically harmed. In Augusta John Emory Bryant was assaulted in the streets, his dog was poisoned, and his family was ostracized. Aaron Bradley was charged with one of the election day killings and ultimately hounded from the state. Tunis Campbell fought on in McIntosh County until finally railroaded into prison and leased to a plantation as a convict laborer.

The Democrats won overwhelmingly. In April, Governor Bullock received 83,527 votes; in November Ulysses S. Grant polled 57,129. The Democratic vote in these two elections increased from 76,356 to 102,707. The Democrats did better virtually everywhere in the state than they had done in April; the bulk of the Republican loss came in the plantation counties. In some cases the effectiveness of the Democratic campaign was truly awesome. Columbia County, located in the old cotton belt near Augusta, cast 1,222 votes for Bullock in April and 1 vote for Grant in November. The Democratic vote increased from 457 to 1,120. Eleven counties reported no Republican votes at all.

The election results, the purge of the blacks from the legislature, and the general atmosphere of violence and intimidation that prevailed in Georgia forced the Republicans to confront the formidable nature of their opposition. The Republicans were attempting to compete within the generally accepted—if somewhat lax—rules of nineteenth-century American electoral behavior. The Democrats approached politics as a form of guerrilla warfare. If not all Democrats engaged in violence or cooperated with the Ku Klux Klan, most did not regard the Republican party as a legitimate opposition and condoned violence by more zealous partisans. After all, stated Robert Toombs, Republicans were nothing but "damn Southern traitors."[37] Joe Brown was accurate in substance when he informed Bullock: "The result of the late elections prove very clearly that the negro vote will not do to rely upon unless there is a white party in the locality of the election strong enough to give them the necessary moral support."[38] The search for a solution to this dilemma completed the breakup of the Republican party in Georgia.

Governor Bullock decided that only a return to martial law could restore order in Georgia. A month after the election, Bullock informed Congress that Georgia lacked "adequate protection for life and property, the maintenance of peace and good order, and the free expression of political opinion."[39] Throughout the following year Bullock worked steadily for a new Reconstruction of the state. The thought of yet another period of military rule threw Democrats into hysteria and angered most moderate Republicans. Bullock and his radical allies labored stubbornly on, lobbying in Washington, testifying before congressional committees, and generally attempting to focus the attention of national politicians on developments in Georgia, a process that the Democrats referred to as "Bullock's Slander Mill."

Governor Bullock was one of the most enigmatic men in Georgia's political history. A compelling person with sparkling eyes and a big red beard, he was described even by a bitter Democratic critic as "a large, handsome, social specimen of a man, pleasant-mannered, and well-liked."[40] Henry W. Grady, a young Rome journalist and an acrimonious opponent of Reconstruction, wrote of Bullock: "We have never . . . seen a man who was gifted with so great an amount of beguiling blarney as is this man."[41]

A native of upstate New York, Bullock became an expert telegrapher and rose rapidly in an express company. In the late 1850s he moved to Augusta to organize a southern branch of the firm, and by the time of the war he headed the Southern Express Company, owned a few slaves, and identified his future with the South. Bullock contributed to the Confederate war effort, serving in the quartermaster corps and attaining the rank of lieutenant colonel. With the end of hostilities Colonel Bullock returned to Augusta to resume his business activities. He helped to organize and became director of the First National Bank of Augusta and served as president of the Macon and Augusta Railroad Company.

According to his own account, Bullock abandoned this promising business career after New York financiers refused a loan to the Macon and Augusta because of the unsettled political conditions in Georgia. Bullock was, his Republican friends and associates later recalled, "strictly a businessman."* He "never dreamt of going into politics" when he agreed to be a candidate for delegate to the constitutional convention; he merely felt "that he could properly represent the business interests of the state." At the convention Bullock championed debt relief and quickly became a leader and a popular favorite among the radical delegates. When they chose him as the Republican gubernatorial candidate, he felt flattered. At the same time, Governor Jenkins and the Democrats heaped scorn on the "mongrel convention" and its work.

*After the conflicts of Reconstruction had been settled and tempers had cooled, Henry Grady became well acquainted with Bullock. Still antagonistic toward Republicanism, Grady set about to learn why a man so charming and sensible as Bullock had been the leader of such a disreputable group as the Radical Republicans. Grady interviewed Bullock's old associates and friends and reported his findings. The quotations in reference to Bullock are from Grady's article.

Bullock's "ambition was awakened and his resentment stimulated." He accepted the nomination.

At first his governorship went well. Bullock took pride in running a "businessman's administration," and even his Democratic opponents admitted that he made competent appointments to judicial and other offices. The "crisis" of his administration came when the blacks were expelled from the legislature. That action offended Bullock's sense of justice and forced him to make a choice. Unwilling to renege on everything his administration stood for, he "had to take sides with the negroes in their contest with the white people of the state."[42] It was a fateful choice. Bullock and the radicals became increasingly isolated in Georgia politics, and the governor spent much of his time in Washington lobbying for national support for his policies.

Bullock's decision to reconstruct Reconstruction was controversial. Surely he was naive in placing confidence in the Republican government in Washington, and probably he never fully appreciated the depth of Democratic hostility to Reconstruction in Georgia. Carpetbagger John Emory Bryant, his biographer concluded, found "the South . . . as different as a foreign country, with strange, totally different values from those in the North,"[43] and this may well have been true of Bullock. The governor's willingness to confront directly such emotionally laden issues as white supremacy and home rule undoubtedly demonstrated courage and integrity; it also carried a hint of political naiveté.

Yet, as Bullock pointed out, the governor did not have authority to remove local officials or to declare martial law, even if he had had a state militia or some other armed body to enforce such actions, and he could get none of these things because the Democrats controlled one of the houses of the legislature. Bullock hoped that a return to military occupation would allow him to gain control of the legislature by reseating the blacks and purging the ineligible Democrats. He sought to maintain white support (as well as to undermine his moderate Republican opponents) through patronage and appointed Foster Blodgett, his chief spoilsman, to head the state-owned Western and Atlantic Railroad, the most abundant source of state jobs. He relied upon the federal military to restore an unfettered ballot to blacks. In an abstract sense, Bullock's program contained considerable merit. If blacks could vote freely, if the bulk of them voted Republican, and if even a small white Republican following could be salvaged, the GOP would be the majority party in the state.

Moderate Republicans refused to support a third Reconstruction and broke with the radical administration. Joe Brown insisted that the proper Republican strategy was to divide the Democratic party by seeking an alliance with the more moderate Democrats. Recent elections "should teach us as Republicans," Brown wrote to Bullock, "that it is impossible to maintain the party in this State, or indeed in the South, without a division of the white vote." "They possess most of the intelligence and wealth of the State," Brown pointed out, "which will always control tenants and laborers." Therefore the policy should be to divide the "intelligence and wealth." Brown argued that the Democrats were already divided and that the Republicans should "conciliate the moderate wing" of the Democratic party and avoid the "blunders" that would "enable the leaders of the crazy wing to apply the party lash so strongly, by appeals to prejudice, as to hold them together."[44] Such a policy would mean effectively abandoning the black Republicans, but that was hardly a sacrifice.

From the beginning moderates like Brown had been concerned with economic rather than social reform. During the early period of Reconstruction, the Atlanta *Daily New Era*, the most important Republican newspaper in the state, had editorialized: "Georgia wants more railroads, more rolling-mills and foundries, more machine-shops, more mining operations, more cotton-mills, more mechanics, more scientific and industrial energy. We have been in the rear ranks of progress long enough. . . . It is to this kind of reconstruction that the attention of the people should be directed."[45] To these Republicans Reconstruction meant an acceptance of emancipation, public education, state aid for economic development, and a national reconciliation that would encourage private investments and public pork barrel projects in Georgia. Whether there was any possibility of convincing a wing of the resurgent Democrats to ally with the declining Republicans remains an unanswered question.

While the right wing of the Republican party went into revolt, the black left wing organized for independent action. Just after the black members were expelled from the legislature, Henry M. Turner organized a black protest rally that met in Macon. From this meeting evolved the Civil and Political Rights Association, which enlisted only black members. All along, Aaron Bradley had argued that blacks should not rely so heavily upon white leadership and guidance or accept the fact that whites received most of the patronage and preferment. By the end of 1868 Turner and other less militant black spokesmen had arrived at a similar position. The Civil and Political Rights Association was

Georgia's first broadly based "black power" organization, although, in practice, it had little option but to support Governor Bullock and the reimposition of military rule.

Congress launched the third Reconstruction of Georgia in December 1869. At first developments unfolded as Bullock and the radicals had hoped. When the state legislature convened in January, the expelled blacks reclaimed their seats and a military board disqualified twenty-two additional conservative Democrats and accepted the Republican candidates who had been defeated in 1868. The legislature ratified the Fifteenth Amendment, writing black suffrage into the constitution, and again ratified the Fourteenth Amendment because it had originally been approved by the tainted legislature containing the ineligible Democrats. The Republicans enacted a common school law providing for segregated but "equal" facilities, although lack of funding and other problems delayed the actual establishment of a school system until 1872. General Alfred Terry, who had replaced the lethargic Meade, demonstrated commendable energy in an effort to restore order, placing seven Klan-ridden plantation counties in south central Georgia under military occupation and dispatching troops to other centers of terrorist activity.

But it soon became evident that these actions had little measurable effect. The conservatives controlled the local governments and law enforcement agencies throughout much of the state. A Jefferson County judge wrote Governor Bullock: "The *same people* who are called upon to administer & vindicate the law, are the *same people* who violate it."[46] Where the Democrats did not hold the offices, local power was usually in the hands of terrorist organizations. Even Bullock's efforts to appoint the "best men" as judges and solicitors often resulted in strengthening conservative control of local affairs. General Terry refused to suspend habeas corpus and establish full martial law, which in order to be effective would have required more soldiers than Terry had available, and the presence of limited numbers of Yankee soldiers seemed only to enrage and embolden the conservatives.

In Chattooga County in the northwestern part of the state, a detail of some thirty Union soldiers arrested a Klansman for murder. Soon afterward about one hundred armed Klansmen surrounded the county jail where the alleged murderer was being held and demanded his release. The young lieutenant commanding the Union detail chose wisdom over valor and surrendered the prisoner. The suspect disappeared, presumably having fled the state, and no one else was arrested, except for the young lieutenant, who was court-martialed. Even radical hopes for controlling the Georgia legislature met with little success. The split between moderates and radicals left the lower house of the general assembly divided about equally between radicals and their opponents.

Thwarted at every juncture, the radicals at least showed perseverance. Governor Bullock now decided that since the legislature elected in 1868 had not been legally constituted until January 1870, its members should serve a full two-year term before new elections would be required. Bullock first asked Congress to extend the term of the Georgia legislature and, that failing, encouraged the general assembly to prolong its own life. It was the ultimate humiliation when members of the Georgia house of representatives defeated a resolution extending their own tenure in office. Georgia was yet again readmitted to the Union in July 1870, and legislative elections later in the year became inevitable.

By this time national Republicans were rapidly losing interest in Georgia and Reconstruction. As Amos Akerman observed from Washington, "the Northern Republicans shrink from any further special legislation in regard to the South."[47] Southern planters no longer represented a threat to the expansion of northern capitalism. The dismal economic conditions in the South, the vigorous industrial and population growth of the wartime North, and the rapid northern occupation of the West left the South a relatively minor backwater province. The raw-material-producing southern states could best serve northern interests simply through the restoration of political and social stability. While hardly anxious to abandon Republican state governments and congressional seats to southern Democrats, northern Republicans no longer had reason to fear a revitalized, nationally powerful planter party and consequently no longer possessed the idealistic zeal for black rights that they had exhibited in the early postwar years.

In Georgia the battered and beleaguered Republican administration was nearing collapse. Petty public quarrels among Republicans undermined what remaining status Bullock's government possessed. Nedom L. Angier, the opportunistic and none-too-scrupulous state treasurer and a Republican moderate, accused Bullock of misappropriating funds. The ambitious, abstemious, moralistic James Emory Bryant had been infuriated when Bullock ignored his efforts on behalf of the party and chose to support for a United States Senate seat the hard-drinking, not noticeably honest Foster Blodgett. Bryant joined Angier and other moderate Republicans as leading critics of the Bullock government.

Unable to avoid the 1870 election, the Bullock Republicans delayed as long as possible by scheduling it for December 1870. Amos T. Akerman, who had been appointed United States attorney general, returned to Georgia to assist in drafting the election law. As passed by the legislature the statute empowered the governor to appoint a majority of the election supervisors in each county, authorized the supervisors to make arrests, placed the county sheriff under their authority, and included a number of provisions protecting voters from challenge or intimidation at the polls. Although the bill contained several articles of questionable constitutionality, it enumerated every protection for voters that the Republicans could apparently conceive.

The law had no observable effect on the conduct of the election. The Democrats–Ku Klux Klan controlled the countryside, and laws passed at the state capitol no longer had any particular relationship to what happened in Georgia. Klansmen, "military companies," and posses organized by county sheriffs dominated the election, even in communities where detachments of federal soldiers were stationed. The Democrats won massively, of course, although a few Republicans survived the onslaught. Henry M. Turner won reelection in Macon; when the legislature convened, it rejected Turner and seated his opponent. Tunis Campbell remained in the senate until 1873; when he was elected to a house seat in 1874, the Democrats awarded the seat to his defeated opponent. Although occasional blacks served in the legislature for the remainder of the century, men such as Campbell and Turner were no longer tolerated.

The new legislature did not convene until November 1871. Thus the Bullock administration limped along for the better part of another year. "He preserved his gorgeous deportment amid it all," the Atlanta *Constitution* observed, "arrayed like a monarch, imposing in presence, smiling and affable, the princely, imperturbable and benignant patron of thieves and adventurers."[48] But Bullock was not so imperturbable as to welcome the impeachment proceedings that awaited him when the legislature met.

If Bullock were impeached, the new governor would be the president of the state senate, and, since the new legislature was Democratic, he would be a Democrat. Therefore, to thwart "Genl. Toombs and his Klan," Bullock hit upon a rational solution to his quandary.[49] He resigned in October 1871 before the new legislature convened. The new governor was thus Benjamin Conley, president of the old senate and a Bullock friend and business associate. Since Conley had not done anything during Reconstruction except to promote state aid for the Macon and Augusta Railroad of which he replaced Bullock as president, the legislature would have no grounds for impeaching him, and the Republican administration could complete its full four-year term. Like so many other of Bullock's abstractly logical solutions, this one proved unworkable. The new legislature quickly arranged for a special gubernatorial election, in which the Democratic candidate ran unopposed. The Reconstruction experiment was over.

In his farewell statement, Bullock blamed Robert Toombs for the downfall of his government. Toombs had in fact plotted feverishly during the years of Bullock's reign, sometimes in alliance with Joe Brown and the Republican moderates. "Politics does make us acquainted with strange bedfellows," he confessed to Alexander Stephens.[50] With Bullock driven from the state, Toombs promptly donated his services to the investigating committees that sprang like weeds from the Democratic legislature. With Toombs playing a leading role, Democratic committees found the Bullock administration guilty of most known crimes.

Generally the evidence fails to support the conclusions of the committees or the popular stereotype of corrupt Republican radicals. The Bullock administration placed too much faith in railroad construction as the panacea that would bind Georgia to the nation and hasten the state's economic development. This policy invited a scramble among promoters for state aid, and Republicans differed little from Democrats in their tendency to ignore conflicts of interest. With a young, besieged, and divided party, Bullock, Blodgett, and their friends came to rely on patronage, and Blodgett's freewheeling management of the Western and Atlantic Railroad produced deficits and contributed to the decision to lease the road to a private corporation.

Yet the Bullock administration was not so inordinately extravagant as Democratic committee reports suggested. The Republicans did slightly increase state taxes from their immediate postwar level, but, as Bullock was fond of pointing out in later years, "the tax rate was less during my term than it has ever been since."[51] The government lived by borrowing. The Georgia state debt at the end of Reconstruction was approximately $10 million, of which $2.8 million was unpaid pre–Civil War obligations, $3.7 million was debt contracted by the Johnson-Jenkins regimes during the presidential Reconstruction of 1865–68, and $3.5 million was attributable to the Bullock administration during 1868–71.

Additionally, Bullock committed Georgia to another $8 million of real or potential debt that the Democrats repudiated. The majority of those obligations were state endorsements of bonds issued by railroads. Bullock's favorite railroad promoter was Hannibal I. Kimball, one of the most daring entrepreneurs in Georgia history. According to the Democrats, the blacks in the legislature conceived a ditty:

> H. I. Kimball's on de floor
> 'Taint gwine ter rain no more.[52]

Kimball wanted to construct railroads and Bullock wanted them constructed, and neither devoted much attention to proper procedure.

The result was new railroads and a large potential state debt. In 1867 Georgia had approximately fifteen hundred miles of rail; in 1871 it had twenty-one hundred miles. To be sure, the Democrats also saw the necessity of restoring and expanding transportation, and the Democratic administrations before and after Bullock aided railroads, although on a considerably less lavish scale. Beyond the bond endorsements the Bullock government issued gold and currency bonds, for which the state received $1.5 million, mostly from New York investors. Toombs and his allies demanded that the entire $8 million be disowned, and the Democrats complied. As a result Georgia encouraged the construction of railroad track and received $1.5 million at no cost to the state.

Whatever the extent of fraud and thievery, few Republicans appear to have benefited. Aaron Bradley died in St. Louis with no bank account and twenty-five cents in his pocket. Tunis Campbell, after being denied the seat in the legislature to which he had been elected, spent six months in prison and a year as a leased convict before leaving the state. Henry M. Turner, also denied the legislative position to which he had been elected, turned to the church, becoming a bishop and a national leader of the "back to Africa" movement. John Emory Bryant labored on, founding the Southern Advance Association as a part of his continuing crusade "to plant American civilization in the South" and participating in Republican factional politics, while his wife and family lived in near poverty conditions.[53] Finally, Bryant returned to the North and became a successful businessman. Foster Blodgett, who actually received a substantial bribe from Joe Brown, Ben Hill, and the other lessees of the Western and Atlantic, was within a few years living in South Carolina and complaining of a dilapidated wardrobe.

Hannibal Kimball, a New Englander who had come to Georgia as manager of the southern branch of the Pullman Company, gained control of a major Atlanta bank, joined with Joe Brown and others to lease the Western and Atlantic Railroad, built the finest hotel in Atlanta at a cost of nearly $700,000, constructed the Union Passenger Depot in Atlanta, established the Atlanta Fair Grounds, served as president of nine railroads, and promoted various other projects. Kimball was somewhat overextended when the Republicans lost control of the state, and his financial empire collapsed. He left for Europe on an unsuccessful expedition to borrow money.

In 1874 a group of Atlanta citizens invited Kimball to return to Georgia to organize an Atlanta cotton factory. In Atlanta he recovered his financial position, established the cotton mill, became director of the Cotton Exposition of 1880, and was almost elected mayor in 1881. When the Kimball House hotel burned, Kimball rebuilt it, with Robert Toombs as one of the investors. Perhaps Kimball was not altogether sad when Toombs lost money on the investment.

Governor Bullock fled to his home town of Albion, New York. "Unfortunately," he wrote Joe Brown, "I am *not* revelling in ill gotten (or other) gains in Paris, London, Egypt or other places named for me by the accommodating newspapers."[54] In 1876 Bullock returned to Georgia under arrest for a variety of charges growing out of the legislative investigations. During January 1878 Bullock faced four separate trials in Atlanta. The presiding judge threw two of the cases out for lack of evidence, and the juries returned not guilty verdicts in the other two. The Atlanta *Constitution* lamented: "But when the witnesses were put upon the stand under oath to confirm their published utterances— and among them were some of the most reliable and honest men in Georgia—they denied that they had ever so testified."[55] Bullock became a prosperous businessman and president of the Atlanta Chamber of Commerce, even allying once again with H. I. Kimball as salaried executives and members of the board of directors of the Atlanta cotton factory that Kimball organized. When Governor Alexander Stephens died in 1881, Robert Toombs, John Gordon, Joe Brown, and Rufus Bullock were among the pallbearers.

Despite these reconciliations, Reconstruction had revolutionary implications. The Radical Republicans challenged the authority of Georgia's planter class and threatened its control of agricultural labor and its paternalistic ideology. The radicals endeavored to create a more dynamic social system based on equality before the law, to elevate the labor force through public education, to encourage railroad and industrial development with public aid, and to centralize and expand the authority of the governor's office. They demonstrated a serious commitment to black rights and strove to protect the interests of small property holders. In short, they championed a political, social, and economic program of capitalist democracy.

The decisive Democratic victory represented the triumph of the landlord class and assured that state power would defend a traditional, paternalistic, and static social order. Although driven from power in national politics, Georgia planters were still the most powerful, most cohesive, and most determined social group in the state. The merchants and professional men of the towns continued their longstanding alliance with the planters, thus, as Joe Brown observed, giving the Democrats "most of the intelligence and wealth of the State." The Democrats assumed the burden of restoring economic and social stability, but, as Brown also pointed out, there was no consensus on how such an elusive goal was to be achieved.

# Chapter Four

## *The Challenge to*
## *Bourbon Democracy*

In its war on Republicanism the Democratic party united most of the state's white citizenry. Antebellum Whigs such as Robert Toombs, prewar Know-Nothings such as Ben Hill, old-line Democrats such as Alfred Colquitt, Civil War heroes such as John Gordon, and erstwhile Republican moderates such as Joe Brown ultimately found themselves in the same party. Many appeared content to rest on their laurels as saviors of the Southland from radical Republicanism. Yet redemption was an ambiguous victory for the old regime, and the Civil War and Reconstruction had unleashed the forces of ideological conflict. Some Democrats were genuine reactionaries who wished to restore as much of the antebellum order as possible. Others, shaken by the state's dire economic difficulties, envisioned a path to prosperity through New South economic modernization under Democratic sponsorship. During the 1870s this uneasy Democratic coalition defined the basic principles that were to underlie the Bourbon system.

Ideological dissension appeared within the Democratic party even before the fall of Bullock's government. At the center of the controversy was the unlikely figure of Benjamin H. Hill. To Joe Brown, Hill belonged with Toombs in "the crazy wing" of the Democratic party.[1] Among the most avid and loquacious of Democratic orators, Hill had ardently insisted: "Never go half way with a traitor, nor compromise with treason or robbery."[2] Then, suddenly, in December 1870, Hill reversed himself, remarking in a public letter that the Thirteenth, Fourteenth, and Fifteenth Amendments were facts that could not be changed and that it was "the duty of every good citizen to abide and obey the Constitution and laws as they exist, precisely as if he had cooperated in establishing and enacting them."[3] Although he had chaired the Macon convention that laid the organizational foundation for the Democratic party less than three years before, Hill attended a dinner hosted by Governor Bullock in honor of a Radical Republican member of President Grant's cabinet and came close to denying that he had ever been a Democrat. "If I ever was a Democrat," Hill stated, "I can honestly say that I did not go to be."[4]

The explanation for Hill's impressive display of freedom from the foolish consistency that plagues little minds concerned railroads rather than Reconstruction. A hapless entrepreneur whose land speculation schemes and business ventures normally went awry, Hill was anxious to recoup his fortunes by becoming a stockholder in the corporation being formed to lease the state-owned Western and Atlantic. Governor Bullock would make the final decision about the lease; therefore, Hill became more tolerant toward the man he had recently characterized as "this stupid express agent" and "a miserable sham Governor." And because the corporation included several prominent Republicans, Hill generously decided to forgive those whom he had called "vile creatures, whose infamy no epithet can describe, and no precedent parallel."[5]

Although railroad profits dictated the timing of Hill's abrupt conversion to a spirit of reconciliation, the conversion itself, at least in part, apparently stemmed from other sources. Hill wrestled with Georgia's crushing economic problems and in the summer of 1871 delivered his analysis of the situation. Addressing the University of Georgia Alumni Society, Hill spoke with surprising candor and considerable insight. Despite Georgia's "vastly superior" natural resources, Hill stated, the "Northern States are all rich and we are poor! They are strong and we are weak!" Hill's explanation for this paradox was not the stock Democratic answer of defeat and emancipation; Hill blamed slavery, which degraded labor and prevented mass public education. Because of slavery, the South had developed an economy based on wasteful and inefficient agricultural practices rather than industry and as a result had lost the Civil War.

With the abolition of slavery, the South stood at "one of those rare junctures in human affairs when one civilization abruptly ends and another begins." The new civilization, Hill insisted, must recognize "that modern progress is chiefly, if not entirely, found . . . in the education and elevation of the masses; in the discoveries and appliances of the physical sciences; in the establishment of schools of science, and in the promotion, enlargement, and results of all departments of industries." Thus Georgians must "honor, elevate, and educate labor"; teach their "own sons . . . to build and operate all machinery"; and "do all in our power to educate, elevate, protect, and advance the negro." With the expansion of education, the development of natural resources, the growth of industry, and the adoption of free labor practices and a more dynamic social system, "wealth will increase, homes will multiply, power become a fact and not a theory, and then, and not till then, we shall see and feel, taking bodily shape and form, those tantalizing, perplexing myths after which we have so long vainly grasped—State rights, State sovereignty, and State independence!"[6] Hill called for economic and social modernization and sought to lead Georgia's "long deluded and now impoverished people" toward a new "civilization."[7] The South should achieve "independence" from Yankee domination by emulating the Yankees.

Hill's frank recognition of the failures of the old regime and enthusiastic support for a new social order offended many Georgia traditionalists. An Augusta newspaper complimented Hill's oratory: "The soundness of abolition principles and the superiority of Yankee civilization were his main topics of discourse. The superior insight of the Radical party into the true policy of the country was made very manifest and our own errors exposed in a masterly way."[8]

Robert Toombs disapproved of the new course being charted by his former ally. Toombs expressed "no interest in men or parties who recognize the 14th and 15th amendments." Instead Toombs's "fixed purpose" was to make Republicanism odious in Georgia and to "expunge" as many Reconstruction accomplishments as possible.[9] Toombs threw himself into the work of the Democratic committees investigating Republican crimes, and so vigorously did he pursue Hill, Brown, and the other lessees of the state railroad that the long-suffering Joe Brown demanded the satisfaction of a duel, a challenge that Toombs declined.

Toombs next directed his attention to the railroads. The expansion of railroad mileage, the breakdown of plantation self-sufficiency, and changing marketing arrangements made railroads more important to Georgia agriculture than ever. Railroads owned some of the most valuable property in the state; more than other Georgia enterprises they had attracted investment capital from outside the state; consolidation had centralized railroad management and enhanced the opportunities for abusing shippers; and the Republicans had treated them generously. All of this gave Robert Toombs ample cause for concern. He insisted that railroad corporations pay taxes at the same rate as other property owners.

Pre–Civil War legislatures, to encourage construction, had offered railroad promoters special tax rates. In 1874 the Democrats enacted legislation requiring railroads to pay taxes at the same rate as other property. Toombs argued that consolidations had voided the original pre–Civil War charters and therefore the companies were subject to the new tax law. Toombs spent ten years battling the railroads. Ultimately he was largely victorious, collecting more than $200,000 in back taxes and establishing the principle that capitalist promoters could expect no special favors in the state of Georgia.

But what bothered Robert Toombs most was the Constitution of 1868, which had been written by people who "with but few exceptions were hungry, hostile, alien enemies, domestic traitors, and ignorant, vicious, emancipated slaves." Perhaps even worse, the constitution stated "that we owe primary allegiance to the United States," Toombs wrote, adding: "We deny it."[10] Toombs launched a drive to hold another convention and to produce a constitution "designed for honest men."[11] In early 1877 the legislature authorized a referendum, and a low turnout of voters approved the convention and elected delegates. The convention assembled during the summer of 1877.

Toombs was the leading advocate for a new convention, and he, more than any other individual, dominated its proceedings. The Atlanta *Constitution* called him "by all odds the most conspicuous figure in the Convention."[12] Toombs was chairman of both the committee on the legislature and the committee on revision, the latter of which controlled the introduction of measures on the floor and prepared the final draft of the document. So pleased was Toombs with the convention's progress that when the delegates exhausted the $25,000 appropriation provided by the legislature he advanced $20,000 of his own money to ensure that the convention continued its work.

The president of the gathering was former Governor Charles Jenkins. When the "mongrel" Reconstruction constitutional convention of 1868 met in Atlanta, Governor Jenkins "after careful consideration and with the clearest conviction" refused to permit the payment of state funds to support such an alien gathering.[13] Finally, even General Meade became sufficiently exasperated to remove Jenkins and to appoint General Thomas H. Ruger as governor. Jenkins took the state treasury and the great seal of the state and fled to New York, where he deposited Georgia's money for the payment of debts. As a result, according to Governor Bullock, the state treasury contained ten cents when his Republican administration assumed office.[14] Taking the great seal, Jenkins went into exile in Nova Scotia. After the Democrats regained power, he returned to the state, bearing the appearance of martyrdom and the great seal unsullied by radical hands. Jenkins shared with Toombs an inveterate hostility toward the work of radical Republicanism.

A mood of reaction permeated the convention. A leading delegate boasted that a local newspaper had described him as "one of those who wish to return to the days of our daddies," and most of his colleagues clearly sympathized with this position. The economic distress of the 1870s, an awareness of Georgia's large public debt, and hostility toward the "excesses" of Reconstruction created a retrenchment mentality among the delegates. A powerful and bitterly reactionary economy bloc, which included representatives from many of the small farmer counties in north Georgia and in the south Georgia pine barrens, sought low taxes and drastically limited state expenditures. A badly outgunned New South group that included a number of urban and business-oriented delegates struggled futilely to permit modest state support for economic development. Strategically placed between the two was Robert Toombs and his planter-oriented old guard following.

The economy bloc dominated much of the debate. The delegates argued endlessly over the maximum salaries that should be paid to state officials and how many clerks they might be permitted to employ and whether to pay jury members one or two dollars per day. Toombs grumbled that the amount of convention time spent "talking of the governor's salary" was costing more "than your children will have to pay in forty years." The convention set judicial salaries so low that one delegate facetiously offered a resolution authorizing superior court judges "to peddle without a license." The proceedings became so dreary that within a month President Jenkins was trying to explain from the podium that he really had not "spoken disrespectfully of the convention, and especially that he had [not] pronounced their work thus far ridiculous" as he had been quoted in a newspaper interview. The final result, however, led Toombs happily to assert: "You have locked it [the public treasury], and you have put the key in the pockets of the people, and I thank God for it."[15]

The product of the convention's labors was the most profoundly conservative constitution in Georgia history. It prohibited virtually anything that might encourage the emergence of a New South in Georgia. The state could spend tax money only for a few specifically enumerated purposes. It could not offer tax exemptions or other favors to encourage industrial development, thereby invalidating an earlier law that permitted new factories to enjoy a ten-year period of freedom from taxes. The state could not borrow money except under the most dire and carefully restricted circumstances. State credit could not "be pledged or loaned to any individual, company, corporation or association," nor could the state invest funds in private corporations as it had done in the antebellum era. With minor variations these prohibitions

also applied to local governments. State aid for economic development, said Robert Toombs, was "theft—spoilation—spoilation under
the forms of the law—the worst of all," and Georgia would have none
of it.[16]

After considerable debate, the convention recognized the existence
of "common schools." Rather than the "thorough system of general
education" provided for in the Constitution of 1868, however, the new
document permitted "a thorough system of common schools for the
education of children in the elementary branches of an English education only." A high school education, one delegate pointed out, only
made a boy "dissatisfied with his lot."[17] Earlier the Democratic legislature had changed the Republican mandate for racially "equal" school
facilities to a requirement that county school authorities "shall, as far
as practicable, provide the same facilities for both races."[18]

While denying state aid to industrial and business enterprise, the
constitution included a number of popular agrarian reforms. It required the legislature "to regulate freight and passenger tariffs, to prohibit unjust discriminations on the various railroads of this State, and
to prohibit said roads from charging other than just and reasonable
rates." Shortly afterward the legislature established a railroad commission that performed effectively and spared Georgia many of the railroad abuses common in other states. The constitution made lobbying
a crime, attempted to guard against conflicts of interest on the part of
public officials, and broadened democracy by shortening terms in office and making a few more positions elective. Toombs successfully
opposed the popular election of judges on the grounds "that the federal government, the conqueror and public enemy of my country, has
injected into the social organization and political body 500,000 sav-
ages, who, whatever their rights, are not fit to exercise the powers of
government."[19]

Although Toombs and others argued that at least one house of the
state legislature should represent population, the convention adopted
a system of legislative apportionment that ensured population growth
in the cities would have virtually no effect on membership in the general assembly. Another provision sought to curtail the political influence of what President Jenkins called this "dangerous element in our
midst" by authorizing a cumulative poll tax that the legislature implemented in the 1880s.[20] As ratified, the constitution both lowered and
limited homestead protection. Georgia voters approved the constitution by a huge majority.

Ben Hill conjured a vision of a land dotted with "schools of agriculture, of commerce, of manufacturing, of mining, of technology, and, in short, of all polytechnics." Robert Toombs promoted a constitution that banned a general system of public high schools. Hill's plea for uplifting and educating black Georgians was answered by segregated schools that were "equal as far as practicable." Hill called for the rapid development of Georgia's natural resources. The Constitution of 1877 prohibited both state and local governments from providing the transportation and other internal improvements that would have made such a program feasible. Hill wanted "the multiplication and elevation of the industries."[21] The constitution denied public encouragement for industrial development. Certainly the constitution was not antibusiness nor did it ban factory enterprise; it merely ensured that public authority would defend social stability rather than promote industrial development.

Only a few months before Toombs and his fellow delegates drafted the Constitution of 1877 in Atlanta, Senator John Gordon and Congressman Ben Hill played key roles in negotiating the Compromise of 1877 in Washington. The compromise contributed to the settlement of a presidential succession crisis but more importantly it symbolized a general understanding between northern Republicans and southern Democrats. The Republicans agreed to abandon their Reconstruction policy of federal intervention in southern states and to support the funding of internal improvements in the South. In exchange, the southern Bourbons tacitly accepted the political order ushered in by the Civil War. With the Compromise of 1877 the South resumed full membership in the Union but did so on northern terms. The southern Democrats won "home rule" and pork barrel projects by acquiescing to an economic and political order dominated by northern industrial capitalism.

The Constitution of 1877 and the Compromise of 1877 established the basic governing principles for the Bourbon Democrats who ruled Georgia throughout the late nineteenth century. The Georgia Bourbons supported a stable social order based on white supremacy, a closed political system resting on one-party politics, and a passive national stance that protected "home rule." Among its other virtues, this system accomplished the fundamental purpose of assuring a subservient labor supply for plantation agriculture. Rarely did political campaign rhetoric question or even stray beyond these accepted fundamentals. The discredited and demoralized Republicans increasingly devoted their energies to party factional squabbles and the quest for federal patronage. During the late 1870s and early 1880s Independent candidates attacked the Bourbons' "machine rule," but they posed little threat to the Bourbon system or to its ideology. For the most part Georgia politics displayed a beguiling harmony.

Having accomplished their counterrevolution launched in reaction to Reconstruction and having defined their basic policies, the Bourbons felt obligated to do little more, except to maintain themselves in office, a responsibility they fulfilled with admirable dexterity. "There are 180,000 voters in Georgia—maybe more," an Atlanta journalist wrote. "But there are 150 politicians who rule the state and hold its offices as absolutely in fee as if they had received a title to the property."[22] White supremacy and the one-party system supported both social and political stability in Georgia.

In 1880 Governor Alfred H. Colquitt, a southwest Georgia planter, Civil War general, and apparent former top-echelon Ku Klux Klan leader, contemplated reelection with some anxiety. So riddled with corruption was his first term that even Georgia's Democratic legislature censured the state treasurer for embezzlement, convicted the comptroller general for thievery, and brought impeachment proceedings against several other members of the administration. In Washington Senator John Gordon, who continued to demonstrate greater natural aptitude for being a war hero than anything else, also suffered anxiety although his problems related to personal finances and impatient creditors, as well as perhaps to some indiscreet correspondence that later became public suggesting that he had accepted bribes from a railroad lobby. In Atlanta citizen Joe Brown, having been driven into private life near the end of Reconstruction, yearned to vindicate himself by returning to public office. Henry W. Grady, an aspiring, talented, and professionally frustrated young Atlanta journalist, had recently become closely associated with the president of the Louisville and Nashville Railroad, which wanted access to the Brown-controlled Western and Atlantic Railroad.

In May 1880, Grady wired Joe Brown: "Williams will pass play certain." When decoded, the message stated: "Gordon will send in resignation certain."[23] Gordon did abruptly resign the Senate seat to which he had recently been reelected in order to accept a retainer as counsel for the Louisville and Nashville; Colquitt appointed Brown to the vacant position; Grady borrowed enough money from a northern capitalist whom he hardly knew to purchase quarter interest in the Atlanta *Constitution*; and the Louisville and Nashville gained access to the Brown-controlled Western and Atlantic and ultimately control of the line. Brown and Gordon vigorously campaigned for Colquitt, and

*Constitution* editor Grady served as manager of his successful reelection campaign. Around such events as these Georgia politics revolved.

Because the Bourbons possessed a limited vision of leadership, it is easy to be overly critical of their performance. Robert Toombs growled in 1882 that they were "as cowardly and venal a lot of place-hunting politicians as ever lived. Like putrid bodies in the stream, they rise as they rot."[24] Actually most of the corruption in Governor Colquitt's administration occurred during his first term. Governor Gordon, who after making a considerable amount of money in railroad promotion promptly lost it in Florida land speculation and felt compelled to re-dedicate himself to public service, served only two terms. Governor Henry D. McDaniel, a Grady favorite and a former Toombs ally in the struggle to tax and regulate the railroads, appears to have been a competent executive, although his policies differed in no noticeable way from those of other governors during the period. Georgia's United States senators—Joe Brown, Alfred Colquitt, and John Gordon served more than one term—were all defenders of southern rights.

There were, of course, political rivalries within the Bourbon leadership. The most persistent was the conflict between Atlanta and the downstate cities. With urban areas serving as transportation, marketing, and service centers for the agricultural countryside, merchants and businessmen preferred one of their own as governor. The Bourbon foursome—Brown, Colquitt, Gordon, and Grady—were all Atlanta-oriented, and Macon and the other downstate cities carried on a tireless and fruitless campaign to break their monopoly of political power. Beyond this, personal differences and conflicting ambitions ultimately led to a widening rift between Brown and Grady on one side and Colquitt and Gordon on the other. Particularly significant was the unfortunate fact that Georgia had only one governor's chair and two Senate seats to offer, and in the late 1880s they were all comfortably filled by Brown, Colquitt, and Gordon, thus leaving the restive Grady without a place. None of this had any known relevance to the vast bulk of Georgia citizens.

Easily the most articulate member of the Bourbon establishment was Henry W. Grady. In addition to being a masterful political manipulator, Grady was a shrewd and effective journalist and orator. The son of an affluent Athens merchant and slaveholder who died in Virginia during the Civil War, Grady held generally conservative and conventional views about life. He was a devoted family man whose avuncular advice to a young friend was never to gamble, never to drink, and to marry young. Although not deeply pious himself, he supported organized religion as a necessary "restraint" for the masses "of simple men and women." Apparently it was this concern for the morality and behavior of "the poorer classes" that led Grady to assume leadership of the prohibitionist movement in Atlanta.[25] Grady launched his journalistic career in Rome, where he was a merciless critic of Reconstruction and a friend and evidently a member of the Ku Klux Klan.

After becoming the highly successful editor of the *Constitution*, the charming, cherubic, ever-industrious Grady quickly emerged as Atlanta's number one citizen and civic leader. The Grady mansion became the social hub of the city, where the rich and powerful of the state and sometimes of the nation partook of hospitality. At one party the entertainment featured a fiddle contest between four state legislators with the prize going to a young first-term representative named Thomas E. Watson. Grady was the foremost exemplar of the "Atlanta spirit," and he was also the leading proponent and propagandist for the New South.

Grady summarized both his optimism about the progress of the New South as a region and the essence of his New South program for development: "The South, under the rapid diversification of crops and diversification of industries, is thrilling with new life." Diversification of agriculture was important to the economic health of the region. "To mortgage our farms in Boston for money with which to buy meat and bread from western cribs and smokehouses," he pointed out, "is folly unspeakable."[26] But Grady's first concern was industrial development. The southern cotton crop "is worth in round numbers $300,000,000," he wrote in 1881. "The same crop when manufactured is worth over $900,000,000."[27] Ensuring that this lucrative transformation took place in the South was Grady's central goal.

Cotton mills alone were not enough. In a column written in the early 1880s, Grady termed himself a "war correspondent" and described the South "fighting against a subjection more grievous" than that threatened by defeat in the Civil War. "The farmers may farm as wisely as they please, but as long as we manufacture nothing, and rely on the shops and mills and factories of other sections for everything we use our section must remain dependent and poor." Georgia and the South needed textile factories, but they also needed the smaller "home industries" that made carriages, watches, matches, and brooms and that canned food. Grady reported that he had found an Atlanta grocer who sold $50,000 of goods per year and imported 95 percent of those products from outside the state.[28]

But usually Grady's writings exuded buoyancy. "Riding through middle Georgia and noting the thriving towns and farms" left the Atlanta journalist convinced that economic success was near at hand. "The truth is the people are contented and prosperous," he wrote, adding: "One more year of improved acreage in grain crops . . . will make our commonwealth absolutely independent of the world, the flesh, and the devil."[29] When Robert Toombs observed that "the sun rose every day on a poorer Georgia than it set on the day before," a horrified Grady attacked the general's "vaporing on this subject" and insisted that Georgia's flourishing growth in industry and agriculture made the state ever more prosperous.[30]

Grady often quoted Ben Hill approvingly, but in fact the strategies of the two bore only superficial resemblances. Hill called for a homemade New South with internally generated capital and mass involvement, a New South that would be independent of outside domination. Grady expected northern investments to finance southern industrialization. Indeed, Grady visualized northern immigrants providing at least part of the skilled labor for factories built by northern capital. The South, Grady stated, "needs peace, stability, capital, immigrants."[31] Consequently, national reconciliation was crucial to Grady's purpose. Southerners, Grady assured a northern audience, "have smoothed the path to southward, wiped out the place where Mason and Dixon's line used to be, and hung out our latchstring to you and yours."[32]

"No commonwealth ever came to greatness by producing raw material," Grady acknowledged, and he opposed sending southern natural resources "to augment the wealth and power of distant communities."[33] Yet his plan to import industrialization from the North while leaving the southern social system relatively untouched promised no escape from colonial and dependent status. Similarly, Grady's panacea for agriculture was for the South "to raise her own provisions, compost her fertilizers, cure her own hay, and breed her own stock." This was perhaps good advice for the most successful farmers—"the planter princes of the old time, still lords of the acres, though not of slaves," as Grady termed them—but it had little relevance for the mass of Georgia farmers.[34]

Most of all, Grady anchored his New South firmly to white supremacy. "Economic issues are as naught, and even great moral reforms must wait on the settlement of this question."[35] Racial inequality, he wrote, "is instinctive—deeper than prejudice or pride, and bred in the bone and blood."[36] An absolute necessity, Grady insisted, was "that the white race must dominate forever in the South." To this end, the one-party system was essential. "The worst thing in my opinion that could happen is that the white people of the South should stand in opposing factions, with the vast mass of ignorant and purchasable negro votes between."[37] Yet, at the same time, a politically solid South with its "electoral votes hurled as a rifle-ball into the electoral college" invited the formation of a solid North, a rigidly sectional political alignment that endangered Grady's hopes for regional reconciliation.[38] Grady recognized the paradox, but his only solution was to plead for northern patience. White supremacy required one-party unity in the South, and that demand overrode all else.

Other urban and small town editors and orators joined Grady in his quest for crop diversification and industrial development. As many townsmen and would-be industrial promoters recognized, the purchase of meat and grain from the Midwest drained investment capital from the state and curtailed economic growth. Similarly, newspaper editors promoted the development of "small diversified industries" that would produce goods for local consumption and keep "at home the money that finds its way North and East annually."[39] The campaign to "bring the cotton mills to the cotton fields" won wide applause.

Yet the cities and towns formed the marketing networks that distributed northern goods to Georgia consumers and collected and dispatched the cotton crop in exchange. Andre Gunder Frank has observed that Latin America "had a colonial class structure which inevitably gave its dominant bourgeoisie an economic self-interest in freely exporting raw materials and importing manufactured products."[40] This description applied equally to the "New South" merchants and businessmen. The prosperity of urban merchants—and indeed the prosperity of the towns and cities—was deeply enmeshed in existing economic arrangements. The Georgia social system prevented the emergence of a free-labor entrepreneurial capitalism, and the dominant planters and merchants—few of whom actively opposed industrial development—found little reason to make serious sacrifices to promote it.

Grady favored industrialization so long as it did not disrupt social stability, endanger white supremacy, interfere with Bourbon one-party rule, or discourage northern sponsorship. Most of his other prescriptions for a New South were equally governed by Bourbon assumptions. During the closing years of his tragically brief life, Grady worried about the economic and political centralization caused by the growth of northern corporate capitalism and the expansion of the federal government. After perceptively discussing the problem, Grady offered to a university student audience the following "remedy": "To exalt the hearthstone—to strengthen the home—to build up the individual—to magnify and defend the principle of local self-government."[41]

The New South portrayed by Grady was "simply the Old South under new conditions."[42] Although a keen observer and a born promoter, Grady was no more successful than the other late nineteenth-century Georgia Bourbons in transcending the South's economic, social, and political dilemmas. By accepting the implications of the Democratic victory during Reconstruction, the Compromise of 1877, and the Constitution of 1877, Georgia Bourbons left themselves with few alternatives except to support the status quo. In truth, the proponents of the New South had lost the war before Henry Grady popularized the term.

The New South as defined by Rufus Bullock or Ben Hill offered no threat to the Bourbon system. Instead the challenge to Bourbon rule emanated from the Georgia countryside. Less than a year after Henry Grady described a South "thrilling with new life," Tom Watson pictured a land where "the fields are worn to sand or seamed with gullies" and a people with "toil-worn faces" immersed in "the battle with poverty." "I would that I could see the glory come back to southern farms," Watson plaintively stated. But the prospects were dim because "it was well-nigh impossible to prosper in the country."[43]

A strange, brilliant, brooding man, Watson was born on the "old plantation home" of his grandfather.[44] Watson's father, an impractical and inept individual of whom Watson was never fond, had just launched his own career as a planter in an area of the old cotton belt northwest of Augusta when the Civil War interrupted. After the war the Watson family fortunes rapidly declined. The plantation that had belonged to Watson's grandfather was the first to go, and in 1873 his father's acres went on the block. Soon Watson's parents and his three sisters lived in a sorry hovel near Augusta and his brother worked as a sharecropper.

During these years Watson struggled to find his own calling in life. He completed his sophomore term at Mercer, then located in Penfield, before the deterioration of his family's financial situation forced him to look for employment. Finding work during the economically depressed mid-1870s was no easy task. Finally, a family friend helped Watson to get a teaching position in a rural community to the south of Augusta. For two years he eked out a bare living teaching by day and

reading law by night. Yet Watson seems to have enjoyed his years in
Screven County. "They have always been good to me—these plain,
country people—and I love them. They gave me a home and work
when I could find none elsewhere."[45]

Admitted to the bar in 1875, Watson set up law practice the following year in Thomson, county seat of McDuffie County, which was also
the site of the old Watson homeplace. An immensely successful lawyer, Watson combined a keen eye for law with hard work and an almost mystical ability to sway rural small town jurors. His lucrative law
practice permitted him to repurchase the family homestead, to restore
his family's fortunes, and to become a large plantation owner with an
abundance of sharecroppers. Although Watson relished walking or riding
over the land and through the woods, he largely left the management
of the plantation to his wife Georgia.

Watson also entered politics. In 1880 he attended the Democratic
state convention, where he established himself as a party maverick by
his outspoken opposition to the renomination of Governor Colquitt.
Watson campaigned for an Independent Democratic candidate in the
election. Two years later Watson won election to the Georgia house of
representatives. As a state legislator Watson compiled a mixed record.
Although he supported such reform causes as higher taxes on railroads
and abolition of the convict lease system, his victories were largely
confined to Henry Grady's fiddle competition. Watson soon returned
to his law practice.

In 1888 Watson campaigned for Grover Cleveland and ran as a
Democratic presidential elector, but by this time it was clear that he
was growing increasingly impatient with the politics of Bourbon Democracy. He became more openly critical of Georgia Democrats and
particularly of Henry Grady, whose optimistic portrayal of the New
South bore little resemblance to what Watson saw in McDuffie County.
Several months before the 1888 presidential election, Watson explained that there were "a thousand dead farms in Georgia" because
of the "burden of unequal taxation, the impossibility of buying or selling except at other people's prices," and a "currency which made the
farmer and his lands an outlaw from its benefits; these and causes
similar to these broke his fortunes and broke his spirit—took his home
and took his hopes." Watson ominously added: *"This system is false
and it shall die!"*[46]

In 1890 an increasingly militant Tom Watson ran for Congress in the
tenth district that sprawled across the old cotton belt from Augusta to
Hancock County. Watson adopted as his platform the program of the

Farmers' Alliance, an organization that spread into Georgia in the late 1880s. With Alliance support, Watson easily bested the incumbent in the Democratic primary. In Congress Watson insisted that southern Democrats elected with the endorsement of the Farmers' Alliance—who campaigned as Democratic/Alliance candidates—should demand that the national Democratic party adopt the Alliance program. When they refused, Watson (later joined by one other Georgia congressman) quit the party of the Bourbons and joined the People's party caucus. Watson thus became Georgia's first Populist. He was also the most articulate critic of the Bourbon position, and he broadened his indictment of the Democrats during the political struggles that followed.

"A magnificent yield of cotton leaves the people unclothed. A magnificent yield of corn leaves them scantily fed. Strange state of things," Watson mused, "when abundance brings want and success means failure."[47] Watson discovered several explanations for these developments. Although farmers far outnumbered other citizens in Georgia, the townsmen "have been organized and have been your masters in every question of finance or state control."[48] A small but powerful clique of politicians monopolized political power while keeping the common people divided along racial lines. The economic system favored manufacturers and financiers over farmers and laborers. And so the list grew. Increasingly it came to center on the policies of the federal government.

"You cultivate the crop with hard work," Watson told Georgia farmers, "and the North and East does all the reaping."[49] The reason was that Congress enacted legislation enriching the Northeast and impoverishing the remainder of the country. "Our leaders," Watson rather accurately observed of the Bourbons, "finding it easy to keep office by submitting to the law as they found it, have allowed the East & North to forge every chain their cupidity wanted."[50] The great failing of the national Democratic party was that it did not "make war on the millionaires and the national banks"; the most outrageous sin of the Georgia Bourbons was that they allowed "the South to be plundered in the interest of the Eastern and Northern plutocrats."[51]

The Democratic party, including most Georgia Democrats, favored lowering the tariff. Republicans wanted to raise it. But, Watson pointed out, the entire debate on the tariff was a sham. "They [the Democrats] say that a robbery of fifty-six per cent under the McKinley [Republican] bill is a national curse, but that a robbery of forty-eight per cent under the Mills [Democratic] bill would be a national blessing." Similarly, the stringent credit system worked great hardships on the masses of Georgians; yet "the Democratic party has made no organized attack on the national bank system for thirty years."[52] The beneficiaries of southern poverty were the industrialists and monopolists protected by the tariff, the money monopoly entrenched behind the national banking law, and the railroad barons and their transportation monopolies.

They were also responsible for the failure of the southern states to fight back. "Just as the English maintain their conquest of India by taking into co-partnership with themselves a certain percentage of Hindus, so the North holds the South in subjection by enlisting Southern capitalists and politicians. . . . United themselves, the Northern capitalists divide the Southerners, and thus rule and despoil the South."[53] The result was the unseemly spectacle of "Southern . . . leaders actually trampling upon each other in their eager haste to help the East plunder the South."[54] The plutocracy of the North had its collaborators in the South, and they in turn maintained their political power behind a smoke screen of white supremacy.

To Watson the Negro question was what southern Democrats talked about "when they come back home after one of their big surrenders at a national convention."[55] "The color question," he insisted, "has been the instrument of our political enslavement." It was what the North used "to compel the South to accept economic doctrines we abhor," what northern Democrats used to rule "the South with a rod of iron," what the "Bosses who have been making slaves out of the whites" used to prevent "the two races from acting together," what the robber used as "a ghost story" to quiet the victim. "We have been led to believe," said Watson, "if we did not vote the democratic ticket some negro would catch us before we got home."[56]

To combat these Democratic tactics, Watson called for an alliance between exploited whites and exploited blacks. One of Watson's most liberal statements on the race issue—and certainly the most widely quoted—appeared in a national magazine during the formative stage of the national Populist party. Referring to black and white southern farmers, Watson wrote: "You are kept apart that you may be separately fleeced of your earnings. You are made to hate each other because upon that hatred is rested the keystone of the arch of financial despotism which enslaves you both. You are deceived and blinded that you may not see how this race antagonism perpetuates a monetary system which beggars both."[57]

Watson frequently made similar observations in speeches in Georgia and elsewhere in the South. In a South Carolina speech, he stated: "I am always glad to see these black people at our meeting for we are one people, united by one economic and social system and what helps one will help another."[58] At the Populist state convention in 1894, Watson announced: "The day has come for the black man to be meted out simple justice as a citizen of the country."[59]

Watson's decision to support legal and political rights for blacks was a calculated political strategy. He had watched the Bourbon organization mobilize black voters to swell the majorities for Colquitt in 1880 and realized that a successful Populist campaign would have to avoid such a fate. Watson was by no means free from racial prejudices, and neither were his rural white followers. In Georgia Watson often reminded his audiences: "Never in my life have I advocated social equality."[60] In practice, the Populists were no more inclined than Democrats to choose black candidates as party nominees, although they did recruit at least nominal black participation on party committees.

Watson called for a sweeping political realignment that would break apart both of the national parties. The Populists would overturn the Democrats in the South and the Republicans in the West and from these bases launch their assault on the Northeast. Tariffs, national banking systems, monopolies, hard money, constricted credit, railroad abuses, and all the other injustices that held southern farmers in bondage would be eliminated. If this strategy required concessions to black southerners, so be it. Tom Watson vowed: "The cause of the South *shall* be heard."[61]

For a time Watson championed the subtreasury plan as a preferred method of transferring the foundations of the political economy from northeastern industrial capitalism to southern and western agriculture. The plan called for the establishment of a federal subtreasury system in all leading agricultural counties. Farmers would store staple crops—cotton, wheat, tobacco, and so on—at the subtreasuries and receive loans equal to 80 percent of the value of the stored crops. The important part of the arrangement was the stipulation that the federal government would print new currency backed by the stored farm products to fund the loans. The subtreasury would, Watson explained, replace the national banking system as "the channels of communication through which the government distributed its money to the people."[62] Rather than a currency based on the magical qualities presumably inherent in silver and especially gold, the currency would rest on cotton and wheat. It was a breathtaking concept intended to shift the center of economic gravity from Wall Street to the agricultural provinces. It was also a difficult strategy to popularize; it horrified conservatives; and, as espoused by Watson, it went well beyond what many other Populists were willing to accept. Ultimately, Watson deemphasized the issue to concentrate on other reforms.

The Populists assailed every Bourbon tenet. By declaring a holy war on northeastern industrial capitalism, the Populists threatened the Compromise of 1877, thereby inviting the federal intervention in southern social relations so dreaded by the Bourbons. On cue, Henry Cabot Lodge, a racist Republican leader in the Senate, introduced a "force bill" calling for federal protection of voting rights in the southern states. The Populists divided white voters, which in Henry Grady's verbal nightmare "would invite the debauching bid of factions" for the "credulous, impulsive—easily led and too often easily bought"— black voters.[63] Grady was at least partially correct; Democrats and Populists were soon competing vigorously for the favor of black voters. In the long term such competition posed a clear threat to white supremacy. And, of course, the Populists had the audacity to question the Bourbon right to rule. It is small wonder that the Democrats regarded the Populists as little better than radical Republicans and fought back ferociously.

The Populist party grew more or less directly from the Farmers' Alliance. Originating in Texas, the Alliance arrived in Georgia in the summer of 1887. On the local level the organization stressed cooperative enterprise. Sometimes this meant no more than suballiances striking bargains with local merchants, promising all their trade to stores that gave special discounts. Often suballiances established their own stores, which were supplied with fertilizers and other goods by the Alliance state exchange. The Georgia state exchange, located in Atlanta, was for a time the most successful in the South. The Alliance promoted cooperative marketing, establishing cotton warehouses, particularly in plantation counties.

The Alliance cooperative program attracted large numbers of north Georgia farmers. Throughout the hills and river valleys, families taught by tradition or experience to be independent increasingly found themselves working another man's land and relying on credit at another man's store. For a once sturdy yeomanry the descent into dependency measured by the soaring growth of farm tenancy was surely traumatic. Cooperative action promised a method for despairing farmers to regain control of their own lives and a weapon with which to fight back against the merchants and townsmen who were the chief beneficiaries of their decline.

In the restive hills the arrival of the Alliance marked a new phase of the continuing struggle between town and countryside, merchants and farmers. During the 1880s townsmen, sometimes supported by more affluent farmers, called for enactment of county fencing ordinances. In antebellum Georgia, farmers fenced in their crops; unfarmed land was a "commons" open for grazing to the livestock of any local resident. Townspeople, tired of swine rooting over their lots and streets, demanded that livestock be fenced, a requirement that many small or landless farmers viewed as yet another invasion of their rights. Fencing laws, along with legislation strengthening property rights relative to trespassing, hunting, and fishing, were debatable issues throughout the state. Following emancipation, many planters supported restrictive legislation as a method to curtail the independence of blacks, and the legislature responded with laws applicable to most of the plantation counties. In the hill country, however, the farmers had by the late 1880s largely won the fencing debate; most of the uplands remained open. Cooperative action offered a path to future progress. The Alliance program, according to a business-oriented critic, meant that "the country people were to be arrayed in fierce hostility to the town people."[64]

The social functions sponsored by the Alliance reinforced its appeal in the hills as in other areas of the state. The twice monthly suballiance meetings featured gospel singing, lectures, ritual, and fellowship. Membership in the Alliance was entirely white, with blacks cloistered in the Colored Farmers' Alliance. In addition to white male farmers, the Alliance recruited women members and welcomed rural teachers, journalists, ministers, and doctors. Classified as undesirable were merchants, bankers, lawyers, and townsmen, a blacklist that seems to have been observed with considerably more seriousness in north Georgia than in the lowlands. Speaking the "language of evangelical Protestantism," the Alliance sought to band together the community of true believers behind a program of cooperative endeavor.[65]

Alliance organizers found no shortage of followers in other parts of the state. The social dynamics so clearly etched in the uplands fueled the general growth of the Alliance; everywhere smaller farmers labored on the verge of bankruptcy. The wiregrass–piney woods region of south Georgia, which was largely unsettled at the time of the Civil War, developed rapidly during the postwar years. Commercial fertilizers made cotton production feasible, and most of all railroad expansion provided access to markets for cotton, lumber, turpentine, and other products. The rapid population growth in the region created social dislocation and inadequate credit, merchandizing, and other services. The Alliance, with its program of cooperative enterprise and social assimilation, thrived in such an environment.

In the plantation belt, the Alliance attracted numerous planters to its ranks. William J. Northen, president of the genteel, prestigious, and planter-dominated State Agricultural Society, and Leonidas F. Livingston, the immediate past president, quickly emerged as Alliance leaders. Intentionally or not, the Alliance offered a vehicle for the reassertion of planter power in an age when the growing towns were becoming the political and social centers of country life. In the plantation counties, towns competed for Alliance warehouses and patronage, and south Georgia railroads gave reduced rates and other advantages to Alliance shippers.

The Alliance roared into Georgia and seemed for a time to overwhelm all before it. By 1889 it boasted eighty-five thousand members and at its height in the summer of 1890 enrolled perhaps one hundred thousand Alliancemen and women. Politicans clamored to find a place on the bandwagon. General John B. Gordon, never one to deny his services to a worthy cause, became an Allianceman, and Henry W. Grady, addressing "for the first time in my life . . . an audience in the open air," spoke at Alliance gatherings.[66] The Atlanta *Constitution* provided the building housing the Alliance state exchange, and the rival *Journal* countered by donating $1,000 toward its operating expenses.

But even in this heady, expansionist atmosphere, it was becoming obvious that cooperatives alone could not break the stranglehold of hard money and stringent credit, crop liens and furnishing merchants, and all the other burdens borne by southern agriculture. Meeting in St. Louis in December 1889, Southern Alliance delegates adopted a radical agrarian program that included nationalization of the railroads, abolition of the national banking system, free coinage of silver, curtailment of governmental spending and taxation, and creation of a subtreasury system of farm credit. A few months later the Georgia Alliance executive committee made the St. Louis platform the basis for a broader Alliance "yardstick" by which Democratic candidates in state contests could be judged.

The Alliance entered politics with a vengeance in 1890. At state and district Democratic conventions and in Democratic primaries, Alliancemen endorsed candidates who supported the main features of the St. Louis program (though not necessarily the subtreasury, which evoked disagreement within the Georgia Alliance) and opposed candidates who did not. The only serious contenders for governor were Alliance leaders. W. J. Northen, a prosperous Hancock County planter, won the office after L. F. Livingston dropped out of the race to run for a congressional seat. A majority of the state legislature elected in 1890 held membership in the Alliance. Georgia sent Tom Watson and five other new congressmen to Washington, and the entire ten-member House delegation measured up to the Alliance yardstick and received Alliance endorsement. The Alliance campaign forced the Democrats to become more attentive to farmer concerns, but, as Tom Watson soon learned, pro-Alliance politicians were not necessarily willing to break with the Democratic party or seriously to disrupt the Bourbon political system.

The record of the 1890–91 "farmers' legislature" further confirmed the limited effectiveness of the Alliance in politics. Alliance intervention produced a more diverse, less affluent, older legislature than the Bourbon Democrats usually elected, but, measured by legislative accomplishments, the general assembly was not remarkably different from any other legislature during the period. It extended the powers of the railroad commission, increased financial support for the common schools, and broadened the fertilizer inspection system; it also strengthened the crop-lien law, approved the first statewide Jim Crow act requiring segregation on railroads, and elected John B. Gordon to the United States Senate.

The failure of the Alliance political crusade increased the pressure for more direct action. Western Alliancemen formed the Populist party in 1890, and the following year Watson bolted the Democratic party to join them. In early 1892 the Southern Alliance and a number of other organizations again met in St. Louis and issued a call urging Alliancemen and other citizens to "hold public meetings . . . and take steps to organize preparatory to electing delegates to a National Convention."[67] Soon afterward the upper piedmont DeKalb County sub-alliance met to organize a branch of the Populist party.

Populism in Georgia was a complex movement that represented at least two separate strains of social protest. Although Watson was the state's best-known and most effective Populist leader, he spoke primarily for one wing of a diverse party. Watson led a sizable group of disaffected Georgia planters centered in the worn and declining old cotton belt. Their goal was to seize control of the state and attack the national political system. Small farmers comprised the bulk of the other wing of the party, and their concerns were essentially local. Concentrated in the north Georgia hills, this branch of Populism grew directly from the Farmers' Alliance. Its leader was William L. Peek, manager of the Alliance state exchange.

Peek's efforts to carry a united Alliance into the third-party movement quickly collapsed. Georgia Alliance president Leonidas Livingston, after considerable vacillation, chose to remain with the Democrats and used his presidential power to retard the Populist revolt. Governor Northen, Senator Gordon, and numerous other Alliancemen remained staunch and unwavering Democrats. The Peek forces countered these defections as effectively as they could. They established a working relationship with the previously ignored Colored Farmers' Alliance. In December 1891 they purchased the *Southern Alliance Farmer*, official voice of the state Alliance and previously a Livingston paper. (By this time Watson had already established his third-party *People's Party Paper.*) Using the Alliance network as their base, Peek and his associates accomplished the formidable task of creating a third-party organizational structure.

The Populists held their state convention in Atlanta in July 1892. The out-at-the-elbow attire of many of the delegates suggested the convention's common folk orientation. The convention nominated a full slate of candidates and chose Peek as their gubernatorial candidate. A substantial farmer from upper piedmont Rockdale County, Peek called himself "a real dirt farmer" and launched a vigorous campaign. The Populists projected a class appeal and sought the votes of black and white farmers and town laborers.

The Democrats renominated W. J. Northen and struck out in rage at the Populist upstarts. The *Constitution* summarized the heart of the Democratic indictment: Populism could only "weaken and divide the Democratic party, and in accomplishing that they tear down the only barrier that stands between the white people and negro domination."[68] To General Gordon, Tom Watson was "this preacher of atheism, this sympathizer with bloody-handed anarchy, this shameless defamer of our spotless, pure and peerless Southern womanhood."[69] Before the campaign, the Democrats redrew the boundaries of the tenth congressional district in an effort to complicate Watson's campaign for reelection.

Violence became almost a standard tactic. Early in the campaign, a mob attacked W. L. Peek, badly injuring his arm and thereby hampering the remainder of his campaign. When James B. Weaver, the Populist presidential nominee, attempted to canvass Georgia, anti-Populist gangs forced him to abandon his tour. In the Georgia uplands, where the conflict between Populists and Democrats reflected the longstanding struggle between farmers and merchants, the campaign sometimes became bloody. In the lowlands violence seems to have centered around clashes between rival groups of planters struggling for partisan control of their counties and particularly for control of the black voting population. By the time the election was mercifully past, at least fifteen people were dead.

In the election the Democrats had the enormous advantage of party loyalty. The Democracy in Georgia was a political church with sacred commitments to white supremacy and home rule and holy symbolism spiritualizing the Lost Cause and the salvation of the state from the sins of Reconstruction radicalism. Heretics, as John Gordon realized, simply had to be shameless defamers of southern womanhood. In real churches, in fact, congregations split apart as Populists or Democrats withdrew to form more faithful assemblies. Such deeply held beliefs also help to account for the Democratic willingness to resort to fraud to defeat the Populists.

Both parties vied for the votes of black Georgians, most of which went to the Democrats. The most obvious explanation for black political behavior is that Peek and the Farmers' Alliance gave their "colored" co-Alliancemen little reason to feel welcome. Edward S. Richardson, the head of the Colored Alliance, was a conservative who favored Negro uplift rather than black militancy and who supported cooperation with whites; yet members of the Colored Alliance could not trade at Alliance cooperatives or buy from Peek's state exchange. Not until the Peek forces began to organize the Populist party did they make overtures to the Colored Alliance. Black leaders divided in the election, with Henry M. Turner, among others, supporting Northen.

But it was also true that the black vote was no longer a free vote. Throughout much of the state, planters and (insofar as they were not the same people) merchants controlled the land, credit, and law. Black people who braved local white opposition to insist on political independence were being foolhardy as well as courageous. They faced not only economic devastation but physical violence. The effective demise of the Republican party left blacks in most counties with little political organization and little reason to feel that the ballot had been of any material benefit. It was small wonder that the combination of economic intimidation, violence, and bribery practiced by planters, merchants, and urban Democratic organizations often influenced the casting of black ballots. Indeed, economic intimidation was not limited to blacks; in some cases, white employers offered political "advice" to white workers.

Georgia did not have a secret ballot law. Instead the parties printed the ballot, and the voter delivered it to the polling booth in the plain view of interested bystanders. Not infrequently planters distributed ballots to their tenants and marched the entire group to the polls to cast them. A county Democratic chairman was stating the obvious when he informed Democratic planters: "It is absolutely necessary that you should bring to bear the power which your situation gives over tenants laborers & croppers."[70] By the late nineteenth century, "the central consideration in southern politics," one scholar has recently concluded, was the "idea of controlling the black vote, especially on the local level."[71] This struggle apparently accounted for much of the violence in the plantation belt.

Finally, of course, it is difficult to draw inferences from election returns. Democratic officials were not always reliable in counting and reporting votes. Watson lost his bid for reelection to Congress as a result of the huge vote against him in Richmond County (Augusta). The approximately ten thousand eligible voters in Richmond County cast well over twelve thousand votes, 86 percent of which went to Watson's opponent.

Northen defeated Peek in the gubernatorial election, Watson lost his congressional seat, and most of the other Populist candidates went down to defeat. Urban areas voted overwhelmingly Democratic, though only Augusta citizens could boast a voter turnout of well over 100 percent. Outside of Watson's district, most Georgia planters and merchants remained loyal to the Democratic party, and, as indicated, most black votes were Democratic. Such a formidable coalition gave Northen a two-to-one majority. Peek ran well only among his hill country farmers, in a few western Georgia Alliance strongholds, and in Watson's plantation counties.

But rather than generating despair, these disheartening results spurred Watson to renewed effort. In July 1893 he began a three-month speaking tour across the state. By this time the national depression of 1893 had turned the already depressed Georgia economy into an economic disaster. Huge crowds of angry, cheering people greeted Watson at every stop. Governor Northen expressed the views of the suddenly hard-pressed Democrats in a letter to President Grover Cleveland: "The conditions of this state are fearful and threatening . . . and we are rapidly losing strength. . . . Ex-Congressman Watson, the leader of the Populists, has taken advantage of the conditions, and is speaking over the State to assemblies never less than 2,000 and sometimes as many as 5,000 people."[72]

As Northen observed, Watson had taken command of the Populist forces. The Farmers' Alliance, already in decline, effectively collapsed under the weight of partisan strife, and its failure combined with Peek's poor showing in the 1892 election strengthened the influence of Watson and his planter following. Watson's *People's Party Paper* was the unofficial voice of the movement, although some thirty-five other Populist papers joined in the clamor to deliver the third-party message. Watson even wrote a song dramatizing the plight of depression-wracked farmers:

> My Husband came from town last night
>     As sad as man could be;
> His wagon empty—cotton gone—
>     And not a dime had he. . . .[73]

The 1894 Populist convention adopted Watson's strategy of minimizing social conflict within Georgia while pressing the attack on national policy. The convention nominated for governor the eminently respectable James K. Hines. Reared on a plantation, Hines studied law at Harvard University and entered politics in a plantation county in Watson's district before moving to Atlanta to pursue a highly successful law practice. Some two dozen black delegates participated in the convention activities, as compared to the two blacks who had attended the 1892 convention, and one, a close Watson ally, was elected to the party executive committee. Watson geared for another assault on the tenth district congressional seat.

In the campaign the Populists eagerly endeavored to broaden their electoral coalition. Watson and Hines sought to augment their rural Populist following by appealing to the votes of townsmen. "Tell me, Mr. Merchant," Watson argued, "if you destroy the prosperity of my farm where will you get your customers?"[74] To Watson, Georgia merchants and shippers had a heavy stake in the struggle against the domination of northeastern industrial capitalism. Borrowing from Democratic strategy, the Populists avidly pursued the votes of black Georgians while accusing the national Democrats of favoring social equality because Grover Cleveland had once supported a mildly anti-segregation policy while governor of New York. Most of all the Populists tried to enlist Georgia planters in their crusade against northeastern capitalism. Georgia planters had once stood against the policies of northern big business; Watson called for them to resume the battle.

Clearly on the defensive, the Democrats responded as well as they could. They nominated William Y. Atkinson, the leader of the younger

Democrats who had long chafed under old guard control of the party, as their gubernatorial candidate. Atkinson denounced the Populists as "western fault-finders" who favored woman's suffrage, breathed "the spirit of confiscation," and championed "the wild and visionary ideas of the mongrel horde from the west."[75] The Democrats called for party loyalty and white solidarity in defense of white supremacy; they appealed to black voters and vigorously worked to corral their votes; and they tightened the control of Democratic local officials over the casting, counting, and reporting of the votes. In the tenth district the party renominated the incumbent who had defeated Watson two years previously.

The campaign was not so violent as the previous one, but it was probably more fraudulent. The voters may well have elected Hines as governor, although election officials declared Atkinson the victor. Democratic managers also counted Watson out in his congressional race, with the approximately 11,500 qualified voters in Augusta casting almost 16,000 ballots and providing the Democratic candidate with a majority of just over 11,500 votes. So fraudulent was the tenth district election that even the Democrats admitted "irregularities" and agreed to another election for the seat. Held in 1895, that election, too, went against Watson.

The reported tally in the gubernatorial race awarded Hines just over 44 percent of the vote. Populist efforts to woo merchants and townsmen produced limited results. The cities, as always, voted heavily Democratic. Hines broke about even in the north Georgia hill country, and his support came from the rural areas. The towns were Democratic strongholds. Most of all the Populists were unable to convert the majority of the planter counties to the third-party standard. Although running far better than Peek had done in the plantation belt, Hines did well primarily in the eastern part of the state among the Watson followers. A substantial majority of blacks voted, were voted, or were counted Democratic. Shaken and divided, the majority of the planters and merchants chose to remain with the Democrats, and that decision doomed the Populist movement.

The 1894 election marked the high tide of Georgia Populism. In the face of the initial Populist challenge in 1892, the Georgia Democracy was divided between the heirs of Henry Grady who had hung out their latchstrings to the Northeast and those Democrats who leaned toward the Farmers' Alliance program and wished to strengthen the party's agrarian appeal. Thus the 1892 state Democratic convention selected a national party delegation friendly to the reactionary and northeastern-oriented Grover Cleveland and paradoxically wrote a state platform that included free coinage of silver, reform of the national banking system, and regulation of railroads and monopolies. The national Democrats nominated and elected Cleveland, whose inept administration was a favorite Populist target and an increasing Democratic embarrassment. At the 1896 national party convention, however, Georgia Democrats joined with other southern and western insurgents to repudiate Cleveland and nominate William Jennings Bryan on a platform of free silver and rural liberalism. Predictably, the Democrats chose a conservative New England banker, Arthur Sewall, as the vice-presidential nominee.

By placing a free silver westerner at the top of their ticket, the Democrats put enormous pressure on the Populists. The national Populist convention chose to endorse Bryan but to replace Sewall with Tom Watson as the vice-presidential candidate. Watson, who did not attend the convention, accepted the nomination on the apparent assumption—or at least the strong hope—that the national Democrats would voluntarily withdraw Sewall and accept the Bryan-Watson ticket or could be forced to do so by the specter of the free silver vote being divided between two tickets. This ploy failed, and Watson's efforts to prevent the Populists from being absorbed or demoralized by the Bryan Democracy proved futile. In Georgia, as elsewhere, the declining Populists ultimately conceded defeat. The Bryan-Watson ticket was withdrawn and Georgia cast its electoral votes for Bryan and Sewall.

The 1896 Georgia state elections took place in October before the November presidential debacle, but even then the third-party movement was clearly on the wane. The Populist gubernatorial candidate, a Rome lawyer and Prohibitionist named Seaborn Wright, presented a respectable challenge to the incumbent Democratic governor, but, when the ballots were counted, Wright's totals were ten thousand votes and several percentage points fewer than the returns for Hines in the 1894 election. The 1898 Populist state ticket documented the party's demise by receiving less than a third of the votes. By this time Watson had retired to McDuffie County to practice law and to write a highly regarded two-volume history of France describing the common folk's heroic struggle against aristocratic privilege.

The Populist crusade rent the Democratic party and provoked sharp social conflict. Third-party partisans, according to an Augusta newspaper, deliberately set "the laborer against the employer, the county against the town, the poor against the rich, the farmer against the merchant, and everybody against the lawyer,"[76] and there was an element of truth in each of these observations. Populist elites, as compared with Georgia Democratic leaders, one recent study has reported, sprang from less affluent families, had considerably less education, and were more likely to be farmers.[77] Among active Georgia Populists were at least a few men of substantial wealth, many planters and lawyers, and doubtlessly merchants and businessmen, but the Democracy remained the party of the privileged in Georgia and the Populists held some claim to being the partisan home of the common man. Such divisions combined with the ideological gulf that divided Populist and Democrat to produce partisan conflict of sufficient intensity to divide communities, churches, even families, and to provoke violence and fraud.

# Chapter Five

## Myth, Reality, and Social Stability in Uptown and County Seat

The Bourbon system that the Populists challenged rested on considerably more than white supremacy and one-party politics. During the late nineteenth century, Georgia settled into its role as a supplier of raw materials and to a lesser extent markets for an extortionate North. The state's eviscerated economy rested upon cheap plantation labor, and the social structure that assured it became increasingly rigid. Tom Watson raised the standard of revolt, but with the failure of Populism the state turned even more inward. Henry Grady may have hung out his latchstrings to the North, but many of his fellow citizens did not, particularly in social and cultural matters. If Populism could not turn back the tide of Yankee values and capitalist market relationships, then mythology, religion, and white supremacy would have to serve.

The plantation remained Georgia's basic economic institution, and its values and most particularly its coercive forms of labor control tended to be those of the state. The days of hundred-thousand-dollar cotton crops were long past, but the first two decades of the twentieth century were prosperous. Evangelist Samuel Porter Jones was not precisely accurate when he announced in 1901 that farmers "were never in so good a condition as today,"[1] but it was certainly true that times were better than they had been since the Civil War. During these years a majority of Georgia's population continued to reside in the plantation counties stretching through the central and southwestern part of the state, and there too were the majority of the towns and smaller cities. In any event the spread of cotton culture into the uplands and pine barrens extended in varying degrees the social relations of plantation agriculture over much of the state.

Successful planters supplemented their agricultural income with general stores, cotton gins, and other enterprises, and successful merchants and businessmen acquired plantations. All became more town-oriented whether or not they actually took up residence there. Many did become townsmen, particularly after the coming of the automobile simplified transportation. Following a tour through central Georgia, Ray Stannard Baker reported in 1908 "that almost any prominent merchant, banker, lawyer, or politician whom I met in the towns owned a plantation in the country."[2] Tenancy required less supervision than slavery, permitting enterprising planters to devote excess time and energy to town pursuits while making town society convenient for their wives and town schools available for their children. The large majority of employed Georgians—62 percent of the work force in 1910—labored in agriculture, the bulk of them as tenants or farm hands. Most of the rest of the work force supplied goods and services to the agricultural sector. At the same time almost one of every three families resided in cities, towns, or hamlets.*

Georgia contained almost 550 villages and small towns in 1910. Planters and merchants provided the nucleus around which many villages emerged. A country store at a crossroads needed only to be augmented by a gin, a church, a school, and perhaps a blacksmith shop and a mule barn (where not only mules but horses, cattle, secondhand guns, and maybe untaxed whiskey could be bought, sold, or traded) to have the foundation for a blossoming community. Some towns were interior cotton centers with presses for compacting the cotton for shipment North; some served as local government centers for the 147 counties in Georgia in 1910; in varying degrees a considerable number conformed to a novelist's description of a southern town where the "proportion of professional people ran high: one went there to have his teeth pulled, his wagon fixed, his heart listened to, his money deposited, his soul saved, his mules vetted."[3] It was also where the surrounding countryside congregated on Saturday afternoon to shop and socialize. An occasional town demonstrated sufficient commitment to progress to raise the funds necessary to launch a cotton mill or fertilizer factory. The latter represented no mean feat because small communities rarely attracted outside capital.

In this environment the daughters of merchants married the sons of planters who themselves became lawyers and bankers. The alliances thus cemented created a small town elite that excluded all blacks and most whites. In a well-known study, Jasper Berry Shannon called it

*Georgia contained 516 villages of less than 2,500 people where 11 percent of the total population resided; 36 towns of 2,500 to 10,000 with 6.4 percent of the state population (of these 14 were larger towns of 5,000–10,000 population and 22 were smaller towns of 2,500–5,000), and 9 cities of above 10,000 with 14.3 percent of the population.

"the county seat governing class." "The political center of gravity of the South," Shannon wrote, "changed from the countryside to the county seat between 1870 and 1900."[4] If county seat governing class is defined broadly to include leading local planters and influential townsmen in neighboring communities, the term is apt. Though individually overshadowed by the greater success of businessmen in Atlanta and other cities, the county planter-merchant-banker-lawyer-doctor elite was the fundamental locus of political authority in Georgia. Disorganized and scattered over a vast area, its members often watched quietly while Atlanta promoters in the Grady tradition ran roughshod over their lackluster rivals in Macon, Augusta, and Savannah—so long, of course, as no vital interests were at stake. When they were, as Tom Watson well understood, the response was different. In 1895 Watson angrily wrote: "The bankers control the voters in the cities and towns just as the overseers used to control slave labor upon the plantations."[5] There was clearly an element of truth in Watson's outburst. The inability of the Populists to win over a sufficient portion of the county governing class or decisively to defeat it was the basic explanation for their failure.

Particularly in the plantation belt, small-town elites retained some of the graciousness of the antebellum South, and the easy availability of black cooks, maids, and yardmen contributed to a comfortable style of life. They also tended to be profoundly conservative, combining the social values of plantation agriculture with the normal conservatism of successful American townsmen. Dependent on cheap labor and surrounded by a sea of poverty, they treasured social stability. Isolated from the mainstream of national development, they were the foremost defenders of what came to be known as "the southern way of life." Their ideology was that of the Lost Cause.

Amid magnolia blossoms and happy, singing darkies the mythology of the Lost Cause encompassed the benevolence of slavery, the chivalry of planters, the righteousness of the South's position during the Civil War, the gallantry of southern white men, the sacrifices of white women, and the loyalty of black slaves. Three recent studies of the Lost Cause have labeled it respectively "a Southern civil religion," "a kulturreligion," and "the dominant faith of a region."[6] Among the most vocal proponents of the creed was Mildred L. Rutherford, a prominent Athens educator who in 1911 became historian general of the United Daughters of the Confederacy.

Rutherford, an Athens writer later recalled, devoted her adult life to "her love of teaching . . . and her determined vindication of the

South, its institutions, its history, its part in the War Between the States and its literature."[7] Her particular concern, like that of the Daughters generally, was "that the truth of history shall be taught in our southern schools." Among these truths was the fact that the Civil War resulted from "the interference with *States Rights*, and slavery happened to be one of the state rights most interfered with." Indeed, there was no Civil War: "It was the WAR BETWEEN THE STATES, for the nonseceding States of the United States made war upon the seceding States to force them back into the Union. Please call it so and teach it so." Even slavery was "a word that crept in with the abolition crusade." Rather than slaves, blacks were "our people, our negroes, part of our very homes." False history "shall be ruled out of our universities, colleges, schools, and libraries," she insisted, although congenially adding, "unless the authorities or communities prefer false history." The South surrendered, according to Rutherford, but the cause was not lost. "There is no New South," she proclaimed. "And the men of today and the women of today are adjusting themselves to the old South remade."[8]

Organized in 1894, the United Daughters of the Confederacy was the most energetic and enthusiastic of the organizations promoting what Rutherford regarded as a not so lost cause. Georgia women met in Atlanta in 1895 to establish a state division, and by 1916 Georgia contained 116 active chapters. The Daughters were responsible for the Confederate monuments that graced virtually every courthouse square, for the ubiquitous pictures of Robert E. Lee and Jefferson Davis in Georgia schoolhouses, and for a variety of other projects. And they were by no means without allies in their endeavors for the cause. Just after the War between the States, Columbus women organized a memorial association and called for setting aside a special day for "paying honor to those who died defending the life, honor and happiness of the Southern women."[9] At the turn of the century the Confederated Southern Memorial Association named Jefferson Davis's birthday, June 3, as Confederate Memorial Day, and it joined Robert E. Lee's birthday as a widely observed holiday.

In 1875 Georgia veterans organized the Survivors' Association of Confederate Soldiers, with, of course, John B. Gordon as president. A decade and a half later it was absorbed by the regionwide United Confederate Veterans, with, of course, John B. Gordon as president. In truth few could match Gordon's oratorical ability to glorify "that old plantation life of the South." Echoing a concern often expressed by proponents of the Lost Cause, Gordon stated: "The great problem of our future is not how to secure material prosperity." It was instead "how to hold to the characteristics of our old civilization."[10] Georgia churchmen shared Gordon's anxiety. One study has concluded that "Christian clergymen were the prime celebrants of the religion of the Lost Cause."[11] By linking the myth with the tribulations of a chosen people, traditionalist ministers rejected northern materialistic versions of progress and offered a formidable defense of the southern cultural status quo. The Daughters, Confederate veterans, Lost Cause ministers, and other groups might not be able to solve Gordon's problem, but they could ensure that the old civilization remained on display as a model for proper behavior.

Political developments in Georgia both recognized the popularity of the Lost Cause and gave the myth a significant boost. In 1886 the hapless Macon political establishment was making yet another doomed effort to place one of its own in the Georgia statehouse. Maneuvering frantically to turn back the threat, Henry Grady decided upon Gordon, who was broke and unemployed following his Florida financial disasters, and launched his campaign by inviting Jefferson Davis to speak in Atlanta. People gathered in the city by the trainloads to see and hear the former president of the Confederacy. "It was," reported the *Constitution*, "a matchless outpouring of enthusiastic humanity." Confederate veterans from all over the state marched through the streets, James Longstreet appeared wearing his Confederate lieutenant general's uniform, Gordon wore his minié-ball scar and looked heroic, and Grady, who orchestrated affairs as master of ceremonies, predicted that "Confederate money will be good before midnight."[12] The contest for the Democratic gubernatorial nomination became almost a referendum on the Lost Cause as Gordon rallied the Confederate veterans to his standard and crushed his downstate rival at the Democratic convention.

Devotion to the Lost Cause became a test of loyalty to the South. By the early twentieth century even Tom Watson was romanticizing southern chivalry, "the womanly ideal," and the heroism and "perfect patriotism" of the Confederacy in a Memorial Day address.[13] In 1859 an obscure New York City minstrel wrote a song that began:

> I wish I was in de land ob cotton,
> Old times dar am not forgotten.

It was a prophetic line; by the end of the nineteenth century it was true.

The mythology of the Lost Cause had wide appeal. It was no doubt psychologically important to many Confederate veterans who returned home to a life of debt and hardships, to long-suffering wives who watched their children grow up with little education and less opportunity, and to countless other citizens who had lost relatives, friends, or fortunes in the conflict and wanted to be reassured that the sacrifice had been worthwhile. Almost any white Georgian and perhaps some blacks could identify with the beautiful belles and gallant gentlemen who peopled the vision. So appealing was the romantic imagery that many northerners accepted it as a pleasant alternative to ever bigger and more grimy industrial cities. But if psychological and romantic explanations help to explain the great popularity of the Lost Cause, its longevity and force rested heavily on its function as an ideological defense of the values of small town-plantation elites. The creed glorified the plantation ideal, justified white supremacy, and supported social stability. The myth of the Lost Cause was firmly grounded in current social reality.

Georgia contained twenty-three communities of more than five thousand population, but by 1910 booming Atlanta had risen far above the rest. Georgia's eight other cities with more than ten thousand people might have been described as oversized towns. Following the Civil War, railroad construction and national governmental policy shifted the flow of Georgia products from the seaport of Savannah to the railroad center of Atlanta. Up the steel rail network came the products of Georgia plantations, forests, mines, and farms through a variety of routes but often from the towns to the larger cities to Atlanta to the factories and trading centers of the North, and back down the tracks came northwestern meat and grain and northern manufactures, with Georgia cities serving as the great distributing centers for the products that ultimately appeared on country store shelves. In 1914 Atlanta's annual commerce was $340 million (compared to an annual production of manufactured products valued at $41 million) and 152 trains passed through the city daily. Atlanta and other cities also provided banking, insurance, and other services to the hinterlands.

Manufacturing expanded. An early twentieth-century Scarlett O'Hara would likely have seen a factory and surely would have known someone who had seen one. Fifteen Georgia firms—eleven cotton mills and four railroad shops—employed more than five hundred workers each. But it would be easy to exaggerate the extent of industrial development in the state. Cincinnati, an Ohio center of the southern trade, had a population that was about the same size as Georgia's nine largest cities in 1910 and was about the equivalent of 14 percent of the total Georgia population. Yet the manufacturing payroll in Cincinnati was greater than all manufacturing wages and salaries in Georgia, and the total value added by manufacturing was higher in Cincinnati. Compared to its own past, Georgia's industrial progress was substantial, but compared to the North, manufacturing remained limited. The huge majority of Georgia factory workers toiled in cotton mills of various types, lumber, turpentine, or resin camps, fertilizer factories, cottonseed oil mills, and railroad machine shops, all of which related directly to cotton, trees, or the transportation thereof.

As Henry Grady had hoped, Georgia cities attracted northern capital. The "usual plan" for launching a factory enterprise in the 1880s, according to Grady, was for local entrepreneurs to raise one-third of the needed capital and to rely on northern investors to supply the rest.[14] By the turn of the century half of the 111 cotton mills in operation or under construction were owned wholly or in part by non-Georgians. These mills included most of the larger operations and most of those located in or adjacent to the larger cities. One study has reported that in 1880 non-Georgians owned 12 percent of the non-agricultural wealth in the state; in 1920 they owned 28 percent. The study did not indicate how much of the remaining 72 percent was mortgaged in New York.[15] Georgia cities served as intermediaries between plantation agriculture and northern enterprise, and northern capitalists invested in such strategic sectors of the urban economy as railroads, factories, and Atlanta banks. This is not to suggest conspiracy—indeed, if anything, the investments hint at returning sectional goodwill and helped to make the South a "favored colony"[16]—but it does indicate the dependent nature of the Georgia urban economy.

At the same time cities and towns were far more prosperous than the depressed countryside. In 1900 a Georgian engaged in agriculture earned during the year $259 in constant 1929 dollars. A Georgian who worked at some calling other than agriculture earned $662. By 1920 Georgia farmers were doing better; in that year their annual income in constant dollars was $442. Yet the condition of nonagricultural workers—generally speaking, townsmen—had also improved, and their average income of $967 was still more than double that earned in agricultural pursuits. Georgia townsmen were not noticeably affluent when compared, for example, to Illinois townsmen. In 1900 nonagricultural workers in Georgia made $662; in Illinois the same group earned $1,366; in 1920 Georgia townsmen received $967 and in Illinois $1,512.[17] But by Georgia standards, townsmen could savor considerable prosperity. Georgia farmers—Sam Jones to the contrary—were among the poorest people in the United States.

The thickness of one's wallet was by no means the only measure of
the growing distance between city and farm. Urban life increasingly
included the availability of electric lights, indoor plumbing, public
transportation, daily mail service, and other conveniences. Some of
these services failed to trickle down to white factory workers and even
fewer to the mass of urban blacks. But for a comfortable and prospering urban bourgeoisie, city life had its advantages. It is little wonder
that Populist spokesmen expressed resentment toward urban areas or
that rural-urban conflict was a central feature of twentieth-century
Georgia politics.

The "uptown" leadership in Georgia cities and larger towns shared
much in common with the governing elite in neighboring small towns.
Rarely did either demonstrate serious lack of faith in the virtues of
cheap labor, low taxes, and social stability. The Lost Cause remained
alive and well along Peachtree Street and flourished in the plantation
belt cities to the south. But there were also differences in wealth, in
style, and potentially even in policy. A town editor wrote: "Atlanta is
certainly a fast place in every sense of the word, and our friends in
Atlanta are fast people. They live fast, and they die fast. They make
money fast and they spend it fast."[18] Even if ultimately dependent on
plantation agriculture, uptown was still a step, or perhaps two or three
steps, up the line from the cotton fields. No matter how devoted an
Atlanta or Augusta businessman was to white supremacy, the issue
was less immediate than it was in Plains or Hahira.

At least in the late nineteenth century, membership in Atlanta's economic elite was relatively fluid. A study of the city's wealthy and presumably powerful found new men persistently pushing their way into
this rarefied company. Although most were southern natives, relatively few were former planters or the scions of planter families. Most
were successful businessmen—mainly merchants and industrialists—
and, the study reported, many built or augmented their wealth by
investing "heavily in real estate in a city where property values esca-
lated at a dizzying pace,"[19] a fact that may help to account for the civic
leadership's preoccupation with population and economic growth.
Similar studies of economic elites in other Georgia cities are yet to be
published, but impressionistic evidence suggests that there was less
social mobility. Henry Grady was not entirely fair, but he did make a
point in commenting about hospitality and leadership in Augusta:
"When this staid city invites a man to involve himself in the melan-
choly pomp and circumstance attending a trip up the canal, you may

be sure that man has a charnel house full of respectable bones aback of him."[20]

No other community matched Atlanta's rapid pace and aggressive leadership. City boosters raised the funds necessary to attract the Georgia Institute of Technology and Emory and Oglethorpe universities, sponsored three major expositions, and formed a manufacturers' association to provide inexpensive factory sites and other assistance for new industries. Local businessmen in some other cities and towns promoted similar programs, and a few corporations, especially railroads, created industrial departments that endeavored to woo northern capital southward. During the late nineteenth century most of these projects were privately funded. During the early twentieth century, however, growth-oriented uptown leaders demanded greater cooperation from their local governments. In 1903 the city of Atlanta contributed to a campaign led by the chamber of commerce to publicize the economic opportunities in agriculture and industry available in Atlanta and vicinity. Such joint public-private projects were to become increasingly common during the 1920s.

The most elaborate of the promotional campaigns was the Forward Atlanta program. In the late 1920s the Forward Atlanta Commission sought to ballyhoo northern investors with arguments that would hardly have surprised Henry Grady. The commission pointed to Georgia's "ample supply" of "native, Anglo-Saxon" labor, low wages, low taxes, abundant resources, and the "absence of labor troubles." Negro workers, the co-chairman of the campaign added, were "well qualified" to perform "the common labor" and were "content" to do so.[21] The points emphasized by the Forward Atlanta program and other such promotional endeavors largely justified the tongue-in-cheek comments of two bemused observers: "The workers are being offered on the auction block pretty much as their black predecessors were, and their qualities are enlarged upon with the same salesman's gusto. Native Whites! Anglo-Saxons of the true blood! All English-speaking! Tractable, harmonious, satisfied with little! They know nothing of foreign-born radicalism! Come down and gobble them up!"[22]

Urban uptown elites joined their small town counterparts in recognizing the virtues of cheap labor, and both demonstrated their concern for social stability. Affluent urbanites watched with mounting anxiety the expansion of the mill villages and tenements that housed the people who ran the factories and the spread of shacks and shanties that measured the growth of the black population. They were disturbed, too, by the social turmoil and high crime rates that accompanied growth. Economically successful whites fled to suburbs and endeavored to defend their prerogatives with property restrictions, which as in the case of Augusta, protected neighborhood serenity and ensured the "absence of objectionable people."[23]

Nowhere was the problem greater than in Atlanta. By comparison the "staid city" of Augusta was socially respectable. Most white factory workers lived in the factory district; the bulk of blacks resided in or near "the territory"; and, sandwiched more or less between, affluent whites found shelter along the prestigious residential streets and in the suburbs. Filling the interstices were the more highly skilled blue-collar workers, clerks and other white-collar employees, small proprietors, and the more successful blacks. But Atlanta was different. The Gate City's exploding population growth created an amalgam of changing neighborhoods. Although there were several black residential areas, there were no substantial ghettos and, indeed, from the viewpoint of Atlanta's political leadership, the amount of integrated housing was depressing. It was no accident that Atlanta became in 1913 the first Georgia city to enact an ordinance promoting racial segregation within city residential blocks. When that ordinance fell victim to a state supreme court decision, Atlanta enacted an even harsher measure that later expired in a federal courtroom.

At this point, Atlanta authorities sought aid from someone more experienced with denying the substance of equality before the law while preserving its form. They hired as a consultant a city planner from Cleveland, Ohio. Atlanta's money was well allocated. The social engineer consultant explained: "It is more desirable that bankers and the leading businessmen should live in one part of town, storekeepers, clerks and technicians in another, and working people in yet others where they would enjoy the association with neighbors more or less of their own kind." It could hardly have been better put, except, of course, for the judicially discreet absence of any specific mention of black neighborhoods. In 1922 Atlanta enacted "a comprehensive zoning plan" embodying many of the consultant's recommendations.[24]

The uptown elite in the cities and larger towns was the most prosperous social group in Georgia. In a study of Augusta, Richard H. L. German described a more comfortable neighborhood at the turn of the century: "Grand and stately homes surrounded by large plots of ground, gardens and trees, were inhabited by the wealthy industrialists, bankers, brokers, merchants, attorneys and other well-to-do residents."[25] By 1930 a rising politician soon to be elected governor could refer without risking misunderstanding to a similar Atlanta residential area as the "silk-stocking, gin-smelling, northside region."[26] Pressed by the problems created by urban growth and concerned about the unruly and possibly sinful behavior of blacks and white factory workers, uptown elites became increasingly reformist. Perhaps no other institution better expressed the uptown viewpoint than the mainline Protestant churches.

To be sure, vast numbers of white Georgians from all walks of life were at least nominal Southern Baptists and Southern Methodists. Southern Presbyterian and Episcopalian churches, while more likely to serve prestigious residential areas, were by no means confined to them. Furthermore, the majority of churches in Georgia were located in rural areas and villages, and, according to a survey of southeastern churches conducted in the early 1920s, three out of five of the most influential members of a congregation were likely to be farmers.[27] Nevertheless, the center of religious gravity had by the early twentieth century clearly shifted to the towns and cities.

Only two congregations in ten could afford a full-time resident pastor, and they were overwhelmingly situated in urban communities and especially in uptown areas. For other ministers life offered hardships. Six out of ten preachers served at least three churches and sometimes several more. A Southern Baptist minister noted in 1917 that his church had nine thousand parsons.[28] Of these, five thousand saved rural souls and served twenty thousand churches. The four thousand urban ministers were responsible for forty-six hundred churches. Five of every ten white ministers worked at other occupations in order to survive until Sunday preaching time. The fact that bright and able young churchmen did not customarily turn down the far higher salaries and more comfortable lifestyles that uptown could offer tended to concentrate denominational talent—though not necessarily piety—in the cities and towns. Under these circumstances the comparatively well-paid, relatively better educated, far more secure uptown ministers came to dominate church councils.

With the shift to the towns and cities came a growing solicitude for proper social behavior. Contrary to popular stereotypes, the leading white Protestant denominations did not become more otherworldly and fatalistic during the post-Reconstruction era; rather, they vigorously endeavored to shape secular behavior. In the Old South, churches disciplined their own members. It was not at all unknown for a Baptist brother to be cast out for "drunkenness and other improper conduct" or "for leaving his wife and taking up with another woman" or for a

sister to be excommunicated "for allowing frolicking in her house" or
for "committing adultery."[29] But antebellum churchmen rarely sought
to discipline the rest of society. A leading historian of American religion may have overstated the point, but his analysis contains some
truth: "In a land with little real poverty, no urban slums or factory
towns, minimal cultural conflict with Roman Catholic immigrants, with
the Indians removed to the West and blacks considered childlike beneficiaries of civilization, the white southerner felt that his region of the
nation was already closer to millennial perfection than any other part
of the country."[30]

Antebellum churches were, of course, ardent defenders of slavery.
Southern Baptists and Methodists broke with their northern brethren
over the slavery issue in the 1840s and Southern Presbyterians did so
in 1861. Freed from Yankee influences, the leading southern denominations enthusiastically supported the Confederate war effort, and, in
the wake of defeat and frustration, they were rewarded with a massive
growth in membership and influence. "Not until the period of Reconstruction," Samuel S. Hill, Jr., the foremost student of southern religion, has observed, "did the churches' near-complete conquest of the
population get underway."[31] Church leaders, with their expanding
membership lists and increasingly uptown orientation, became pre-
occupied with the moral conduct of the blacks who no longer benefited from the "civilizing" influence of slavery, with the poor whites
congregating in mill villages and tenements, and with Georgians generally who faced the corrupting intrusions of Yankee capital and culture. "I want to see the day come," said Samuel Porter Jones, "when,
if Christians haven't got faith enough in the Lord Jesus Christ . . . to
bind them to decency and right, that the law will help us to make our
members decent."[32]

The church had a duty "to create right sentiment," according to Jones,
and the state had a duty to enforce it. After all, "no man has a right to
an opinion on a moral question." "A man who thinks as he pleases,"
Jones pointed out, "will not be long in determining to do as he pleases."[33]
Drunkenness, especially by a presumably settled married man, headed
the list of the threats Jones perceived to decency. One solution to the
problem was: "Any husband who is known to have been intoxicated
. . . should be consigned to a place of refuge and guarded and protected for at least five years."[34] Jones sometimes stated his views more
vigorously than his fellow ministers, but a consensus was emerging
during the late nineteenth century that government should sternly
prohibit alcoholic beverages, prostitution, gambling, and other vices.

People should be made to be decent whether or not they liked the notion.

Like many other evangelists of the era, Jones had firsthand knowledge of alcoholic husbands. Born the son of a lawyer-businessman in Alabama, Jones experienced a series of traumatic shocks during late childhood and adolescence. His mother, a woman with a strong personality and deeply held religious convictions, died when Sam was nine. He and his brother and sister were packed off to Cartersville, Georgia, to live with grandparents. Two years later Sam's father remarried, moved to Cartersville, and reclaimed the children. Hardly had Sam had time to settle down in another home with a different mother when his father left to fight with Lee's army. Sam was apparently largely unsupervised during the war years and had already developed a fondness for alcohol before Sherman's hordes descended on Cartersville in their advance toward Atlanta. Sam became detached from the rest of his family and while they fled southward, Sam drifted behind Union lines and ultimately made his way to Kentucky. There a business acquaintance of his father sheltered the teenager for the remainder of the war. Jones returned to Cartersville, where, despite a blossoming drinking problem, he completed high school and then read law.

In 1868 Jones passed the bar examination and married the girl he had wooed in Kentucky. While Republicans and Ku Kluxers battled for control of the fate of Georgia, Jones and his new wife moved around while he unsuccessfully attempted to start a law practice. Jones was also unsuccessful in controlling his appetite for alcohol. By 1872 Jones and his growing family had returned to Cartersville, where they lived in a hovel while Jones worked long hours as a manual laborer at a local furnace. Then Jones underwent his conversion. Just emerging from a lengthy drinking spree, he was called to the bedside of his dying father, who chided the young man about his drinking. Jones vowed never to drink again and soon afterward preached his first sermon at his grandfather's church.

For the remainder of the 1870s Jones was a Methodist circuit rider serving a series of predominantly rural circuits. Usually he was minister of four or more churches at a time. In the early years it was a hard life. "I would work on the farm when I was not preaching and make a few bales of cotton, carry them to town, sell them, and apply the money on my debts." But Jones had now found his profession; he was a richly gifted preacher with an eye for folksy anecdotes and an ability to summarize his thoughts in catchy epigrams. "Every barroom is a recruiting office for hell." "Politicians have no more heart than a Florida alligator or a society woman." "A woman can be a perfect lady and dance but she cannot be a Christian and dance."[35]

Soon Jones's reputation spread, and other Methodist ministers invited him to preach at revivals. At one of the earliest of these, Tom Watson was a member of the audience. Watson later wrote: "In the good year 1877, Sam Jones lit down in this veritable town of Thomson and began to go for the devil and his angels in a manner which was entirely new to said devil."[36] The Methodist hierarchy recognized Jones's success in 1880 by appointing him fund-raising agent for a church orphans' home, which effectively left him free to devote full time to his evangelical work.

During the next quarter of a century Jones became one of America's foremost evangelists. In one of his earliest forays outside the state, Jones went to Brooklyn, where the resident minister looked him over, quickly escorted him to a local clothing store, and purchased him a new suit as a "gift" before permitting Jones to appear before the worshipers. But Jones soon established a sophisticated organization and many of his revivals were enormously successful. In Nashville, Tennessee, he converted a wealthy steamship entrepreneur who promptly removed the bars and casinos from his riverboats and replaced them with chapels and who soon afterward in alliance with Jones put up most of the money for a Jones-Ryman auditorium designed to serve as a tabernacle but which gained fame as the longtime home of the Grand Old Opry. His preaching, lecturing, and writing and ultimately the returns from his investments in a variety of enterprises made him relatively wealthy. "I am the best paid preacher on the continent," he stated in 1899, and he probably was.[37] Jones continued to live in Cartersville, a flourishing town located on the Western and Atlantic about midway between Atlanta and Chattanooga.

Jones was by no means a typical Georgia minister. Unlike many other clergymen of the period, he had little interest in theology. "I despise theology and botany," he often observed, "but I love religion and flowers." Rather strangely for an evangelist, Jones disliked religious emotionalism—"heart religion," he contemptuously called it. In one sermon he stated, "Repentance don't mean blubbering and crying." He showed scant interest in Lost Cause mythology, and he placed limited emphasis on white supremacy. Even in his Atlanta newspaper column aimed at a predominantly Georgia readership, Jones not infrequently made clear his values: "I would rather see a sober negro in office than a dirty drunken saloon keeper."[38] With a national reputation to protect, it is hardly surprising that he minimized sectional appeals, but he seems to have had little interest in either theology or mythology even before he gained renown.

Great numbers of people in Georgia and elsewhere no doubt agreed with much that Jones taught, but his basic audience was southern, middle class, white, and urban. Although often making forays outside the South, Jones remained essentially a southern evangelist whose successful revivals were overwhelmingly concentrated in southern and border state cities. Although never losing the circuit rider's ability to communicate with ordinary people, he espoused the social if not necessarily the theological views of urban elites. He was Georgia's foremost uptown minister.

The social gospel according to Sam Jones was reasonably typical of the teachings of other churchmen in the major white Protestant denominations in Georgia. Jones was sympathetic toward workers and appealed to the paternal charity of management; he was sympathetic toward farmers and advised them to work hard, diversify, and stay out of debt; he was sympathetic toward women who fulfilled their proper role, which Jones summarized in the title of a favorite sermon as "Mother, Home, Heaven," and toward blacks who stayed in their place; he was sympathetic toward industry and economic growth so long as they did not encourage rum, Romanism, or moral laxity. The last point presented Jones with a vexing problem. "I know the roar of commerce and rush of trade, and the whistle of the engine, and the click of the telegraph have well-nigh drowned out the voice of God," he lamented.[39] Yet Jones approved of the very economic and technological innovations that were threatening to shout down the Creator. His solution was more vigorous promotion of "social purity," by which he meant the purity of the home, of womanhood, of moral living, and, of course, of right sentiment.

Sam Jones was by no means alone in his struggle to reconcile urban growth and economic progress with social stability and paternal values. He feared the corrupting effects of materialism among the affluent and the social and moral consequences of scarcity among the poor. In the time-honored European tradition, he sought to reinforce the old system by strengthening morality among the rich and poor. "Society is corrupt at the top and at the bottom," Jones stated. "The one with its frills and flowers, and the other with its rags and ruffians."[40] He frequently expressed sympathy for lower income groups: "If there is anybody I want to see go to heaven it is poor white folks and niggers. The Colonels and those big fellows who have had such a good time here can sort of afford to go to hell."[41] The affluent must avoid the vices of "high society" and "fashion" and must then ensure the social purity of the "poor white folks and niggers."

State government should police right behavior, but unfortunately the people who ran state government were entirely untrustworthy. Like many other uptown spokesmen of the era, Jones distrusted politics. He expressed an almost ferocious hostility toward politicians, often describing hell as a place where office seekers canvassed relentlessly for votes. Jones seemed convinced that politicians—all of them, apparently—rode "into office on the shoulders of whiskey" or at least with financial and other backing from liquor interests. The fact that politicians also rode out of office "into hell on the same shoulders" may have been consoling but it did not solve the immediate problem.[42] To that end, Jones used his revivals to organize Law and Order Leagues, which were predominantly uptown citizen groups that pressed for strict enforcement of existing antivice laws and for the enactment of new ones. Although Jones initiated many such leagues in Georgia, they appear to have been short-lived.

In his sermons Jones verbally constructed a two-lane route to salvation and right sentiment. It required the following individual commitment: "I have quit the wrong; I have taken hold of the right."[43] Inevitably, "right" turned out to mean an enthusiastic belief in social purity and an active church membership. Jones directed most of his efforts to combating the foes of Christianity, and they were, in the words of one scholar, those who "indulged in, or condoned, dancing, card-playing, gambling, circuses, swearing, theater-going, billiards, baseball, low-cut dresses, society balls, novel reading, social climbing, prostitution, and above all else, drinking alcoholic beverages."[44]

Given the extent of his hostility to alcohol, it is in one sense ironic that Jones held traditional views about the place of women in society.* Historians are generally in agreement that the prohibition crusade must in considerable part "be attributed to the efforts of temperance-minded women."[45] During the Civil War southern women experienced, in the words of Anne Firor Scott, "what was for many of them a new condition: life without a man around to make decisions."[46] That experience along with the shortage of marriageable age males during

---

*Jones did not publicly oppose women's suffrage; he merely insisted that a woman did grander work and achieved more satisfying results by raising several male children. Despite the irony, there was nothing inconsistent in Jones's position. He supported prohibition in large measure because he perceived liquor as a threat to mother, home, heaven, and social purity.

the immediate postwar years, urbanization, and other factors encouraged considerable numbers of women to participate in activities outside the home. Women became increasingly involved in church work and influenced their denominations to support the quest for social purity that Sam Jones so eagerly sought. By the 1880s the Woman's Christian Temperance Union (WCTU) was energetically engaged in the fight for prohibition. It is particularly ironic that Georgia's most outspoken feminist—and an ardent prohibitionist—was Sam Jones's neighbor in Bartow County.

Born into a wealthy plantation family, Rebecca Latimer grew up in comfort and attended Madison Female College. Her graduation speaker was Dr. William Felton, a prominent planter, doctor, minister, and sometime state legislator who lived three miles outside Cartersville. Following their marriage, Rebecca Felton began her career as mother and plantation mistress. While it seems clear that she was not entirely the home and motherhood type, she might have adjusted to the role had it not been for the Civil War. With the approach of Sherman's army, the Feltons sought refuge near Macon.* There both of their surviving children died of illnesses. Although Rebecca had given birth three times, only a stepdaughter remained in the family circle. The Feltons returned to north Georgia to find their house still standing but the plantation badly dilapidated.

To make ends meet, they opened a school in Cartersville, where they both taught. Sam Jones was one of their students. During the Reconstruction years, Rebecca bore two more children, one of whom died in childhood. But by this time, whether because of the continuing succession of family tragedies or the nature of her personality, Rebecca's interests no longer centered—if, indeed, they ever had—exclusively on home and family. In 1874 William announced his candidacy as an Independent Democrat for Congress, and Rebecca effectively became his campaign manager. They made a good team. William was a veteran politician and an eloquent speaker; Rebecca was a capable organizer and an indefatigable correspondent. Felton defeated the local Bourbon organization and served three terms in the House of Representatives. Rebecca carried on much of the family political correspondence and managed his reelection campaigns.

During these years Rebecca Felton developed an avid interest in politics and in a variety of public causes. One was John B. Gordon.

---

*William Felton, who was some fifteen years older than Rebecca and did not enjoy good health, chose to oversee his slaves rather than to fight in the war.

Just after William first announced for Congress, Rebecca wrote to leading Democratic politicians asking if they intended to come into the seventh district to campaign for the regular Democratic nominee. Although Gordon's reply was somewhat ambiguous, it clearly indicated that he had other commitments. But, Rebecca wrote on the back of Gordon's letter: "The Consummate Liar was in Rome the next Saturday—abusing and reviling Dr. Felton." By the time Gordon led an all-out though unsuccessful effort to unseat Felton in 1878, Rebecca's hostility toward the war hero was implacable. "There was something almost heroic," her biographer noted, "in her hatred for him." A third of a century later, Rebecca began a chapter in her memoirs with: "It is not a pleasant task for me to express my opinion of General Gordon." She managed to overcome her displeasure sufficiently, however, to devote a hundred pages to sketching some of the general's shortcomings, which included all extant varieties of public malfeasance, dishonesty, and corruption. Henry Grady was right when he reported that Felton never forgot a political injury nor allowed her husband to forget.[47]

Gordon and several of his highly placed Bourbon associates leased convicts, and that alone was enough to make the practice anathema to Rebecca Felton. She was also genuinely offended by the cruelty and immorality of the convict lease. In some camps women—even white women—were sexually abused by guards or by male convicts. Rebecca Felton did not condone such behavior, and she launched a campaign to abolish the system. Felton was an early proponent of temperance, and she could rival Sam Jones in blasting John Barleycorn. "If it is morally wrong to kill one's neighbor by the bullet," she insisted, "it is morally wrong to kill him by the grogshop."[48] In 1886 she joined the Woman's Christian Temperance Union, both to pressure the Georgia chapter to take a stand on convict lease and to express her prohibitionist views. She was successful on both counts and became a regular WCTU lecturer.

From the war on rum Felton moved on in the twentieth century to be the leading Georgia champion of women's suffrage and other feminist causes. As she aptly observed, "Woman suffrage had its inception in the fight against saloons." Her favorite argument on behalf of suffrage was to point out to men that they had failed to elect politicians who supported prohibition. "When you tell me to embroider muslin and fondle poodle dogs," she snapped, "I tell you I am afraid my child and my neighbor's child might go to perdition while I was at it."[49]

But Felton's defense of women's rights went well beyond the quest for social purity. She starkly stated: "The marriage business is a lottery. You can draw a prize but you are more apt to draw a blank." Large numbers of wives in Georgia, she angrily informed a committee of the state senate, "are only permitted to live, wait on their masters, bear children and . . . are really serfs, or common treadmill slaves in the homes, where they exist until they die."[50] By 1915 Felton was championing a lengthy feminist program that ranged from prohibition to equal pay for equal work.

Felton's feminist pronouncement did not go unchallenged. Mildred Rutherford of the United Daughters of the Confederacy leaped to the defense of "the manhood of the South, and the true rights of Southern women." Felton attempted to dismiss Rutherford and her friends: "To these I can only say if they prefer to *hug their chains* I have no sort of objection."[51] Nevertheless, Felton stood with the minority. Georgia was the first state to reject the Nineteenth Amendment.

Rebecca Felton was Georgia's premier woman as well as its most prominent feminist. She was a shrewd political strategist and a leader in a variety of public endeavors. She was often selected to serve on national committees when a female representative seemed appropriate and was appointed the first woman ever to serve in the United States Senate. Felton was a prolific writer (of books, articles, an Atlanta newspaper column, public letters, and a large private correspondence), a frequent speaker (before prohibition meetings, women's groups, legislative hearings, and other public events), and on occasion a newspaper editor (in Cartersville), an insurance agent, and a real estate speculator. A substantial inheritance from her father provided her with financial independence beyond the substantial holdings of her husband. She personified many of the contradictions and paradoxes that accompanied the changing place of women in a paternalistic society.

Felton, like many of the uptown women with whom she was frequently allied, rarely questioned the broader paternalistic class structure of Georgia social relations. Although no particular friend of public schools, Felton fretted about the scant educational and other opportunities available to rural white girls, especially those living in the predominantly white counties of northern Georgia and the southern wiregrass, and of the possible effect of poverty on their moral development. "What nobler work" could southern ladies perform, asked Rebecca Felton, "than the uplift of the poorer classes of their own sex, race and color?" It was a rhetorical question and, as usual, Felton was ready with a solution: "I believe, ladies, we must prepare to demand compulsory education for this class of apathetic and illiterate people and with this compulsory education we must contrive to inaugurate some system of manual training to arouse interest in their minds." Like Booker T. Washington on blacks, Felton had little confidence in the intellectual capacities of common white folk. In fact, Felton specifically compared her plan to provide "manual training" for white farm girls with Washington's educational program for blacks; after all, she stated, "no pupil of his school has ever been in the chain gang or penitentiary." "To a class like this," she explained, "book education does not meet conditions at all."[52]

Her solutions to the problems of blacks were similar. Because the appeal of prohibition extended across class and racial lines, blacks often attended prohibition rallies. At the end of a standard prohibition speech, Felton offered "a word to my colored friends here present." Her central advice to blacks was to "look up and determine by your own efforts of industry-economy-intelligence-sobriety-and-virtue that you will make yourselves and your race respected."[53] And, of course, they should vote for prohibition. The white ladies in Felton's audience would doubtless have agreed.

But on numerous other issues involving race relations, Felton diverged markedly from other vocal women. Generally women activists were an important force in promoting such humanitarian and family-oriented reforms as regulation of child labor. Felton opposed child labor legislation on the grounds that the cotton mills might replace white children with blacks. Generally women's groups, especially after the organization of the Association of Southern Women for the Prevention of Lynching, opposed Negrophobic barbarities and supported paternalistic racial moderation. Felton applauded the lynchers.

Rebecca Felton was the first prominent Georgian to defend lynching as a public good. During the late 1890s she frequently reiterated: "If it requires lynching to protect women's dearest possession from ravening, drunken human beasts, then I say lynch a thousand negroes a week, if it is necessary."[54] Felton first made the statement in a speech entitled "The Needs of Farmers' Wives" delivered before the State Agricultural Society. Apparently she regarded the lynching of black men as an appropriate method for protecting white farm women. Such a view was paternalism run rampant. In her defense of lynching Felton offered an ingenious explanation for the cause of rape that tied together black voting, whiskey, dishonest politics, and the lust of black men for white women. White politicians "equalized themselves" with black men by "honey-snuggling" them at the polls and then purchased their votes and enraged their lust with liquor. Therefore, the way to discourage rape and promote honest politics was to disfranchise blacks and establish prohibition. It was a compelling argument for reform.

Except for her animosity toward old-line Bourbon politicians, Rebecca Felton was an avid defender of the established order in Georgia. She sided with the north Georgia merchants against the Farmers' Alliance and, like Sam Jones, was deeply suspicious of the Populists. Her aging husband could not, however, resist one final assault on his Bourbon enemies and became the Populist candidate for Congress in the seventh district. Rebecca Felton took little interest in his unsuccessful campaign. She was a consistent defender of cotton mill owners and lauded their generous and humane treatment of employees. For white rural girls, she favored vocational training; for the daughters of affluent white families, she favored the admission of women to the University of Georgia. Otherwise, she had "never been an admirer of our public school system": after all, "it is a well-established fact that many of our greatest criminals are among the best educated."[55] She was almost as insistent as Sam Jones upon right sentiment. When an Emory University professor wrote a harmlessly moderate article on race relations for a national magazine, Felton led the campaign demanding his dismissal. The foes of Christianity were the same for Rebecca Felton as they were for Sam Jones.

The women's reform campaign in Georgia encompassed much of Felton's outlook and some of her programs. By the early twentieth century substantial numbers of women participated in organizational activities outside the home. Wives of the county governing class worked with missionary societies to "aid their heathen sisters" abroad and in other church programs and perhaps were members of the local United Daughters of the Confederacy chapter, the garden club, and the community temperance or literary society. Uptown women participated in similar activities except that they were more likely also to be active in specialized women's clubs and to support or at least sympathize with home missionary activities, woman suffrage campaigns, and the WCTU. Affluent urban black women often focused their club work on the uplift of the less fortunate of their race under the slogan "Lifting as We Climb." These activities no doubt widened the interests and social awareness of a considerable number of women and at the same time made worthwhile contributions to community welfare.

Most Georgia women were little affected. The black women who tended the children, kept the houses, and cooked the dinners while white ladies attended meetings were unable to participate, but perhaps it was just as well because black women would not have been welcome. The Georgia Federation of Women's Clubs early adopted a whites-only policy, and Rebecca Felton stated: "Freedom belongs to the white woman as her inherent right."[56] Nor did the ladies' organizations include the wives and daughters of factory workers, tenants, agricultural laborers, and small farmers—that is, the bulk of white sisterhood in Georgia—who would likely have been too busy to participate even if they had owned the proper clothing and anyone had thought to invite them. The latter was distinctly unlikely because social exclusiveness was a part of the appeal of women's organizational activities.

Urban elites formed the core of the women's reform movement. Their organizations were relatively far more numerous and more active than those in the counties, and they provided much of the state leadership. Urban clubwomen often supported suffrage and other feminist causes; they campaigned for prohibition and social purity; and they advocated a range of community improvements, many of which stressed charitable and religious uplift directed toward "the promotion of helpful Christian work among the poor of the city."[57] Like Henry Grady before them, uptown women tended to view religion and prohibition as necessary restraints for the masses "of simple men and women." Many of the projects sponsored by women's groups were of considerable social merit, but the growing Georgia cities spawned social problems that quickly outpaced the best efforts of well-intentioned volunteers. Public agencies gradually assumed responsibility for the urban health and welfare projects that had once been largely within the private charitable domain, and uptown women looked elsewhere for new challenges. During the early twentieth century their reform enthusiasm increasingly focused on the pressing problems faced by rural Georgians. As Rebecca Felton observed, farmers and their wives and daughters are "irrevocably bound to the soil and burdened by hopeless poverty" and thus are "enslaved by their own apathy and adverse conditions."[58]

To alleviate this dire state of affairs, uptown women's organizations launched a program intended to improve life in the country. Women's groups created traveling exhibits and libraries; they supported home economics and hygiene programs and the work of home demonstration agents; they provided scholarships for rural girls and arranged for rural girls to visit in uptown homes; and they established several "model" rural schools stressing vocational training and several schools for mountain whites. The Federation of Women's Clubs termed this program "urban-rural cooperation." One scholar has referred to it as the "ruralization" of women's organizational activities. The president of an Atlanta women's group explained that "farm women have been able to lighten their drudgery by incorporating ideas into their work, ideas which club women in the cities through their advantages have discovered and are broadcasting through the newspapers."[59]

A leader of the "urban-rural cooperation" campaign was Nellie Peters Black, Georgia's most prominent clubwoman. A wealthy Atlanta widow who was the absentee owner of a plantation raising among other things thoroughbred livestock, Black was three times president of the Georgia Federation of Women's Clubs. Active in a variety of civic projects, Black favored the expansion of women's rights, especially those that would broaden opportunities for uptown women, and she worked devotedly for improvements in educational facilities, especially the establishment of free kindergartens in urban communities. Black organized a series of rallies sponsored by the Georgia Federation and the state Department of Agriculture that were designed to inform and uplift farmers and their wives. In her speeches at these meetings during 1915 and 1916, Black stressed the importance of diversified farming, vegetable gardens, and a "diversified pantry." Tom Watson saw all of this as further evidence of an uptown attitude: "We country people have no pride and no self-respect and no sense and no experience; and therefore we gladly welcome these city folks who modestly take it upon themselves to come out into the country, and teach us how to farm and our wives how to cook."[60]

Interestingly, Black seems to have become involved in what Watson chose to describe as "these benevolent Atlanta ladies who are rotating around the state, to teach farmers' wives how to milk and churn and cook and keep house" as a result of an effort to sell oats grown on her plantation. Black consulted Atlanta grain dealers who informed her: "No, we prefer to buy western oats."[61] Further inquiries by Black demonstrated that there was little outlet for local foodstuffs in Georgia. The transportation and marketing system was designed for exchange with the North, not for self-sufficiency in the South. Angered, Black wrote several public letters that touched off some newspaper comment. Everyone seemed to agree that markets for foodstuffs might encourage agricultural diversification, but no one explained how this goal might be achieved. The solution that ultimately emerged from uptown deliberations was the campaign Black led to instruct farmers' wives on the virtues of a "diversified pantry."

The quest for a diversified agriculture foundered on the same shoals that grounded the search for rapid industrial growth. In the mid-1890s Edward Atkinson, a Boston capitalist who took a sympathetic if somewhat disdainful interest in southern economic development, pointed out that southern promoters tended to view industrial progress in terms of a large textile factory. Actually, Atkinson explained, healthy industrial growth was "a single great factory surrounded by a hundred little work shops." The lack of the "hundred little work shops" was a crucial economic problem in Georgia, and the explanation for this absence was the "idea of caste and class."[62] With regard to capitalist economic development, Atkinson was acutely correct. The "single great factory" did not threaten social stability and the patriarchal order; the "hundred little work shops" suggested a free-labor capitalism and a more dynamic social system that might wreak havoc on the "idea of caste and class."

Diversified agriculture and workshops had little place in the Georgia social order. County governing elites defended plantation labor relations under the banner of the Lost Cause. Uptown elites favored economic growth but not to the extent of sacrificing social stability and disrupting marketing arrangements. Textile factories could be built, at least in part, with imported capital; too many workshops required social changes at home. It was better to dangle cheap laborers before northern capitalists and to encourage farm wives to stock their pantries.

# Chapter Six

## *Myth, Reality, and Social Stability in Plain Black and White*

B y the early twentieth century the chasm between town and country was a fundamental fact of Georgia society. The "country people" became almost synonymous with the "poor people." A twenty-two-year-old DeKalb County woman poured out her heart in a letter to Tom Watson in 1921. "Country children never have the chance that town children have," she lamented. Her father was poor and, she predicted, always would be. "I wish I had been raised in town so that I could have gotten the schooling that every child ought to have."[1] Despite the best efforts of uptown ladies, the poverty-stricken rural countryside, where 68 percent of Georgia's people resided in 1910, provided neither the social services nor the opportunities that were more generally available in the towns and cities.

Not all rural Georgians were poor, of course. Of the approximately two hundred thousand whites gainfully employed in agriculture in 1910, almost eighty-five thousand owned their own land. During the early twentieth century and particularly during the halcyon years of the World War I era, even tenants had an excellent chance to "cash out" in the black. In a variety of ways, country living, in addition to its travails, had positive features. It was usually simpler than life in the cities. Birth, color, and sex largely determined one's place in society, and economic scarcity, a rural environment, and Georgia's patriarchal social structure encouraged strong family and kinship ties, which further reinforced social stability. Isolated from uptown's ceaseless struggle for status, life on the farm was less pressured, less achievement-oriented, more family-centered, and, no doubt, in many ways more satisfying, provided, of course, the crop would only cash out when it came time for settling up. Work was hard, but it was regulated by the sun and the weather and not by a clock or a factory machine. And when the work was done, hunting, fishing, and other inexpensive rural recreations, the Saturday afternoon visit to town, and an occasional revival or political rally helped to keep life interesting. Outside visitors often found the country poor to be passive and fatalistic, but, as one historian has recently pointed out, fatalism was not necessarily an irrational attitude for a poor and powerless people to hold.[2]

Rural churches were ramshackle structures when compared to the brick edifices in uptown and county seat, but many of them possessed a simplistic dignity. In an autobiographical novel, the wife of a former rural Methodist circuit rider might have had Sam Jones in mind when she wrote: "The very gifted, highly educated pastor of a rich city church feels it down to his spiritual bones that his gospel is worth more than that of the simple-minded itinerant on a country circuit." When her husband was assigned briefly to a town church, she found appalling the "mock spirituality" of "these teething saints" with "their very narrow moral margins and too few steadfast convictions of any sort."[3] Country Christian life could be deadly monotonous, but the circuit rider's wife found it a more sincere and honest existence than that of uptown.

Perhaps, as the circuit rider's wife suggested, "the voice of God" was more audible in the country, where "the roar of commerce and rush of trade" were but a faint echo. Even if uptown controlled the conferences and conventions of the major denominations, rural churches maintained their own character, and poor Georgians who did not feel comfortable in the big churches could avail themselves of a bewildering variety of Pentecostal Holiness, Free-Will, Primitive, Wesleyan, Nazarene, and other sects that were happy to make worshipers welcome whether or not they owned a white shirt and tie or a stylish dress. The white country congregations included the people who were the backbone of the Populist movement, and they would probably have supplied more Populist recruits had it not been for the cumulative poll tax. Further disfranchisement measures and declining opportunities for the expression of political dissent during the early twentieth century may have encouraged the religious dissent that the small sects represented.

Like the gospel according to Sam Jones, country theology stressed religious individualism, but beyond that, the differences were substantial. Lower-class churches and especially the sects placed heavy emphasis on emotional involvement and audience participation. Many of these churches tended to base status on religious behavior rather than on material wealth and to award recognition to depth of faith and degrees of grace. Country religion was escapist in the sense that it credited the mysterious ways of God rather than social injustices as the cause for suffering, and it was otherworldly in that it stressed the rewards of afterlife rather than the virtues of material acquisitiveness. In extreme form it created the backwoods prophets who were to become standard characters in southern novels. At the same time the churches provided emotional and social solace for a hard-pressed people.

More hard-pressed were the congregations in neighboring black churches. As a black saying had it: "Hit might be hard fer er rich man to git to heaben but hit's jest natchly hard fer er po' man ter git any-whares."[4] Of the 255,000 blacks gainfully employed in agriculture—which was seven out of every ten employed blacks—only 16,000 owned their own land in 1910 and nine out of every ten families did not own their own houses. The church was virtually all that rural blacks possessed and controlled, and, more than in the white community, it was the center of social as well as spiritual life. As in the white churches, services rarely convened more than twice a month; congregations were often small; and ministers usually had limited religious training. Often, as one critic has observed, "The Church was more likely to help the Negro adjust to his inferior station in life than to encourage him to change it."[5]

But even more than in the white churches, black religion was a positive force. Large numbers of church offices permitted almost any adult to become an officer, and burial societies and local charity missionary societies performed important services for a poverty-stricken people. Black Christianity, a study by Samuel S. Hill, Jr., has reported, "featured expressiveness, joy, fellowship, moral responsibility, pious feelings, and the hope of heaven. It de-emphasized guilt and punishment, ecclesiastical forms, and learning."[6] To the horror of better educated black ministers in the towns, most black churches did indeed feature expressiveness: "The great shout, accompanied with weird cries and shrieks and contortions and followed by a multi-varied 'experience' which takes the candidate through the most heart-rendering scenes" was a frequent occurrence.[7]

The relentless pressure of population growth on the farms forced migration to the city. Nevertheless, it was a tribute to the paternal order in the countryside that migration was limited and gradual. During an era when the North imported a largely non-English-speaking peasantry from Europe, relatively few Georgians left the land. No doubt the tendency of northern capitalists to look to the South for cheap raw materials rather than cheap labor was a factor, as was northern racism. But more fundamentally, the stability of the social system at home apparently kept them on the farm. The sense of place, the hold of kinship, the love of the land, and a rigid social structure based on caste and class and buttressed by patriarchal values proved to be profoundly resistant to change.

Manufacturing in Georgia expanded within the prevailing social order. The labor relations of plantation agriculture carried over—indeed were deliberately carried over—into the industrial sector. As W. J. Cash pointed out, a southern factory was frequently "a plantation, essentially indistinguishable in organization from the familiar plantation of the cotton fields."[8] The cotton mill village was the most obvious example of industrial paternalism, but similar arrangements were common in the turpentine and lumber camps and often less comprehensively in other types of mills and factories.

Farmers, who lived in another man's house and worked another man's land, moved into the mill villages to live in another man's house and work another man's machine. Yet, despite the almost identical labor relationship and social dependency, the two positions were crucially different, and the migration from farm to factory was often a wrenching experience. "I thought it was terrible to spend six days of every week in a mill," wrote one observer. "I had never spent all of a day in any house in my life."[9]

Long after factories and mill villages had become a part of the Georgia landscape, a working-class minister reminisced in his Sunday sermon: "A long time ago you could hear the horses biting corn out of the trough, and see the firelight in the stove in the kitchen. . . . And smell the cornbread cooking. Many things happened on the farm, you know. Dogs barking. My it's so beautiful out there."[10] Social practices "that possessed . . . a simple dignity on the farm, were crude and uncouth in the village."[11] A visiting journalist, doubtless with some exaggeration, described one mill village where "jest ter make things sorter homelike" mill workers "kicked out the panels of the doors, smashed the windows, riddled the walls, and cut up the floor for kindling."[12]

Mill employment complicated family life. Even if the whole family had worked the farm, they had done so as a unit; there was something different about the wife and child who also worked at the mill drawing their own wages. Emotional strains could arise if the husband was laid off and had to live on the earnings of his "dependents." The social snobbery of the townspeople and particularly the uptownsmen reminded mill workers of their inferior status. "It would be as unthinkable in most uptown homes," one writer has observed, "to invite a 'common millhand' to dinner as it would be to invite a Negro."[13] Most of the people who went on the factory payroll had never enjoyed high social standing and may have been accustomed to being dismissed as country people by townsmen, but being a not very successful individual in the country was not the same as being disdained as a linthead in the city. It is little wonder that many first-generation lintheads struggled to save enough money to buy land and return to the farm.

Few actually went back. Most adjusted to the factory and the crowded neighborhood. Factory wages in Georgia were pathetically low when compared with those in the North but not when compared to a sharecropper's income. Factory workers ate and dressed better than did the majority of Georgia rural dwellers. Probably even more than in the country, the church in the mill village or factory district served as a center of social life. Like the country churches, working-class religion, especially the sects, encouraged participation from the congregation, which was what Sam Jones seems to have had in mind when he condemned "heart religion" with its "blubbering and crying."

Except perhaps in the very largest factories the relationship between workers and management was more personal and paternal than contractual. A former Athens mill worker explained how the owner "visited every house and knew every man, woman, and child that lived in his village by their first names." Often the entire extended family labored in the mill. In the Athens cotton factory, the mill worker's grandmother "kept house" and everyone else—"my grandfather, my mother, two uncles, and three aunts"—held positions in the mill. The Athens mill worker had a particularly solicitous and patriarchal boss. "If he found that some member of a family had been sickly for a while, he would have men, wagons, and teams go there while the family was away at work and move their things to some house that he considered a healthier spot. When that family would come back from work they'd find a note from him on the door telling them where to go, and when they reached there they found everything in its place; even the wood was in the wood box."[14] The Athens mill village—or at least the former mill worker's recollections of it—was an extreme example, but it did suggest the paternal labor relationships that underlay New South industrial progress.

"It is a grand sight to look upon that thickly settled quarter of Augusta, with all these well-equipped homes for factory people, and see the care and humane endeavors of these mill owners to promote the well-being of those they employ,"[15] wrote Rebecca Felton, and it was a view that most affluent Georgians would likely have endorsed. Other observers have not been so kind. Richard H. L. German, who investigated the same quarter of Augusta, described the factory district somewhat differently: "Tall two-story brick and wooden tenement houses, crowding several families into one building with dark, ill-ventilated, dreary tiny apartments were a common distinguishing feature." These and the "small wooden frame houses" mainly owned by the mills provided living quarters for most factory workers.[16]

In 1914 the Atlanta *Constitution* described a mill village in that city as "dreary, drab, monotonously the same, row after row of houses. Behind them, sanitary conditions which are a menace to the city's health. Laborers live here."[17] Atlanta's firms were less likely than those elsewhere to provide housing for employees; workers found shelter wherever they could afford the rents. "Living in row houses, tenements, or shanties, the city's workingmen found inadequate," a recent study has reported, "not only the roofs over their heads, but also city government's unconcern for their neighborhoods." The city's mercantile leadership felt "that commercial priorities came first."[18]

Another writer described a more isolated mill village: "Flung as if by chance beside a red clay road that winds between snake fences, a settlement appears. Rows of loosely built, weather-stained frame houses, all of the same ugly pattern and buttressed by clumsy chimneys, are set close to the highway."[19] Only its permanence differentiated such a mill village from the sawmill settlements and turpentine camps that were most numerous in the southern part of the state. Frequently they were located on plantations and were operated in conjunction with cotton and other crop production. During the early twentieth century, the devastation of Georgia's trees led to a decline in the production of lumber and naval stores. Nevertheless, more than six of every ten Georgia factory workers in 1909 produced cotton goods, lumber products, and turpentine and resin.

About 15 percent of industrial wage earners in Georgia were women, the majority of them employed in cotton mills. Women consistently received less pay than men, even when performing the same job, although the gap narrowed during the twentieth century. There was ample justification for the sentiment expressed in an early twentieth-century Georgia mill song:

> I worked in the cotton mill all my life,
> I ain't got nothing but a barlow knife,
> It's a hard times, cotton mill girls,
> Hard times everywhere.[20]

But cotton mill girls earned considerably more than household servants, almost all of whom were black women. At the turn of the century Georgia still had more maids, cooks, and washerwomen than factory workers of both sexes. A considerably higher percentage of Georgia black women were gainfully employed than was true nationally. In 1910 three of every ten women sixteen to forty-four years of age in the United States earned an income; six of every ten black women and two of every ten white women in Georgia did so.

The number of factory workers grew steadily, and working conditions gradually improved during the first two decades of the twentieth century. Cotton mill wages seem to have declined during the last two decades of the nineteenth century. Management propagandists sought to justify low wages by arguing that living expenses were low in Georgia. Various studies, however, failed to document any substantial differences in living costs of factory workers North and South, primarily because higher food and clothing costs in the South offset savings on other items.[21] During the World War I era, mill village welfare programs, improved housing, and better living conditions became more common. High wartime taxes encouraged mill owners to invest surplus profits, and they chose to improve worker welfare rather than to pay higher wages. Such improvements presumably strengthened paternalistic bonds and undermined the appeal of labor unions.

Black workers did not live in the villages nor, except in the most menial capacities, did they work at the mills. They did, however, provide much of the labor for the lumber and cottonseed oil mills and the fertilizer and brick factories, and they repaired more than their share of the track and loaded more than their share of the trains that carried the cotton North and of the ships that docked at Savannah and Brunswick. Blacks moved to the city at almost the same pace as whites, and they suffered the same trauma of transition from rural to urban life. By 1910 the counties containing Augusta, Columbus, Macon, and Savannah were all approximately one-half black in population, and one-third of Fulton County's people were nonwhite.

At the time of emancipation, skilled blacks were numerous, although often their skills reflected jack-of-all-trades plantation competence rather than craftsmanship. At any rate black workers had limited opportunity to develop their trades. During the late nineteenth and early twentieth centuries, the number of skilled black workers declined relative to the number of skilled white workers. A study of occupational mobility in Atlanta found that not only did black workers during the late nineteenth and early twentieth centuries start out on a lower rung of the occupational ladder but they were much less likely to advance to higher status positions than were white workers.[22]

The result of this process was to concentrate blacks in "nigger work," which by standard definition meant the jobs that were the lowest paying, the hardest, and the dirtiest. Statistical comparison of black and white workers in Atlanta, where blacks were probably better off economically than anywhere else in the state, is indicative (Table 2). The occupational categories are roughly ranked from lowest to highest status, and, although the groupings are crude, they illustrate the extent to which black workers were dependent on household service and manual labor in manufacturing and transportation for subsistence. And blacks inevitably received less pay for the same work than whites.

Not surprisingly, only two in ten urban black families owned their own homes in 1910. One writer has described the black residential district in Augusta at the turn of the century: "Rows of low-rent tin shanties, ramshackle buildings, wooden shacks and older, former white residential homes lined the dusty roadways, streets and alleys." W. E. B. DuBois noted that in Atlanta the alley was "the nucleus of Negro population." Along Atlanta's unpaved, often muddy alleys were houses and shanties that lacked running water, electricity, or most any other convenience. It was in such neighborhoods that, "while sociologists gleefully count his bastards and his prostitutes, the very soul of the toiling, sweating black man is darkened by the shadow of a vast despair."[23]

Even for prosperous blacks, housing was a problem. Because of their scarcity, good homes available for purchase by blacks usually cost more than houses for whites, and almost inevitably they were residences in formerly white neighborhoods. In reaction Heman E. Perry con-

## Table 2: Occupation by Race in Atlanta, 1910

|  | Blacks | | Whites | |
|---|---|---|---|---|
|  | number | percent | number | percent |
| All workers | 27,225 | 100 | 30,981 | 100 |
| Domestic and personal service | 17,233 | 63.4 | 1,411 | 4.6 |
| Manufacturing, transportation, and communications | 6,637 | 24.3 | 11,786 | 38.0 |
| Trade | 1,883 | 6.9 | 8,904 | 28.7 |
| Clerical | 568 | 2.1 | 6,715 | 21.7 |
| Public and professional service | 904 | 3.3 | 2,165 | 7.0 |

Source: Adapted from Thomas Mashburn Deaton, "Atlanta during the Progressive Era" (Ph.D. dissertation, University of Georgia, 1969), 135.

structed a middle-class housing development in western Atlanta that soon became the center of black affluence in the city. A daring entrepreneur and for a time the most successful black businessman in the state, Perry established the Standard Life Insurance Company in 1912 and from this base branched into banking, numerous service industries, and construction. His empire became overextended and collapsed in the mid-1920s, but his enterprises served as a training ground for a growing black bourgeoisie and provided comfortable homes for the black merchants, businessmen, professionals, mail carriers, craftsmen, and educators who could afford them.

In the late nineteenth century successful black entrepreneurs usually catered to a white clientele. By the turn of the century the growth of the black urban population, worsening race relations, and the desire of many blacks to escape dependence on whites encouraged businessmen to exploit the Negro market. Alonzo F. Herndon, one of Atlanta's most successful black entrepreneurs, was proprietor of a barber shop catering to an exclusively white trade; in 1905 Herndon founded the Atlanta Mutual Life Insurance Company that relied on black customers. This shift toward ghetto economics offered limited but significant opportunities for blacks to achieve affluence within a broader society characterized by white supremacy.

During these years black businessmen generally endorsed the program of racial solidarity, self-help, and economic nationalism championed by Booker T. Washington. When Washington's National Negro Business League held its annual meeting in Atlanta in 1906, some twelve hundred delegates attended, and many Georgia blacks applauded its emphasis on racial opportunities and economic growth. Black entrepreneurs struggled to launch ghetto business enterprises, and in 1908 black Atlanta women created what was probably Georgia's most socially active women's group, the Neighborhood Union, to improve black neighborhoods in the city. These efforts generated considerable optimism among bourgeois blacks. "Concerned with material success and social advancement, convinced of the value of hard work, appreciative of social order and self-discipline, and hopeful about the future of their children," Blaine A. Brownell has described the black entrepreneurial class, "the members of this Negro commercial-civic elite shared many of the goals and attitudes of their white counterparts."[24]

In Augusta the center of black business enterprise was the Gwinnett Street neighborhood, the home of such black-owned firms as the Pilgrim Insurance Company and the Penny Savings Bank and the site of the Tabernacle Baptist Church presided over by Charles T. Walker, whose sermons were said to attract "larger crowds than any other Negro of his time."[25] In Atlanta, Auburn Avenue—"Sweet Auburn"— was the heart of a business district with sixty-four black-owned firms and seven black professional offices in addition to fourteen enterprises owned by whites. Near Auburn Avenue lay Decatur Street, which many "respectable" blacks regarded as a "street of shame."[26] There dives, prostitutes, and blues music flourished, and Gertrude "Ma" Rainey filled engagements at the Eighty-One Theater. There, too, Thomas A. Dorsey played and sang blues music, composed songs, and ultimately became Ma Rainey's piano accompanist.

Born near the turn of the century in the hamlet of Villa Rica west of Atlanta, Dorsey referred to himself as the son of "a country preacher."[27] He displayed a precocious talent for musical instruments and soon drifted into Atlanta to perform at theaters and dance halls along Decatur Street and to write "those kind of double-meaning songs that made big hits at stag parties."[28] One of these efforts was "It's Tight Like That," a bawdy, catchy, country blues song. Dorsey teamed with Hudson Whittaker, an Atlanta guitarist and vocalist who also accompanied Ma Rainey, to record "It's Tight Like That," which became a popular hit and made Dorsey's reputation. By that time "Georgia Tom" Dorsey and "Tampa Red" Whittaker had moved to Chicago, where Ma Rainey made her home.

Dorsey suffered a major illness during which he reevaluated his religious convictions and became interested in gospel music. In the late 1920s Dorsey played and wrote blues songs while struggling to find a market for his gospel compositions. During the 1930s he teamed with Sallie Martin and Mahalia Jackson. A native of Pittfield, Georgia, Martin completed an eighth-grade education before moving to Atlanta to work at odd jobs and to develop a talent for music. Together Dorsey, Martin, Jackson, and Rainey were largely responsible for making Chicago the mecca of gospel music. By this time Dorsey was becoming known as "the greatest personality" in gospel music, a man "whose talents as a composer, publisher, performer, teacher, choir director and organizer" shaped the American gospel tradition to the point that gospel songs were often referred to as "Dorseys."[29]

Dorsey left Georgia, but every Sunday morning the Georgia countryside reverberated with his music. Through church choirs and congregational singing virtually all Georgians both white and black learned the lines of such "Dorseys" as "Precious Lord":

When my way grows drear
Precious Lord linger near, . . .
Take my hand precious Lord and lead me home.

Red Foley's recording of Dorsey's "Peace in the Valley" became a highly popular song, transcending church audiences. Whether Dorsey was thinking of growing up in Georgia or living in Chicago, "Peace in the Valley" promised better days:

> There'll be peace in the valley for me some day,
> There'll be peace in the valley for me I pray,
> No more sadness, no sorrow, no trouble I'll see,
> There'll be peace in the valley for me.[30]

Georgia Tom, Tampa Red, and Sallie Martin migrated to the North, but the urban black street life from which they sprang was a prominent aspect of social behavior in Georgia's growing cities. Segregation and an urban environment permitted the black underclass an "impulse freedom" that was a far cry from the propriety of uptown and of middle-class blacks, the latter of whom particularly made something of a fetish of social decorum in order to distinguish themselves from the black common folk. John Dollard compared lower-class black social behavior with that of middle-class citizens in a relatively small southern town: "His impulse expression is less burdened by guilt," and "he is more free to enjoy, not merely free to act in an external physical sense, but actually freer to embrace important gratifying experiences."[31]

Blues was the music of lower-class black urbanites. Its emphasis on self and on individual expression was an indication of an individualistic ethos that was gradually undermining the paternalistic ideology. As Lawrence W. Levine has argued, "there was a direct relationship between the national ideological emphasis upon the individual, the popularity of Booker T. Washington's teachings, and the rise of the blues." Black street life had an earthy quality, and blues music recognized "the physical side of love which, aside from tepid hand holding and lip pecking, was largely missing from popular music" admired in uptown or even from the country ballads of the upland white folk.[32] Ma Rainey belted:

> If you don't like my ocean, don't fish in my sea.
> Don't like my ocean, don't fish in my sea.
> Stay out of my valley and let my mountains be.[33]

Sam Jones, Rebecca Felton, and Nellie Peters Black would hardly have found such lines entertaining.

Sam Jones worried about the social purity of the "poor white folks and niggers," and so did a considerable number of other whites. Black street life and white factory districts created social settings that often appeared threatening to the paternal order, as indeed did the very anonymity of urban life. To white purists, urban blacks frequently appeared aggressive, uppity, at times downright frightening, and certainly sinful. Blacks and whites jostled each other on the walkways and on public streetcars. Working-class blacks competed with whites for jobs, and black artisans marketed the same skills as white artisans. White workers, torn between their antagonism toward blacks and their desire to join with other workers to improve their position in the marketplace, demonstrated on occasion a militancy that was difficult to explain within the context of a paternalistic ideology. Rebecca Felton thought even home life was menaced by the modern age "with its dizzy pace of commerce and its dizzier whirl of distractions."[34]

"The city of Atlanta is rearing a generation of young negroes, both boys and girls," former Governor William J. Northen lamented in a speech in 1911, "that will give trouble, great trouble, at no distant day in criminal and vicious living."[35] Freed from the "civilizing" influence of slavery, blacks were reverting to barbarism. "The depth of the negroes' debasement," an Atlanta writer insisted, "is shown in the impurity of the women." With each new generation, the writer continued, the Negro race "becomes more disinclined to work and its vagrants multiply; each generation is more prone to live by crime, more unchaste, and more quick to desert their conjugal partners and children."[36]

White workers, themselves insecure in a state with an overabundance of laborers, sought to defend their position from black encroachment. Augusta workers, one of their number informed Tom Watson in 1906, "are forming a Society of good moral-law abiding citizens to devise the best method of protecting ourselves from Negro predomination."[37] In Atlanta "a typical Southern white workingman of the skilled variety" wrote: "All the genuine Southern people like the Negro . . . and so long as he remains the hewer of wood and carrier of water, and remains strictly in what we choose to call his place, everything is all right, but when ambition, prompted by real education, causes the Negro to grow restless and he bestir himself to get out of that servile condition, then there is, or at least there will be, trouble, sure enough trouble." Should a trained black worker attempt "to take my work away from me," the writer continued, "I will kill him."[38]

Racial tensions were by no means confined to the city. The growth of towns and the expansion of railroads spread Georgia's version of a market economy throughout the state, even though village–small town folk culture, plantation labor relations, and Lost Cause ideology proved to be formidable bulwarks of the old order. Everywhere the "childish," "exuberant," "inferior but lovable" black of slavery days seemed to give way to "the 'uppity,' 'insolent,' 'pushy' Negro who did not know his place, who was out to compete with the white workers and to rape white women."[39] Like many other whites, Rebecca Felton lauded the "old time ante-bellum negro" who "are yet remarkable for their orderly and law-abiding conduct," but she found little to admire among "the younger class of negroes" who had been influenced by Yankee "man and brother" propaganda.[40] Negroes, Tom Watson pronounced from McDuffie County, "simply have no comprehension of virtue, honesty, truth, gratitude, and principle."[41]

Whites responded to these developments with increasing hostility and violence. The Atlanta race riot of 1906 was the bloodiest event in a general campaign of white racial aggression. Between 1889 and 1930, there were more than 450 lynchings in the state, and this number does not include the "legal lynchings" that resulted when an angry white community held a hasty trial, returned a quick verdict, and scheduled the prompt execution of an accused black. Although lynch mobs were often recruited from the lower strata of white society, their existence depended upon the willingness of county governing elites to tolerate and to a considerable degree to encourage them. Racial violence was nothing new in postemancipation Georgia, but not since Reconstruction had it been so prevalent and never had it been so brutal.

The rape of white women was the standard justification for lynch law. It was too cruel to compel a wronged woman to compound her shame by testifying in court; better that the men deal directly with the matter. The problem with this rationalization was, of course, that the bulk of lynchings did not involve rape or white females. Governor Hugh M. Dorsey reported in 1921 that during his two-year administration 135 cases "of the alleged mistreatment of negroes in Georgia" had been called to his attention. Of these, two involved "the 'usual crime' against white women."[42] Lynchings most often resulted from black assaults on white men, and thus they served as a crude but important form of labor control. By justifying lynching as a defense of white womanhood, white men linked the vulnerability of women with the behavior of black males; "the fear of rape, like the threat of lynching," one study has concluded, "served to keep a subordinate group in a state of anxiety and fear."[43] Lynchings buttressed the patriarchal system but in so doing they exposed the extent to which traditional social relations had come to depend on external force rather than internal compulsion.

But there was also a ritualistic quality to lynching. The practice was sometimes more than simple mob violence; it was a popular spectacle. On a Sunday afternoon in 1899 in the county seat town of Newnan, approximately two thousand people watched a black be tortured, burned at the stake, and mutilated. Many in the audience were Atlantans who had ridden special excursion trains that enterprising railroad officials had pressed into service for the event. One published report gleefully described the affair: "They trotted Mr. Nigger to the shade of a nice pine tree, bound his body to the trunk, and the fun began. Some fagots were heaped around him, a gallon of kerosene was poured upon the fuel to make the fire a little bit hotter, then a match was applied, and soon Georgia had a cooked nigger. His ears and nose and other portions of his anatomy were cut off for souvenirs. . . . The nigger made a confession implicating two other coons both of whom were lynched the following day by the mob. Excitement is intense and a race war is imminent."[44] The Newnan atrocity and the report of it were beastly even by Georgia standards, but lynchings did seem to serve as a ritualistic reaffirmation of white solidarity in an age of class and social conflict.

Less spectacular but more consistently effective in maintaining patriarchal practices was the machinery of law enforcement. In Georgia the caste, class, and sex of offender and victim, not the crime, determined punishment. Virtually any criminal act with a black male perpetrator and a white female victim was a major and often a capital offense. Almost equally as weighty on the scales of justice was black aggression toward a white gentleman of good standing. Black violence toward a lower status white man was serious but depending on circumstances might be treated more leniently. White aggression toward blacks normally merited little or no official notice, and Georgia courts were usually tolerant when sentencing blacks convicted of crimes committed against other blacks, particularly if the accused had a white protector to put in a favorable word on his behalf. By demonstrating limited concern for black-on-black crimes, law enforcement officials effectively encouraged blacks to channel their hostilities toward whites into aggression toward other blacks. Similarly, the law was often relatively lenient toward violence between whites so long as they were whites of similar social standing. Official tolerance of private vengeance remained an important factor in Georgia justice, and self-defense was a time-honored plea by the defense. A planter rarely committed a serious offense by violating the legal rights of a tenant; in the mid-twentieth century the fact that a landlord was convicted of murder for brutally killing a former white tenant who had stolen a cow was such a rarity that it seemed to merit book-length study, particularly since the conviction resulted in part from the testimony of blacks.[45] Georgia was not the only place where social status and color influenced justice, but law in Georgia was a particularly accurate measure of the patriarchal hierarchy.

In these circumstances, black leaders had difficulty formulating a strategy, if indeed, an adequate response was possible. Bishop Henry M. Turner insisted that the only alternative was to return to Africa. "Without multiplying words, I wish to say that hell is an improvement upon the United States when the negro is involved." Although a few hundred Georgia blacks did in fact embark for Africa, Turner's program won limited popular support. A far larger number of blacks continued to support the Booker T. Washington program of self-help and racial solidarity. The foremost spokesman for this philosophy in Georgia was Benjamin J. Davis, editor of the Atlanta *Independent.* "Our growth, if permanent and substantial, must like the white man's, issue from material development," Davis editorialized. "Let us have faith in our own possibility and construct our fabric upon the fundamental principles of morals, self-help, self-reliance, race resources and race pride." Like Washington, Davis accepted without serious protest the increasing restrictions on black rights. On black disfranchisement, Davis wrote: "The negro must begin at the bottom and learn the rudiments of the responsibility of the ballot before he can comprehend its importance or enjoy its protection. The further the negro removes himself from politics the more self-reliant he will become."[46]

In many ways Davis was a living embodiment of the Booker T. Washington strategy. Through discipline and hard work, Davis had risen from modest circumstances in a small southwest Georgia county seat town to become a successful businessman and editor of the state's most prominent black newspaper. To a gradually growing number of other black Georgians, however, Davis pointed toward a path that led to despair rather than progress. His son became a leader in the Communist party. Born in Dawson—"The whole town had the atmosphere of a feudal plantation,"[47] he later wrote—Benjamin J. Davis the younger studied law and became attorney for Angelo Herndon, the Communist organizer who was the defendant in a widely publicized trial in Atlanta. So disgusted did Davis become with the Georgia version of legal justice, that he joined the Communist party, moved to New York, became the Communist councilman from Harlem, and served as a leading national spokesman for the party. Like his father, Davis became a newspaper editor, although perhaps the *Daily Worker* could not appropriately be compared with the Atlanta *Independent*. During the anti-Communist crusade that followed World War II, Davis became an inmate of a federal penitentiary.

The central stream of revolt from Booker T. Washington's leadership centered around neither Turner's escapism nor Davis's radicalism; its leader was W. E. B. DuBois. An Atlanta University faculty member, DuBois grew increasingly dismayed with "Mr. Washington's programme," which "accepts the alleged inferiority of the Negro races" and "counsels a silent submission to civic inferiority." Although crediting Washington with being "the most distinguished Southerner since Jefferson Davis," DuBois demanded "a stoppage to the campaign of self-depreciation." DuBois launched his public "Parting of the Ways" with the Tuskegee leader with the publication of the enormously influential *The Souls of Black Folk* in 1903. "By every civilized and peaceful method," DuBois wrote, "we must strive for the rights which the world accords to men, clinging unwaveringly to those great words which the sons of the Fathers would fain forget: 'We hold these truths to be self-evident: That all men are created equal.'"[48]

In a parable on Washington, DuBois described a white man who kicked a "Black Leader" down a flight of stairs and pitched a quarter after him. "'My friends,' said the Black Leader, 'the world demands constructive work: it dislikes pessimists. I want to call your attention to the fact that this White gem'man—I mean gentleman—did *not* kick me nearly as hard as he might have: again he wore soft kid boots, and finally I landed in the dirt and not on the asphalt. Moreover,' continued the Black leader as he stooped in the dust, 'I am twenty-five cents in.'" As this story suggests, DuBois became increasingly strident in his attacks on the "Black Leader" from Tuskegee. Washington, DuBois reminded his friend John Hope, "stands for Negro submission and slavery."[49]

Atlanta soon became the center of opposition to the "Tuskegee machine." In 1904 DuBois and his allies established the *Voice of the Negro*, edited by Jesse Max Barber. During its relatively brief existence, the *Voice* was the leading outlet for anti-Washington sentiment. DuBois was a leader in the creation of the Niagara Movement and later of the National Association for the Advancement of Colored People. In 1910 he left Atlanta to become editor of the NAACP's *The Crisis*. DuBois found kindred souls among educated blacks in Atlanta, including John Hope, president of Atlanta Baptist College, and Max Barber, editor of the *Voice*. Elsewhere in the state his most prominent ally was William J. White, the militant editor of the Augusta *Georgia Baptist*. Numerous other blacks who followed Washington or who simply felt that the most practical black strategy was cooperation with paternalistic whites remained critical of DuBois; according to Benjamin Davis and the Atlanta *Independent*, "the poor devil is crazy and ought not to be taken seriously."[50]

The divisions between black and white workers, the abundance of cheap labor available to employers, and the prevailing paternalism in labor relations ensured the absence of a mass labor union movement. They did not, however, ensure docile workers. The Knights of Labor arrived in Georgia in the 1880s and promoted among workers much the same program that the Farmers' Alliance spread among farmers. Although small compared to the Farmers' Alliance or to the total number of nonagricultural workers, the Knights enlisted perhaps nine thousand members during the mid and late 1880s. In Augusta the Knights supported a massive cotton mill strike that kept all nine of the city's mills closed for three months. Most Knights in Georgia were whites, but the union's willingness to accept blacks and even to organize rural black workers led to violence and the murder of a union organizer. A decade later, the National Union of Textile Workers (NUTW), an American Federation of Labor affiliate, began a membership drive in Georgia. Far from being an alien invasion, the NUTW was headed by Prince W. Greene, a Columbus weaver, and Georgia produced some of the union's most able organizers. By the turn of the century, Atlanta, Augusta, and Columbus had experienced major NUTW-supported strikes by cotton mill operatives.

Most of these strikes were defensive in nature. Georgia factory workers normally joined a union and walked off their jobs when wages were cut, new work requirements were imposed, blacks were hired or promoted, or some other previously held right was violated. Similarly, blacks were more likely to respond when existing prerogatives were threatened than to join with DuBois in an effort to gain new or expanded rights. When in the 1890s Atlanta, Augusta, and Savannah enacted ordinances requiring segregated seating on streetcars, blacks in all three cities organized boycotts and forced the city governments to repeal the enactments. Even in religion, the sects seem to have been at least in part a resistance to the growing town control of the denominational churches.

Strikes by factory workers rarely succeeded. Usually they collapsed when management began to evict workers from mill-owned housing. In fact, mill and factory workers normally won only one kind of industrial conflict. During the late nineteenth and early twentieth centuries, workers on a number of occasions walked off the job when management hired, promoted, or otherwise placed blacks in positions above what was normally deemed "nigger work." Usually these strikes were short and successful; the workers enjoyed the support of the white community; and management normally conceded and fired, demoted, or segregated the offending blacks. When strikers demanded restoration of wage reductions or union recognition, however, a truculent management almost inevitably responded with lockouts, evictions, and determined resistance. Following yet another unsuccessful strike in Augusta in 1902, union efforts to organize textile workers and, indeed, factory workers generally largely disappeared.

Skilled craftsmen had greater success in their organizational efforts. In the mid-1880s typographers forced the Atlanta *Constitution* to recognize their union, and organized workers set to type some of Henry Grady's most impressive New South articles. During the 1890s skilled artisans created central trade associations in the larger cities and in 1899 organized the Georgia Federation of Labor. During these years strikes were not uncommon in the state. A census bureau official counted 210 strikes involving twenty-seven thousand employees between January 1887 and June 1894. Of these 42 succeeded, 55 were compromised, and 113 failed.[51] By the late 1890s the Atlanta *Constitution* was no longer reporting strikes on the grounds that publicity encouraged the strikers and gave the state an unfavorable image.

The railroad brotherhoods, the largest of Georgia's unions and the most strategically placed, carried off half a dozen major strikes during the late nineteenth and early twentieth centuries, usually forcing management at least to compromise outstanding issues. In Atlanta, where by 1920 almost half of all union members resided, labor organizations enjoyed a period of significant political power. Between 1894 and 1916, James G. Woodward of the typographers' union was elected mayor four times. But despite the rumblings of an inchoate labor movement, only a tiny fraction of Georgia's nonagricultural work force belonged to unions after the decline of the Knights at the end of the 1880s.

The craft unions were essentially conservative. Unlike free blacks and factory workers, skilled tradesmen had traditionally held a secure place in the Georgia social order, and their unions endeavored to protect this position and to encourage a sense of fraternal community among the labor elite. "The trades union is not an agency of antagonism but of sympathy and charitableness," stated the *Journal of Labor*, which was the voice of both the Georgia Federation of Labor and the Atlanta Federation of Trades. "It does not aim to array man against man, but to unite them in the bonds of truest brotherhood."[52] The craft unions were reformist in the sense that they supported improved public education, woman's suffrage, and similar measures, and any labor activity at all no doubt seemed threatening to management, disruptive to uptownsmen, and downright seditious to county governing elites.

Rural poverty, black indigence, and meager factory wages, all of which were bound up with and exacerbated by lack of capital, a dependent colonial relationship with the North, and Georgia's own social structure and social ideology, accounted for the state's failure to develop the crucial home market that would have permitted the takeoff into rapid economic development. During the Civil War the Confederate armies had provided an insatiable market, and the Georgia economy had responded with an impressive flow of foodstuffs and manufactured products. After the war, the economy had, by comparison, stagnated, and the diversified farms and the "hundred little work shops" had failed to materialize. As a *Journal of Labor* writer commented, "it does not pay to pay small wages because small wages pay nobody because nobody can pay anything for the things which ought to be paid for when they have nothing to pay with."[53]

Georgia remained poor and "backward," and its people sought solace in religion, family, folk culture, Lost Cause mythology, and whatever else promised security or simply aided survival. Towns, markets, and railroads slowly eroded ideological paternalism. Planters became more town-oriented, and uptown leaders became ever more removed from direct contact with the lower orders of Georgia's people. Despite serious efforts by mill owners and managers to maintain paternal labor relations, the twentieth-century trend was toward less personalized practices. The efforts by uptown women to reassert upper-class stewardship through charitable work and the ruralization of the women's clubs was a notable endeavor, but its lack of focus not to mention its failure confirmed the continuing breakdown of old values in uptown. Labor unrest, religious dissent, the emergence of a feminist movement, the behavior of urban blacks, the ritualization of lynching, and the declining social position of blacks were all linked to the decreasing acceptance of paternal responsibilities by reigning elites and to the dispersion in varying degrees of an individualistic ethos among the general population. With the deteriorating sense of paternal obligations by those in a position to exercise them came a growing tendency to defend the established system through coercion in such forms as lynch mobs, segregation laws, and campaigns for public enforcement of social purity.

# Chapter Seven

## *Progressivism and the*
## *End of an Era*

Following the Civil War, social conflict, civil strife, and ideological dissension periodically disrupted Georgia life, and the events of the 1890s shattered the shaky political peace established by the Bourbon counterrevolution that followed the upheavals of Reconstruction. The Alliancemen with their cooperatives and political yardsticks, the Populists with their attack on the Bourbon system, and the cities with their social problems and nonconformity kept Georgia in turmoil for more than a decade. Such behavior challenged the verities of the Lost Cause and threatened the sense of moral order in uptown. By the early twentieth century, cotton prices were up and Georgia enjoyed relative prosperity. The Populists had been routed; the textile unions had been driven from the state; and Booker T. Washington in his "Atlanta Compromise" address of 1895 had advised fellow blacks to abandon political participation and the quest for social equality. In these circumstances the Democrats launched a program designed to sustain the established order that took the name Progressivism.

The Progressive movement was complex, and it emanated from a variety of sources. At heart, however, as John Dittmer has concluded, "Progressive reform in Georgia was conservative, elitist, and above all racist."[1] In 1890 Tom Watson observed: "Men in prosperity do not want reform. Reforms commence from below. . . . They begin with the 'outs,' not the 'ins.'"[2] Populism, or at least one wing of it, was a revolt from below. Progressivism in the main was the work of the "ins" and particularly the "ins" in the cities and larger towns. Their goals included a stable, clearly delineated social order resting on white supremacy; morality and propriety in personal conduct including temperance; an honest, "responsible" political system based on disfranchisement and one-party rule; and good government that provided as many urban social services to whites as low taxes and the Constitution of 1877 permitted.

During the last years of the nineteenth and the early decades of the twentieth centuries, urban governments enacted a flood of Jim Crow ordinances. Legislation requiring segregation in restaurants, bars, parks, zoos, theaters, fairs, jails, chain gangs, and nearly everywhere else people might come together became common. These laws required separate seating at such events as shows and lectures; different time periods when blacks might attend such events as fairs; and exclusion of blacks from swimming pools, libraries, and other public facilities where segregation was not feasible. Atlanta established the bizarre requirement that courtrooms have "white" and "colored" Bibles for swearing in witnesses. While most of this legislation merely codified previously existing practices, some of it extended segregation into areas where it had not previously been practiced. By further sanctifying segregation with public authority, the laws encouraged more discrimination by employers, proprietors, and whites generally. It seemed almost logical when an Atlanta black who purchased an automobile was asked: "Whose road are you going to drive it on?"[3]

Black resistance to these measures was ineffective. In several cities blacks resumed their boycotts when new streetcar segregation ordinances were enacted, but this time the city fathers in Atlanta, Augusta, Rome, and Savannah refused to reconsider. The boycotts ultimately collapsed, and blacks moved to the back of the streetcar. By this time federal court justices were busily interpreting the Fourteenth and Fifteenth Amendments—at least as they applied to blacks—out of the United States Constitution, and national politicians, led by the Republicans, were enthusiastically applauding a "splendid little war" of imperialism against Spain and taking up "the white man's burden" in the Philippines and elsewhere. Bereft of allies and intimidated by state-supported white terrorism, most blacks sought whatever safety they could find by strengthening their identification with a white protector of the "better class" or by withdrawing as far as possible from contact with whites.

Leading Georgia political figures vigorously supported the drive to buttress the patriarchal system. "The field of agriculture," stated a turn-of-the-century governor, "is the proper one for the negro."[4] The governor perceived a relationship between the amount of education blacks received and the crime rate in the black community. Governor Hoke Smith, the state's most prominent Progressive, commented: "Those Negroes who are contented to occupy the natural status of their race, the position of inferiority, all competition being eliminated between the whites and the blacks, will be treated with greater kindness."[5] On another occasion, Smith observed: "Kindly, but firmly, the large majority of the negroes must be supervised and directed by the white man."[6] Like Rebecca Felton, much of Georgia's political leadership longed for the idealized "old time ante-bellum negro."

With the spread of Jim Crow segregation came the push to remove blacks from politics. In 1898 the Georgia Democratic party adopted the statewide primary, and in 1900 it became a white primary. In the early years of Bourbon control the Democrats normally nominated candidates at party conventions. Soon, however, opposition to "ring rule" led party organizations to adopt local primaries, some of which permitted blacks to participate and some of which were white only. The establishment of a statewide white primary in 1900 eliminated this ambiguity. At least in primary elections, there would be no more "honey-snuggling" blacks at the polls. "It was gratifying to see the voting booths free from noisy crowds," observed the Augusta *Chronicle* just after that city adopted the white primary in 1899.[7]

Georgia law and the Constitution of 1877 required payment of a cumulative poll tax, and the Democratic party required a white skin. But even these measures were not enough. In 1908 Governor Hoke Smith promoted, and the state's voters ratified, a constitutional amendment requiring that registrants must also pass a literacy test. The amendment offered a number of exemptions: an illiterate who was a military veteran or the descendant of a military veteran, who possessed a specific amount of property, or who was of "good character" could be added to the voter rolls, provided, of course, that he had paid current and past poll tax assessments at least six months before the election. In the aggregate these provisions—poll taxes, white primaries, literacy—ensured that virtually no blacks and few lower income whites would disrupt the orderly political process in Georgia. So successful were these reforms in stabilizing one-party rule and responsible electoral participation that the Democrats permitted a secret ballot in 1922.

The racist tide was so overwhelming that few publicly opposed it. William H. Rogers, a representative from McIntosh County and the only black in the general assembly, objected to the disfranchisement amendment and, following its passage, announced his resignation from the legislature. He was the last black person to participate in the lawmaking process for more than half a century. Like a voice from the past, former Governor Rufus Bullock fruitlessly reminded white Georgians: "Every man in the confederate service gave his parole to 'obey the laws in force where he resided' and the equal rights of black citizens is the very foundation of the law which we have given our honorable parole to obey."[8] Black leaders in Atlanta and Savannah attempted to organize Suffrage Leagues to oppose ratification of the amendment, but by 1908 few blacks voted and the effort was ineffective.

Segregation, disfranchisement, and other forms of racial proscription grew from indigenous roots, but the emerging champions of these and other "reforms" were the Georgia Progressives. The generally recognized leader of the movement was Michael Hoke Smith. Born in North Carolina, Hoke Smith moved with his family to Atlanta in 1872. A teenager at the time, Smith began to read law in an Atlanta office. During 1873 he taught school in the southeast Georgia county of Burke, departing only a few weeks before Tom Watson arrived in an adjacent county also to teach and study law. After passing his bar examination at the age of eighteen in 1873, Smith struggled as a young and unknown lawyer to establish himself in a city where the legal profession was crowded and highly competitive.

Smith turned to personal damage law, representing those who had grievances against corporations, particularly railroad corporations, in exchange for a percentage of the claims awarded. The Atlanta *Constitution* may have had Smith in mind when it editorialized: "But while we have a very able bar, we have quite a lot of shysters, who make money by hunting up cases."[9] In any event, Smith was extremely good at it and soon became a richly successful attorney. In 1887 he purchased a majority interest in and became president of the Atlanta *Journal*, which he and some talented editorial associates rapidly expanded. By 1890 the *Journal* had overtaken the *Constitution* to become the most widely circulated daily in the state. During these years the friendship between Hoke Smith and Henry Grady dissolved into bitter rivalry.

Smith also became an enthusiastic participant in state factional politics. During the late 1880s he sided with John B. Gordon and Alfred Colquitt as they drifted apart from Grady and Joe Brown, although, except for minor differences over tariff policy, everyone involved seemed to agree upon all outstanding issues other than who was most qualified to hold office. With the coming of the Farmers' Alliance and the growth of political discord, Smith quickly emerged as a leading reform Democrat, a proponent of free silver, rural credit, low tariffs, and similar measures. He carried on a friendly correspondence with Tom Watson and in a public letter to William L. Peek endorsed the subtreasury or some better system that would produce a "currency with non-perishable agriculture products as a basis."[10]

Smith was the leader of the Grover Cleveland forces and headed the state's pro-Cleveland delegation at the national Democratic convention in 1892. Cleveland reciprocated by appointing Smith secretary of the interior. During the mid-1890s Smith was the foremost spokesman for the Cleveland administration in Georgia. In numerous speeches he defended the gold standard and hard money, attacked visionary soft money schemes promoted by Populists and reform Democrats, and generally identified himself with administration policies. At the height of the depression of the 1890s, Smith noted: "I have never seen the South look so prosperous, especially Georgia." When he did choose to recognize the existence of economic problems, he suggested that "relief from panics has always come through restoration of confidence, not through bad money." Despite the increasing number of lynchings, Smith insisted: "Today we have no race problem in the South, but the white man and the colored man work side by side in peace."[11] By 1896 Georgia Democrats had had enough of Grover Cleveland and of Hoke Smith. The former secretary of the interior retired to his Atlanta law practice.

For almost a decade Smith was largely outside the Georgia political arena. He remained a conservative Cleveland Democrat. During the 1904 presidential campaign Smith made a number of speeches. When Watson, the Populist candidate for president, spoke in Augusta, Smith gave an answering address criticizing Watson's campaign and defending the Democratic candidate. But political currents in Georgia were in flux, and by the following year Smith and his Atlanta *Journal* friends had perceived the opportunities awaiting a strong "reform" candidate in the 1906 gubernatorial election. As the *Journal* phrased it, Georgia needed "a big conservative man, who is resolved on seeing that justice is done to the railroad interests as well as to the public; one who will have force enough to give the proper direction to the present public sentiment, but who will have poise enough not to let himself be carried into any wild-eyed position."[12] At 245 pounds, Smith was just the man.

More than a year before the 1906 gubernatorial election, Smith announced that he would "under no circumstances be a candidate." He then proceeded to launch his campaign for the Democratic nomination for governor. Smith called himself "the people's candidate" and promised to disfranchise the people who were black. He advocated a program that he later termed "progressive democracy," which included modest proposals to strengthen railroad regulation and to improve the common schools for whites. "The negro child," he explained, "should be taught to work."[13] Above all, Smith championed white supremacy. His ally in this crusade for reform was Tom Watson.

Following his ill-fated campaign for vice-president in 1896, Watson had retired to McDuffie County to write a history of the plain people of France, biographies of Napoleon, Jefferson, and Jackson, and a novel. Like Smith during these years, Watson also pursued a lucrative law practice, and he became a popular and expensive lecturer. Watson retained the loyalty of many of the "Old Pops," and, as the threat of Populism receded into history, even his former enemies expressed admiration for his literary accomplishments. By the early twentieth century Watson was becoming something of an elder statesman, "the Sage of Hickory Hill." He remained, however, a prominent spokesman for those "outs" in Georgia who were white.

While in political exile Watson brooded over the lost battles of the 1890s. He concluded that only by disfranchising blacks could a Populist alternative be rebuilt in the state. "The democratic party in Georgia did not dare disfranchise the Negro," he stated in a 1904 speech; "they must keep him where they could use him in order to beat us with." So long as blacks voted, Democrats would use the race issue to hold whites together, and so long as Democrats bought or coerced the votes of bribable or economically vulnerable blacks, honest elections in Georgia would be impossible. "For more than a generation," he told an audience in Thomson, "they have kept you under the rod of Eastern Plutocracy by their cry of Negro Domination."[14] Watson was not alone in linking economic reform with black disfranchisement; the theme ran through the correspondence of other Populists. W. L. Peek informed Watson that he wished "to make this a white man's government and for the people to rule in place of the corporations."[15] The war on the Eastern Plutocracy now included an assault on black political participation.

Watson accepted the Populist presidential nomination in 1904. One of the planks in his platform was: "I stand for White Supremacy and the principle of Home Rule."[16] During the campaign he promised to support any reform Democrat who would pledge to work for enactment of a disfranchisement amendment. Smith seized the offer to work with Watson for "the development of policies we discussed nearly fifteen years ago, about which we entirely agreed."[17] The alliance was concluded. Ironically, the leader of the outs had become the ally of the ins.

Smith conducted a virulently racist campaign for governor. Democrats had long employed racial demagogy to defeat Republicans, Independents, and Populists; Smith was the first—though certainly not the last—to use the tactic against fellow Democrats. Watson and much of the old Populist leadership, including former gubernatorial candidates Peek, James K. Hines, and Seaborn Wright, campaigned vigorously for Smith. In a blaze of antiblack, antirailroad rhetoric, Smith swept past four opponents to win the Democratic primary overwhelmingly.

Governor Smith promptly presided over the adoption of the disfranchisement amendment. A few north Georgia members of the state legislature opposed the measure on the grounds that it would disfranchise illiterate whites as well as blacks. Their argument appears to have been correct, although so many factors were involved that the impact of the amendment on voter turnout is difficult to measure. In elections during the hectic 1870s a majority of male adults consistently appeared (or at least were counted as appearing) at the voting booths. Participation fell sharply in response to the insipid, one-party politics of the 1880s. The appearance of the Populists revitalized electoral participation. Approximately half of the potential Georgia electorate turned out for the 1892 presidential election and for the 1892 and 1894 gubernatorial contests. Turnout sagged following the decline of the Populists, and then the adoption of the white primary removed almost half of the potential electorate from meaningful political participation. Large numbers of whites, however, remained politically active. Almost six of every ten white adult males helped to elect Hoke Smith in 1906 and more than six in ten helped to defeat him in 1908, the last primary before disfranchisement. Although the 1910 gubernatorial primary featured the same two candidates as in the 1908 contest, about twenty thousand fewer whites voted, which may in part have been the result of a relatively lackluster campaign but surely was also influenced by the more stringent registration provisions.

Thereafter voter turnout fluctuated steadily downward. At no time between 1920 and 1944 did as many as a quarter of the adult population appear at the polls, and rarely did more than a third of the potential white electorate cast ballots. The disfranchisement amendment strengthened the assumption that political participation in Georgia should be confined to those sufficiently affluent to pay poll taxes, sufficiently white to vote in white primaries, and sufficiently literate to read and write excerpts from the state or federal constitution. The poor, the black, and the unschooled need not apply.

Prohibition was a kindred reform. In the 1870s counties and other civil jurisdictions began to petition the legislature for local laws prohibiting the sale of alcohol, and in 1885 the general assembly enacted a local-option prohibition law. By the time of Hoke Smith's governorship, white concern about the "drunken" behavior of blacks and the remarkable tendency of whites to blame white violence during the Atlanta race riot on besotted blacks gave urgency to the prohibition issue. In 1907 the legislature banned the manufacture and sale of alcohol. "It was the deliberate determination of the stronger race to forego its own personal liberty on this as on other lines of conduct," a leading Progressive explained, "for the protection of the weaker race from the crimes that are caused by drunkenness." After all, according to Rebecca Felton, liquor dealers "are willing to fire up the black demon's blood that he may assault your young maidens."[18] Unfortunately, Sam Jones died the year before the law's enactment.

Actually Jones would likely have been disappointed. The 1907 law prohibited the manufacture or sale of alcoholic beverages in the state, but it did not deter their importation or possession. Locker clubs catering to the more affluent quickly appeared in towns and cities, and court interpretation allowed saloons to sell "near beer" to their customers. The legislature gradually tightened the law and finally in 1916 enacted an ironclad, bone-dry measure with heavy penalties for violators.

Progressivism spawned a variety of other reforms, some of which established important precedents. At the turn of the twentieth century, Georgia government stressed local control of local affairs. The Constitution of 1877 circumscribed the range of community action, but within its limitations localism flourished. Federal revenue agents might harass upcountry farmers who decided to turn their corn into moonshine, but the state of Georgia did not. The railroad commission regulated freight and passenger rates and inspectors checked the content of fertilizer—these were statewide concerns too important to ignore. But locally chosen sheriffs, constables, and town police enforced the law; locally elected assessors and collectors gathered the state's taxes; and local school boards spent the state school fund. The state supreme court ensured general interpretation of the law, but for the most part communities did about what locally dominant elites wanted them to do.

Yet much of the spirit of Progressive reform emanated from uptown, and, although its goals were inchoate and limited, its thrust was in fundamental ways urbanizing, centralizing, rationalizing, and "modernizing." The consequent tension between uptown and county seat threatened at times to produce political dissension, and this, too, made

Progressivism cautious. Like the path to prohibition, reform measures often came piecemeal, usually offered wide latitude for local interpretation, and normally made little provision for enforcement until, ultimately, the legislature became convinced that there would be no serious local objections to a bone-dry approach. Thus Georgia enacted a child labor law in 1906, gradually expanded its provisions for a decade, and then in 1916 hired a factory inspector to see if employers had paid any attention to it. Also in 1916 the legislature enacted a compulsory school attendance law containing so many exceptions that local authorities were largely free to ignore it, to enforce it for whites and ignore it for blacks, or whatever. To be sure, in this instance some short-term benign neglect was perhaps necessary; if Georgia had required all its children to go to school, there would have been no place for them to sit. Not until the 1940s did a more adequate compulsory attendance law appear.

In 1908 Georgia abolished the convict lease system. Yet another legislative committee investigated the lease system and uncovered conflicts of interest and corruption, and Governor Smith fired the chief warden for accepting bribes. Uptown newspapers, the state Federation of Labor, Rebecca Felton, and others demanded an end to the practice. With the growth of the state's budget, the money received from leasing convicts became increasingly negligible, and continuing reports of the chilling brutalities in the camps remained an embarrassment. During the late 1890s the legislature established a state farm and a reformatory and assigned women, disabled men, and boys to them rather than to the lease camps. With the abolition of the convict lease, however, Georgia did not build new prisons; it scattered the state's felony convicts among the county misdemeanor prisoners, thereby providing more labor for the the county chain gang crews and no doubt improving the criminal expertise of the locals.

More important than the ban on leasing state prisoners was a concurrent law requiring counties to work misdemeanor prisoners on public projects. Since the Civil War it had been common practice in Georgia for planters and other employers to pay the fines of people convicted in local courts and to require them to work long enough to repay the cost of the fines. But in 1905 the United States Supreme Court upheld and broadened the federal antipeonage law, and thereafter the national government began actively to prosecute debt peonage offenders, including several in Georgia.

Federal interference in Georgia affairs encouraged reform sentiment. So, too, did the automobile, which brought the need for better roads, and roads, of course, were local responsibilities. In many counties, chain gangs performed whatever repairs and improvements the roads received. The prison reforms of 1908—the end of convict lease and of "fining out" local prisoners—thus increased the labor available for road work. The foresightedness of these reforms was fully demonstrated when Congress in 1916 provided federal funds on a matching basis for road repair and construction. In most counties, convict labor was Georgia's contribution for matching federal funds. Despite the fact that prisoners were probably not much better off than they had ever been, debt peonage declined rapidly (even though some counties ignored state legislation and permitted employers to pay misdemeanor fines well into the twentieth century). Ultimately, these developments strengthened state governmental authority at the expense of the counties. In 1916 the legislature created a state highway department, which was a requirement for participating in the federal program. The original state highway commission included all three members of the prison commission in addition to three other appointees. The legislature reorganized the commission in 1919 and established a state road system.

During the Progressive era the school fund was the largest item in the state budget. Like other turn-of-the-century Georgia governmental programs, popular education was a miscellany rather than a school system. Local school systems formed one part of the educational mosaic. They differed from the rest of the common school program because they levied local taxes to support the schools. Just after the Civil War a few cities and urban counties established their own locally supported systems. The state accepted these systems when it created the common school program in the early 1870s and awarded them a share of the school fund. Before ratification of the Constitution of 1877, the number of local systems gradually increased.

In the mid-1880s Atlanta, Augusta, Columbus, Macon, Savannah, and a number of other cities and larger towns were a part of a city or county local system. These areas contained the better public schools in the state. Possessing an adequate tax base and the authority to use it, they augmented state funds with local taxation and supported school terms that often ran nine months or longer. By 1900 there were approximately fifty local sytems. Since state funds could be spent on "the elementary branches of an English education only," the local systems contained all of the public high schools, which in reality were uptown institutions. The twelve public high schools in the state in 1905 were all white, and the large majority of that year's graduates went on to college.

The bulk of Georgia's students were outside the local school systems; they attended schools more or less financed by the common school fund. The state allotted the fund according to the number of school-age children residing in a county or system. Local boards of education decided how the money would be divided. For whites in heavily black plantation counties, this arrangement had its advantages. By allotting most of the state funds to white schools, local county elites could provide reasonably adequate schools for whites without local taxation. The black schools in the plantation counties were the most financially starved in the state, but then, it was said that blacks and sharecroppers did not need an education.

Particularly in predominantly white counties, the schools were often a combination of public and private. The school fund provided salaries for teachers for three months in the 1880s and five months after the Farmers' Alliance legislature of 1891 raised school taxes. For a longer school year, parents had to pay teachers' salaries. The result was essentially a continuation of the old field schools of antebellum days with greater state support.

Throughout the state black schools fared less well than did white schools. Black teachers received less pay, and school terms were frequently shorter than at neighboring white schools. Dorothy Orr, the historian of Georgia public education, calculated that in 1910 Georgia spent $1.76 per black child in the state for black teachers' salaries and $9.58 per white child for white teachers.[19] Generally, discrimination was most extreme in the plantation counties and seems to have been least so in the urban local systems. For educational opportunities beyond the elementary level, blacks were dependent on private schools. Even after the state began to construct high schools, the disparity remained large. In 1936 Georgia had 431 white public high schools and 40 that enrolled blacks.

The Constitution of 1877 permitted communities to levy local school taxes. First, however, two grand juries had to recommend the move, and then two-thirds of the locality's registered voters (not just two-thirds of those voting) had to endorse the action. A 1904 constitutional amendment eased these restrictions by requiring only a two-thirds vote by those participating in the election. The result of this amendment was to broaden the disparity in educational opportunities between town and country. Within a decade after ratification of the amendment several counties, some seventy-five towns, and numerous militia districts had their own local systems. Overwhelmingly these were the more affluent communities capable of providing a local tax base, and their withdrawal from the county systems further weakened rural schools.

Throughout the Progressive era city and town white schools improved, while, by comparison, country and black schools declined. A series of constitutional amendments between 1900 and 1920 eliminated "elementary branches of an English education only" from the constitution, made high schools a part of the state system, required counties to levy school taxes, and permitted local systems to impose taxes for education without elections. Usually the newly constructed high schools were located in the towns and cities, and the growing reliance on local taxation benefited urban and wealthy areas. By the early 1920s it was little wonder that Tom Watson's young correspondent wished that she had grown up in town "so that I could have gotten the schooling that every child ought to have." Not until 1926 when the legislature created a small school equalization fund to aid the poorest counties and districts was there any effort to counter this trend.

Progressivism generally benefited the towns and cities, and local municipal reform was a central feature of the movement. In 1897 Augusta voters elected Patrick Walsh, editor and owner of the Augusta *Chronicle*, as mayor, thus launching a "Good Government" movement that ultimately produced such projects as the $2.2 million Augusta levee. In the same year Lucius H. Chappell, former president of the Columbus chamber of commerce and—in the words of a local historian—"the Father of our Modern Columbus," became mayor of that city.[20] During the 1920s Atlanta constructed a series of viaducts that raised a new automobile-oriented city atop an older railroad city. During these years, Georgia cities, like those elsewhere, created planning commissions, introduced at least rudimentary civil service procedures for the employment of police, fire department personnel, and other local government workers, and generally pursued a policy of close cooperation between municipal government and chamber of commerce.

Other legislation covered a variety of subjects. The railroad commission became the public services commission with its membership elected and its power extended to cover public utilities. Georgia's restive textile workers received a sixty-hour maximum workweek. A contract-enforcement law strengthened the crop-lien system by making violation of a lien contract prima facie evidence of fraudulent intent, and other legislation increased the penalties for "vagrancy." An underfinanced and inadequate state board of health appeared in a land of malaria, pellagra, hookworm, and venereal disease. Indigent and maimed Confederate veterans and the widows of veterans received greater financial support. In these and most other areas the pattern for Georgia Progressivism took shape during the gubernatorial administrations of James M. Terrell (1903–1907) and Hoke Smith (1907–1909, 1911).[21]

Despite all of this activity, the proponents of Progressivism took precautions that taxes and spending did not get out of hand. A 1904 constitutional amendment set five mills as the maximum state property tax. Since higher levies had been common during the late 1890s and early 1900s, this measure assured that property owners would not be unduly harassed by public requisitions from Atlanta. The amendment appeared to have had some effect on collections; perhaps the most revealing aspect of state taxes during the prosperous 1900–1920 period was how little collections increased (Table 3). Despite the lowering of state property taxes, however, Progressive measures encouraged higher local taxes. By shifting much of the tax burden from the state to the community, Progressivism further widened the gulf between town and country. In any event, the localized system of assessing taxable property and collecting taxes left county leaders effectively free to set whatever rates they wished to pay through property assessments.

Throughout the late nineteenth and early twentieth centuries, Georgia's basic tax was the general property assessment. Farm spokesmen often complained that agricultural property was taxed at an unfairly high rate, a claim which a study of published tax sources does not technically support. Yet the farmers were essentially right. The basic problem, as Alton D. Jones had pointed out, was the system established by Robert Toombs and his friends in 1877: "The tax on property, as provided by the constitution, was *ad valorem* only, and at a uniform rate, with all property bearing the same millage regardless of the income it produced."[22] Property value often failed to measure income-producing capacity. This was particularly true of farm property, which might produce limited earnings, when compared to the property owned and the income earned by professional people, service-oriented businessmen, real estate speculators, corporate stockholders, and, perhaps to a lesser degree, manufacturers and railroad owners.

Nevertheless, taxes were low for everyone in Georgia. And on the basis of the ability to pay taxes, they were lower during the Progressive era than during the Bourbon years. After World War I the general property tax rapidly declined in importance. By the early 1920s Georgia had placed a sales tax on fuel oil and had established a motor vehicle registration fee. These two taxes quickly replaced the general tax as the backbone of state tax collection, and in 1930 they produced well over half of all state income. This fact alone suggests that few other items bore crushing tax burdens. As Table 3 indicates, however, the gasoline, motor vehicle, property, and lesser taxes did greatly increase state revenues during the 1920s.

Table 3 summarizes trends in state expenditures over half a century. It lists the programs that dominated budget outlays in given years. The state debt largely explains state spending policies for three decades after the Civil War. The Bourbons have often been described as parsimonious, and perhaps they were, but the failure to repudiate more or all of the state debt during the early 1870s largely guaranteed that state services would suffer. In 1893 the school fund replaced the state debt as the number one item on the budget, and it remained so for more than two decades. During the early twentieth century, pensions and other aids to Confederate veterans and widows were major state expenses, although they amounted to only a trifle in comparison to the billions paid to Yankee veterans over the years by the federal

## Table 3: Government Expenditures, 1880–1930

| | State Disbursements Allotted to Selected Items | | | | | |
|---|---|---|---|---|---|---|
| | 1880 | 1890 | 1900 | 1910 | 1920 | 1930 |
| Public debt* | 69.1 | 36.9 | 12.6 | 8.0 | 3.1 | 0.1 |
| Common schools* | 6.9 | 23.2 | 40.0 | 38.8 | 30.2 | 19.8 |
| War pensions* | 2.9 | 8.7 | 19.0 | 19.1 | 12.0 | 4.7 |
| Highways* | 0 | 0 | 0 | 0 | 16.2 | 45.1 |
| Other* | 21.1 | 31.2 | 28.4 | 34.1 | 38.5 | 30.3 |
| Total | 100.0 | 100.0 | 100.0 | 100.0 | 100.0 | 100.0 |
| | Per Capita Disbursements (in Constant 1920 $) | | | | | |
| | $ 3.19 | $ 2.55 | $ 3.86 | $ 4.07 | $ 3.82 | $14.51 |

*Actual disbursements (bookkeeping duplications and balance-on-hand eliminated).
Source: Calculated from *Annual Report of the Comptroller General*.

government. By the late 1920s highways were the principal beneficiaries of state largesse. Analysis of these budgetary priorities may
suggest that Progressivism was more important for its social and political innovations than for its breakthroughs in governmental economics.

The alliance between Hoke Smith and Tom Watson was short-lived.
The Populists had favored such programs as prohibition and abolition
of the convict lease; Watson had become a fanatic on the disfranchisement issue; and Smith appointed James Hines as counsel for the railroad commission, offered Watson a position on the University of Georgia
Board of Trustees, and consulted him on other administration patronage. Consequently, Watson had reason to be pleased with Smith's performance. Actually, Watson became increasingly critical. Within a few
months after Smith's inauguration, Congressman Thomas W. Hardwick, a friend to both men and something of a go-between for them,
was pleading with Watson to adopt a more "positive" attitude, to demonstrate "that you can be not only *destructive* but *constructive*."[23]

One point of sharp contention emerged when the Atlanta-oriented
Smith tampered with the county unit system. Traditionally, at Democratic party conventions, delegates voted by county, with each county
casting two votes for each representative in the lower house of the
legislature. All counties had at least one representative, and thus two
convention votes, and the more populous counties had two or three
representatives and four or six county unit votes. This system was
biased against the larger counties, and as the cities grew the discrimination became greater. Fulton County had the same number of votes
as three sparsely peopled rural counties. When the Democratic party
adopted primary elections to nominate the party's candidates, the county
unit system was retained.

Following their 1906 victory in the gubernatorial campaign, the Hoke
Smith forces abolished the county unit method of counting votes. Future primary elections would be determined "by direct popular vote."[24]
This action, when actually implemented by the Democratic Executive
Committee before the 1908 election, strengthened urban electoral influence at the expense of small county governing elites and of rural
voters generally. Hoke Smith's political enemies found the decision
ideal for splitting the Smith-Watson alliance. Watson, who had been
carrying on a friendly correspondence with the opposition all along,
was soon busily plotting to overturn the Democratic rule change. Clark
Howell, editor of the Atlanta *Constitution*, agreed with Watson "that
this abrogation of the county unit system is by all odds the most rev-

olutionary measure that has ever been thrust upon the people of Georgia." According to the Atlanta editor, it "transcends all other issues . . . , will destroy rural influence," and was "forced down the throats of the people."[25] Beyond this, the county unit question promised to be an appealing political issue in the next gubernatorial contest.

Fittingly enough, the actual break between Smith and Watson concerned the fate of an Augusta factory worker. During the 1890s Arthur P. Glover was an active and militant Populist who lived in the Augusta factory district. "When politics reached the shooting stage—as they not infrequently did in the 'nineties'—Glover was generally on hand," Watson's biographer has observed, "his trigger-finger a-twitch."[26] Glover had been accused of shooting a Democratic deputy sheriff in an election day fracas. On another occasion when a Democratic mob threatened to attack Watson at an Augusta campaign rally, Glover and other Populists leaped to his defense. The latter incident resulted in the only meeting between Watson and Glover during those years.

In 1906 Glover killed a female mill worker with whom he had been having an extramarital affair. There was no question that Glover committed the crime; he freely admitted that he "killed the Dean woman." But the case quickly became complex. Glover pleaded not guilty because of insanity, and clearly there was prima facie support for the contention. Glover had grown up in a poverty-stricken broken home from which his mother had fled, leaving the youngster under the care of a brutal and alcoholic father. Glover was born with a misshapen, elongated head that his mother had tightly bandaged before her departure in a futile effort to warp the baby's head into a more normal dimension. All of this had taken its toll; there could be little doubt of Glover's mental instability. Even Hoke Smith, after studying the case, admitted that Glover was "below normal mentality."[27]

The case was also beset by political complications. The prosecuting attorney rushed the case to trial with such untimely haste that Glover's lawyer had no opportunity to prepare a defense. So blatant was this miscarriage of justice that a higher court ordered a retrial. At the second trial in the spring of 1907, Glover received a fair hearing, but the jury again delivered a guilty verdict. Nevertheless, the presiding judge and the prosecuting attorney were both old-line Democratic leaders who had been prominent in the battle against Populism and who had helped to count the votes in Augusta during Tom Watson's contests in the 1890s. Glover insisted that "it is not what I have done so far as the killing of Maude Dean is concerned but it is my past political life that is what they are after me so hot about."[28] Glover's lawyer agreed, and so did Tom Watson. Watson launched a vigorous lobbying campaign to convince Hoke Smith and his prison commission to commute Glover's death sentence.

The case presented a classic confrontation. To prosecuting attorney Boykin Wright and other uptown Augusta political elites, Glover symbolized the dangers lurking in the factory district. Glover was unstable, disruptive, immoral, and violent. Outward appearances suggest that Wright and his friends sought to make an example of Glover, and certainly they lobbied against commutation of his sentence. To Watson, Glover was a victim of the economic system he had so long struggled against. It is not clear why the ever-flexible Smith chose to accept the advice of his prison commission and permit Glover to be executed. Surely Smith empathized with the uptown views of Wright and the Augusta establishment, and by this time his relationship with Watson had cooled perceptibly so the governor probably saw little to be gained from further efforts to placate Watson. And Smith may not have understood why anyone would be concerned with what happened to a factory worker.

Watson joined the opposition. Just after Glover's death, Watson dispatched an emissary to encourage Joseph Mackey Brown to oppose Smith in the 1908 gubernatorial primary. The son of former Governor and former Senator Joe Brown, Joseph Mackey Brown was born to wealth and married wealth. Beyond this his accomplishments were meager. He had failed to establish a career in railroad management, and his business ventures were seldom successful. He had excellent connections, however, and in 1904 Governor Terrell appointed him a member of the railroad commission. There he crossed swords with Hoke Smith. The issue was one of the most hotly debated subjects in early twentieth-century Georgia politics—railroad freight pricing policies.

Earlier the railroads had established and the railroad commission had accepted a distinction between "port rates" and "interior rates." Goods arriving in Georgia by sea received the lower "port rates," giving Savannah and other port cities an advantage over Atlanta and other interior centers. In 1904 the Atlanta Chamber of Commerce, the city Freight Bureau, and the Atlanta *Journal* launched an attack on these pricing policies. The Atlanta shippers asked that port rates be established as the base for all state freight charges. The attorney for the Atlanta Freight Bureau was Hoke Smith. The following year the railroad commission, by a two-to-one vote, ruled against the Atlanta petitioners. Joseph Mackey Brown voted with the majority.

Hoke Smith launched his gubernatorial campaign with railroad regulation as one of the central planks in his platform. By calling for a reduction in railroad rates, Smith was able to broaden the local concerns of his Atlanta clients into a general reform position. None of this had any particular relevance to average Georgians, but, then, neither did a good many other Progressive reforms. During the 1906 campaign, Brown defended the railroad commission and attacked Smith in a series of public "cards" to the people of Georgia. After Smith became governor, he fired Brown, who retired to his home north of Atlanta to write more cards.

Brown had his own reasons for favoring the status quo in pricing policies. Apparently contrary to the letter of the law regarding membership on the railroad commission and certainly contrary to its spirit, Brown was deeply involved in a railroad promotion scheme to build a line to Savannah. "Probably much of Brown's opposition to the controversial Atlanta port rates," his biographer states, "stemmed from a secret railroad project in which he was interested."[29] Although the project collapsed in 1906, Brown was already committed to his anti-Smith position, and his abrupt dismissal from the commission made him appear a martyr. A deeply conservative man who seemed genuinely offended by Smith's aggressive governmental activism, Brown was another strange ally for Tom Watson.

Indeed, the election of 1908 was a strange contest. Brown was a small, timid man with a weak voice. Rather than public speeches, he published his cards to explain his position on the issues. He insisted that Smith's railroad reforms would frighten investment capital from the state and would injure "thousands of Georgia women and orphans" whose well-being was miraculously dependent on profitable returns to railroad shareholders.[30] Brown created an effective campaign organization by establishing Joe Brown clubs over the state and by using the services of surrogate speakers. Brown championed the county unit system, conservative government, and the existing structure of railroad freight rates. Tom Watson, the Atlanta *Constitution*, and anti-Smith political leaders supported his effort.

Hoke Smith campaigned vigorously, but he had difficulty grappling with an opponent who would not meet him on the hustings. "The combination of the liquor interests and the negro," Smith lamely observed, "threatens white civilization in Georgia."[31] An economic slowdown as a result of the Panic of 1907 also hampered the incumbent's campaign; his opponents insisted that somehow or other Hoke Smith's reforms were responsible for business distress. Smith nevertheless was able to defend a successful first term, and not since the Constitution of 1877 had established two-year gubernatorial terms had the electorate failed to grant an incumbent a second tenure.

The campaign was no doubt an embarrassment to Tom Watson. He did not so much support Brown as he vented spleen on Hoke Smith. Since Brown represented the Atlanta *Constitution*–old guard faction, Watson was hard-pressed to explain his strategy to his followers. One former Populist wrote: "I in common with many of your friends up this way, am entirely at sea to know what to think of you." Watson's new allies, in Congressman Thomas Hardwick's words, were "the same 'old gang'—they are reactionaries of the most violent type."[32]

The election nevertheless produced genuine electoral enthusiasm. In the white primary almost two-thirds of the white electorate appeared at the polls to nominate Brown governor by a narrow margin. Despite the dearth of legitimate issues, the contest hinted at real social cleavages. To be sure, Progressive politics in Georgia revolved around the really important matters: patronage, preferment, personality, and political power. Yet, at the same time, a series of early twentieth-century elections touched upon the broader divisions in white Georgia politics.

Smith represented the uptown position. His concern with social stability, lower freight rates, urban progress, and anti-county-unit, anti-black "direct democracy" mirrored the views of growth-oriented, commercial-civic elites in the cities. Smith, of course, was much too shrewd a politician to allow himself to be isolated in uptown; his racism and county connections gave his campaign wider appeal. Brown sought to represent the county governing class. His support for the county unit system, for an inert government that did not seek to "centralize" programs in Atlanta, and for downstate railroad pricing policies and his growing hostility to all forms of labor militancy won applause from spokesmen for county elites. Tom Watson led the white "outs." Large numbers of farmers, small proprietors, workers, and other common citizens continued to cast ballots, even while disfranchisement reforms took a further toll on the white underclass of sharecroppers, laborers, and factory workers. In the mercurial, one-party politics of Georgia, these divisions were often more easily sensed than documented; yet they formed the underlying cleavages in Democratic party politics.

These divisions lay at the base of a series of heated political contests. Brown won the governorship in 1908. In the spring of 1910 Hoke Smith issued a "final statement" categorically denying any further gubernatorial ambitions. Veteran observers saw another Brown-Smith contest in the making. Smith won the rematch by a small margin, but he served less than a year before being elected by the legislature to fill an unexpired term in the United States Senate. Brown returned to the governor's mansion in a 1911 special election. As governor, Brown did very little except to demonstrate an almost unseemly eagerness to call out the National Guard to put down striking workers. His followers restored the county unit system, thus making the primary election of 1908 the only one during the first six decades of the twentieth century to be decided by a direct, popular vote. In 1917 the legislature made the county unit system mandatory in primary elections for state offices. The last of the Brown-Smith confrontations took place in 1914, when Brown attempted to unseat Smith in the senatorial primary. Again it was a bitterly fought election in which more than half the white electorate cast ballots. Brown stressed his "law and order" antipathy for organized labor, insisted that unions led workers "into negro affiliation and racial degradation," and even, incredibly, accused Smith of being pro-Negro and pro-union.[33] It must have been too much; voters returned Smith to the Senate by a two-to-one margin.

Progressive reform offered little to Tom Watson's "outs" or to rural and village dwellers generally. To the contrary, it tended to widen the gulf between the larger towns and the countryside. With its commitment to disfranchisement, segregation, and white supremacy, Progressivism enthroned a nativism that could easily be extended to other politically defenseless groups. While uptownsmen organized their Kiwanis, Exchange, and Rotary clubs to discuss urban growth, commercial expansion, and business profits, Tom Watson helped to create the Guardians of Liberty, a group that was soon expending its energies in the battle against "the encroachments of the Roman Catholic Hierarchy."[34] C. Vann Woodward has movingly recounted the course of Watson and his allies from Populist radicalism to nativist demagoguery. Unable to cope with northern corporate capitalism and its government, many rural and small town Georgians, often joined by workers and other out-groups in the cities, retreated into a defense of traditional white southern Protestant culture. "A frustrated man and a frustrated class," Woodward wrote, "found their desires and needs complementary."[35]

These were difficult years for Tom Watson. In 1908 he again accepted the presidential nomination as the Populist candidate. "I am the only man in the race," he insisted, "standing squarely for *white supremacy*."[36] Few seemed to care. Watson received only a scattering of votes, and, most disappointingly, only seventeen thousand in Georgia, where he had concentrated his campaign. Watson remained neutral in the 1910 gubernatorial campaign in order to focus his efforts on unseating Congressman Thomas Hardwick, an old friend and ally who had fallen into disfavor. Hardwick won renomination easily. Watson launched an attack on Hoke Smith, accusing Smith of an impressive variety of marital infidelities. The charges were unfounded.

Watson won victories, too. After his return to the Democratic party in 1910, he sometimes emerged triumphant in the continuing factional squabbles. But in Georgia's increasingly issueless and meaningless one-party politics, triumphs were transitory and futile. Watson grew ever more antiblack, anti-Catholic, anti-Semitic, and, it seemed at times, anti almost everything else. There was truth in Hoke Smith's observation: "He hates everybody. He slanders everybody. He preaches no doctrines but bitterness and strife. He is radical and dangerous."[37]

The Leo Frank case exemplified the emerging trends. In April 1913 an assailant murdered Mary Phagan, a thirteen-year-old Atlanta factory worker and the daughter of a sharecropper who had moved to Marietta to become a mill hand. The girl's youth and the brutality of the crime lent themselves to sensationalism, and the Atlanta press had a well-established reputation for not permitting squeamishness—or journalistic responsibility—to interfere seriously with the sale of newspapers. The Atlanta police, already under heavy criticism for incompetence, cast about desperately for a criminal and chose Leo Frank. Having committed themselves to the conviction of Frank, Atlanta Chief of Detectives Newport Lanford, prosecuting attorney Hugh M. Dorsey, and the Atlanta police appear to have manufactured evidence, bribed and coerced witnesses, and suppressed information that did not aid the prosecution. Hostile crowds demonstrated in the streets while a jury found Frank guilty of murder in August 1913. Frank did not attend the sentencing whereby it was decreed that he would hang because the presiding judge feared that he might be lynched.

Although born in Texas, Leo Max Frank grew up as a part of an affluent Jewish family in New York. Frank moved to Atlanta when his uncle offered him the opportunity to help establish and to manage a branch of the National Pencil Factory. Soon afterward Frank married the daughter of a wealthy and prominent Jewish family in Atlanta. Well educated and soft-spoken, Frank seemed to epitomize uptown virtue, except perhaps for his Jewish religion. He was a successful and rising businessman who participated in the flow of northern capital into the South and who profited from the sweatshop labor of Mary

Phagan and others like her. Frank retained one of the most prestigious law firms in the city and employed his own private detectives to gather evidence. Three appeals to the Georgia Supreme Court and two to the United States Supreme Court failed to overturn the verdict. In contrast to the drumhead justice often meted out to blacks and sometimes to poor whites, Frank's conviction was sufficiently valid to withstand repeated scrutiny by higher courts. Yet, of course, Frank had not had a fair trial, and in fact much of the evidence pointed toward a different culprit.

Appalled by the judicial process in Georgia, national Jewish organizations launched a campaign demanding a retrial or at least the commutation of Frank's death sentence. Numerous non-Jews throughout the nation joined the crusade. Even some southern state legislatures passed resolutions in favor of commutation, and Frank received more than a million letters from throughout the United States and elsewhere. Rarely had Georgia been so prominent in national affairs. Uptown soon felt the pressure. Whether because of a dilatory sense of justice or—as cynics might imagine—a rising concern for the state's image in the wake of such massive and uniformly bad publicity, urban elites joined in the call for commutation and possible retrial. Several urban Georgia newspapers adopted this position, and some ten thousand citizens signed petitions circulated primarily in uptown areas. This campaign brought Tom Watson into the fray. In the spring of 1914, approximately a year after Mary Phagan's death, the Atlanta *Journal* editorially urged a retrial.

Tom Watson was enraged. His old enemies—Yankee respectability, uptown bankers, the *Journal*, and by implication Hoke Smith—were banding together to protect the "lustful," "New York jew." It was a case of "the little factory girl" and the numerous others "who, in so many instances are the chattel slaves of a sordid Commercialism that has no milk of human kindness in its heart of stone!" Watson raged in his *Jeffersonian*: "It has shown us how the capitalists of Big Money regard the poor man's daughter. It has shown us what our daily papers will do in the interest of wealthy criminals. It has shown us how differently the law deals with the rich man and the poor."[38] Leonard Dinnerstein, the leading student of the Leo Frank case, stated: "In 1913 the people of Atlanta, many of whom had been coaxed from the countryside with the promise of a better life, rose up and attacked a symbol of the new industrial culture which had reneged on its promise."[39] Atlanta Jews and Leo Frank came to personify "the subversive values of the emerging urban, commercial, and industrial age."[40]

In June 1915, Governor John Marshall Slaton commuted Frank's death sentence. The act touched off a wave of revolt. Crowds demonstrated throughout the state, and a battalion of the state militia was hard-pressed to turn back the mob attacks on the governor's mansion. Slaton, who bravely made his decision in the closing days of his term, left the state and remained for several years on an indefinite vacation until tempers cooled sufficiently for him to return safely to a private law practice in Atlanta. In Phagan's home town of suburban Marietta, the Knights of Mary Phagan vowed to avenge the girl's death. In August 1915 a band of twenty-five Knights invaded the state penitentiary at Milledgeville, kidnapped Frank from his hospital room (where he was convalescing from a knife attack by another prisoner), drove halfway across the state to Marietta, and carried out the court's original sentence. Jubilant crowds celebrated in the streets of Marietta, Atlanta, and elsewhere; Watson extolled the lynch band; and soon afterward the Knights of Mary Phagan formed part of the nucleus for a resurrected Ku Klux Klan.

The 1920s brought the first serious crisis for the old order and intensified the defense of traditional values. In 1920 cotton prices dropped precipitously, and, worse, the fields teemed with boll weevils. The terrifying insect arrived in Georgia in 1913 but not until 1919–20 did it become a problem and not until the early 1920s did it become a plague. Weevil eggs, laid in the small leaves encasing the cotton blossom, prevented the boll and consequently the cotton from developing. The destruction from 1921 to 1923 was devastating. Georgia's annual cotton production (in 500-pound bales) during these years was: 1918, 2,122,000; 1920, 1,415,000; 1921, 787,000; 1922, 715,000; 1923, 588,000; 1924, 1,004,000; 1926, 1,496,000. The extent of the destruction varied. In Greene County, located in the old cotton belt between Atlanta and Augusta, a 1919 cotton crop of 21,500 bales became a disastrous 326 bales in 1922. "Not since the days of the Civil War," one farmer stated, "have the people of our county been confronted with so serious a problem as now, namely that of the boll weevil." "Cotton is pitiful," wrote a central Georgia planter in 1923. "Drowned red, grassy, and full of Weevils." The same planter commented: "I get so discouraged at times that I feel like throwing up the sponge and quitting the game."[41]

Of necessity, many farmers did throw up the sponge during the early 1920s. By the hundreds of thousands they moved to the towns or, more frequently, left the state. Georgia suffered a net migration loss of nearly half a million people between 1920 and 1930. Almost two out of every ten citizens cast their lot elsewhere, and a substantial majority of the state's population loss was black. By 1930, for the first time in Georgia's history, a majority of the labor force worked in non-agricultural occupations. The decimation was greatest among small farmers and tenants. As a neighboring South Carolinian observed, many "of the strongest tenant families left the cotton fields. Only the old and the young and the determined stayed on."[42]

As if to mock the economic catastrophe of the countryside, uptown and neighboring environs remained relatively prosperous. The number of wage earners employed in manufacturing increased by more than one-fourth, and by 1930 three of every ten Georgians lived in an urban community of twenty-five hundred or more people. Although real factory wages declined significantly during the 1920s, uptown and even many lower-middle-class urban neighborhoods enjoyed good times. While most Georgians wrestled with varying degrees of economic destitution, a suburban real estate promoter in Atlanta explained to a reporter: "I doubt if today there is not in the heart of every young man and woman an ambition and hope to someday own a little home out in a subdivision on some charming wooded hill-side."[43]

Atlanta launched its massive viaduct construction project, and during the late 1920s the "Forward Atlanta" campaign advertised the city's hospitality to new industry to a national audience. Uptown won a signal victory in 1924 when voters ratified a constitutional amendment permitting local tax exemptions to new or expanded factories. Although the amendment seems to have been a response to general economic distress, it greatly facilitated the cooperation between government and chamber of commerce that civic-commercial elites had long favored. Soon towns and cities throughout the state were offering tax exemptions to factory enterprises, sometimes in conjunction with free factory sites and other concessions.

These circumstances formed the backdrop for the revival of the Ku Klux Klan. "Colonel" William J. Simmons, a medical school dropout, defrocked Methodist minister, insurance salesman, and fraternal society devotee, organized the Klan's rebirth. "Mints and cloves wrestled with the bourbon on his breath," Atlanta journalist Ralph McGill wrote, "causing the knowing to speak of him with . . . phrases reserved for the amiably fraudulent who manage to be equally at home leading prayer, preaching, taking a dram, or making a fourth at poker."[44] Simmons dreamed of Klansmen galloping across the walls of his bedroom, and the avidly pro–Ku Klux Klan motion picture *Birth of a Nation* helped to rekindle interest in the hooded order. The Klan foundered during the early years following its inaugural meeting on Stone Mountain near Atlanta in November 1915. Not until the emotional hysteria of World War I and the postwar demand for 100 percent Americanism—100 percent idiocy Tom Watson called it—did the Klan begin its remarkable growth. During the early 1920s it became a formidable national phenomenon.

For a time the Klan enjoyed great political power in Georgia. At one point the governor, the chief justice of the supreme court, the state superintendent of education, the mayor of Atlanta, and numerous other important officials were Klansmen or at least were closely associated with the order. But like Watson's earlier victories, political success meant little. The Klan had no program, no strategy, no vision beyond sterile mythologies and putrid animosities. It could only strike out at those who were vulnerable and, like Tom Watson, rail at unwelcome changes while accepting them. The revolt of the outs had come to signify resentment toward the affluent, hatred toward blacks and other minorities, and a mood but not a viable policy of truculent social reaction. In Georgia as elsewhere the Ku Klux Klan, bedeviled by internal conflicts over money and power, declined rapidly after the mid-1920s.

Watson lived long enough to enjoy the Klan's blessing. He bravely, if not always consistently, opposed Woodrow Wilson's war; he struggled against the wartime emotionalism that ultimately banned his *Jeffersonian* from the mails; and he fought the "100 percent idiots," their Red Scares, and the League of Nations. In 1920 he enjoyed one last political triumph. He won the Democratic nomination for the United States Senate, retiring to private life his old opponent Hoke Smith. It was doubtless a satisfying accomplishment. Although apparently never a Klansman, Watson was persona grata with the organization. A Mississippi Klan group named Watson "the man most feared by the papists of this country," and the Georgia Klan sent a huge cross of roses to the funeral when Watson died in 1922.[45]

During these years Georgia government was more notable for its antics than for its accomplishments. The legislature chose once again not to sponsor rapid development by rejecting in the mid-1920s a proposed constitutional amendment that would have permitted a $70 million bond issue for highway construction. The legislature also rejected a bill permitting local governments to establish public libraries. Representative Hal Kimberly, a leader of the opposition, explained that people needed only three books: "Read the Bible. It teaches you how to act. Read the hymn-book. It contains the finest poetry ever written.

Read the Almanac. It shows you how to figure out what the weather will be. There isn't another book that is necessary for anyone to read, and therefore I am opposed to all libraries."[46] The legislature blithely dismissed bond issues and public libraries as it did efforts by the Ku Klux Klan–supported governor to reform the tax system by shifting the burden of payment from real estate to income. Finally, during the fiscal crisis of the Great Depression of the 1930s, the general assembly enacted a modest income tax.

Georgia's governors were sound and conservative men. Lamartine G. Hardman, who served from 1927 to 1931, was perhaps the most memorable, although his fame rested more upon his astonishing physiognomic insights than upon his executive leadership. Two men had been convicted of murder and sentenced to death. A third person then confessed that she and a male confederate had actually committed the fatal crime. Lawyers for the two condemned men begged Hardman for a stay of execution until the new evidence could be evaluated. The governor settled the matter by studying photographs of the two men, concluding that they were definitely criminal types, and permitting their execution.

Economic conditions improved during the late 1920s, and cotton production returned to near pre–boll weevil levels. At the same time low market prices failed to restore prosperity. The system built upon the plantation remained intact, but it was increasingly a shell. Alienated and frustrated, the "outs" followed Tom Watson and Klan charlatans down the murky byways of racial and religious bigotry. Families and factions within the county seat elite dickered for power, increasingly joined Watson and other spokesmen for the "outs" in their nativist crusades, and otherwise sought to defend "the southern way of life." Politics grew increasingly remote from the profound social problems generated by a decaying social and economic order. Many blacks, exercising about the only option open to them, left the state. But the worst was yet to come.

The Great Depression of the 1930s was a crushing economic disaster in the countryside. As David R. Goldfield has observed, southern cities "were the nation's 'basket cases' during the 1930s,"[47] but conditions were even worse in rural areas. Georgia's exhausted and eroded soil and its inefficient, labor-intensive methods could no longer compete with newer cotton-producing areas in the western part of the nation, and the Depression further reduced the pathetic income of an already hard-pressed and battered people. The same planter who considered throwing up the sponge in the 1920s did so in the early 1930s.

"I never dreamed," he wrote to his wife, "that I could not support you and the children."[48]

Federal price supports soon offered some assistance to larger landowners, but times remained desperate for small farmers, tenants, and laborers. A Georgian who returned to the state after residing outside the South was horrified: "I could not become accustomed to the sight of children's stomachs bloated from hunger and seeing the ill and aged too weak to walk the fields in search for something to eat."[49] In Erskine Caldwell's fictional *Tobacco Road*, Jeeter Lester explained: "My children all blame me because God sees fit to make me poverty-ridden. . . . I worked all my life for Captain John. I worked harder than any four of his niggers in the fields; then the first thing I knowed, he came down here one morning and says he can't be letting me be getting no more rations and snuff at the store."[50] So it was for a great many blacks and whites who had spent their lives in agriculture, and the bankruptcy of the system was not confined to the economy. It was also evident in politics and government.

The new champion of the outs was Eugene Talmadge. The son of a planter and cotton gin operator, Talmadge grew up in modest affluence. He received a college education and a law degree from the University of Georgia and married a widow who owned a large farm in the south Georgia county of Telfair. Talmadge practiced law, although he failed to establish a practice, and farmed, although he was not particularly good at it and did not seem to like it. Turning the family's agricultural operations over to his competent wife Mitt, Talmadge entered politics as the champion of the farmer. After serving three terms as commissioner of agriculture, he became governor in 1933.

The Talmadge administration—the self-appointed spokesman for the wool-hat boys, the dirt farmers, and the common folk—bitterly opposed the New Deal. With rising intensity, Talmadge assailed relief, minimum wages, agricultural price supports, and the use of federal highway funds in Georgia. Although Red Cross rations and federal relief measures saved a great many Georgians from starvation, Talmadge insisted: "If the government keeps handling relief, manicuring ladies' nails and giving relief people cars to ride around in, it will stifle religion in the country and all religion will just dry up. Let the communities take care of relief through their religious organizations."[51] The Roosevelt administration, in reaction to the hostility of Talmadge and other state officials, federalized Georgia relief operations in early 1934 and continued to provide them outside of state influence. To Talmadge this meant domination by "foreigners" from North Dakota,

Minnesota, and elsewhere, and the Georgia House of Representatives resolved approval of the governor's position. The federal government did employ in Georgia social workers from elsewhere, largely for the rather obvious reason that Georgia had virtually no people with any training, but Georgia politicians who had little interest in relief certainly understood patronage.

Perhaps even worse from Talmadge's view, these modern-day carpetbaggers wanted to pay blacks and poor whites thirty cents an hour for relief work, and the National Recovery Administration and the Federal Bureau of Roads suggested even higher minimum wages. "I do not believe the money collected in taxes should be spent at the rate of 40 cents an hour for Negro highway laborers and boys who drive trucks," Talmadge fumed, "when the folks, white men and women, work in the field alongside these same roads for much less than 40 cents an hour, some of them for only 40 cents a day."[52]

On the minimum wage issue, Talmadge had the support of most of the Georgia congressional delegation and leading urban newspapers. Increasing pay levels for Georgia workers would presumably disrupt the agricultural labor system and retard industrialization, and paying blacks as much as whites threatened to encourage serious social maladjustments—plowhands, cooks, washerwomen, and other menial laborers might become demoralized by such riches. Southern politicians were largely successful in saving the region from higher minimum income. Relief workers were soon drawing fifteen cents an hour minimum, and highway workers were toiling at prevailing local wages. The National Recovery Administration succeeded in raising minimum factory pay and in generally eliminating child labor in industry despite the whining of Talmadge and his friends. But such measures could be expected from a federal agency that Talmadge called "a combination of communism, frenzied financing, and wet nursing."[53]

Talmadge rejected farm price supports as "the first move toward making peons of the farmers of America." He and his allies refused to permit Georgia to participate in old age assistance, aid to dependent children, and all the other social welfare programs largely funded by the federal government because they would "add on nearly every Negro of a certain age in the county to this pauper's list" and would "eradicate state lines and centralize all power in Washington."[54] There were, of course, legitimate criticisms that could have been and were leveled at much of the New Deal structure, but few emanated from Georgia.

Talmadge was instrumental in crushing another wave of labor militancy that swept across the state. In his 1934 reelection campaign, the governor vowed: "I will never use the troops to break up a strike." But that was before the great textile strike of 1934. The United Textile Workers had enjoyed considerable success in its organizing drive during the early 1930s. In August 1934, shortly after Talmadge made his nonintervention pledge, textile workers in Alabama began to walk off the job, and the strike soon spread to Columbus and elsewhere in Georgia. The textile union declared a general strike in September, a massive nationwide effort that perhaps three-quarters of Georgia textile workers joined. Talmadge dispatched four thousand National Guardsmen to "all sections of the state where rebellion or violence or insurrection is going on that local authorities are unable to handle."[55] The Guard arrested traveling "flying squadrons" of organizers and other militants and imprisoned them in a barbed-wire internment camp near Atlanta. These tactics broke the strike and once more spared Georgia workers the perils of mass unionization.

The patriarchal system provided the ideological and social structure upon which Talmadge's concepts of good government rested. In a sense, perhaps, his policies could even be explained in terms of pressure group politics. Planters, who readily accepted farm price supports, could appreciate the governor's efforts to prevent the New Deal from spoiling sharecroppers and field hands. Talmadge enjoyed the support of many textile mill owners and other low-wage employers, who no doubt appreciated his battles against minimum wages and unions. But Talmadge's basic popular following was not the county governing class and certainly not uptown elites. Although Talmadge enjoyed Atlanta and seems to have made enthusiastic use of its social advantages, on the stump he was the scourge of the cities. In smaller masculine groups, Talmadge invited the wool-hat boys: "Come see me at the mansion. We'll sit on the front porch and piss over the rail on those city bastards."[56] Before larger rural audiences, he merely observed that he did not want any votes from a town large enough to have a streetcar. Talmadge was the inheritor of Tom Watson's outs and the enemy of uptown progress and Yankee influence. In the theater of the absurd that had become Georgia politics, the protection of rural and village usages and customs meant striking out at virtually anything that was not inherently native to the Georgia countryside. Those who might have disagreed—the blacks and the white underclass—had little to say in such matters.

Georgia government was almost as inadequate as Georgia politics. Talmadge declared martial law in the state capital and used the National Guard to gain control of his own administration. Backed by armed troopers, he dismissed the popularly elected public service commission and two of the three members of the state highway board. Two years later, the state legislature, whose leaders were locked in a bitter quarrel with the governor, adjourned without passing a state budget; Talmadge ran the government during 1936–37 without legislative appropriation, although this required a further resort to martial law and the heavy-handed replacement of the state comptroller general and treasurer.

Talmadge had his own concepts of model administrative procedure, but his antics in government cannot be dismissed as individual foibles. In 1936 Georgia voters rejected a Talmadge lieutenant to elect as governor Eurith D. Rivers, a proponent of the New Deal. Rivers promoted the legislation and constitutional amendments that permitted Georgia to share in New Deal programs. He also endeavored to shore up the state's foundering school system. But, as President Franklin D. Roosevelt observed from Warm Springs, "this state cannot raise money for education because there is nothing to tax."[57] The Rivers administration was soon facing bankruptcy and declaring martial law at the state capitol in order to force the highway department to surrender road funds for other pressing financial emergencies. In 1940 the voters returned Talmadge to the governor's office.

Much of the rest of the nation watched all of this in wonder. During the 1920s, as George B. Tindall has demonstrated, the "image of the benighted South" came to maturity, despite cheery "Forward Atlanta" publicity campaigns. H. L. Mencken may have been too critical when he described Georgia and the rest of the South as the "bunghole of the United States, a cesspool of Baptists, a miasma of Methodism, snake-charmers, phoney real-estate dealers, and syphilitic evangelists."[58] In 1931 Mencken wrote a series of essays seeking to identify "the worst American state" on the basis of such indicators as wealth, education, health, and public order. Georgia was in the running all the way, although Alabama, Mississippi, and South Carolina ultimately nudged the state into fourth place.[59] From its arrogant tone to its contemptuous conclusions, the article was in many ways unfair. It was also true.

In the mid-1930s Arthur F. Raper intensively studied two Georgia plantation counties. "The decadence of this civilization is far advanced," the study concluded. "The collapse of the plantation system, rendered inevitable by its exploitation of land and labor, leaves in its wake depleted soil, shoddy livestock, inadequate farm equipment, crude agricultural practices, crippled institutions, a defeated and impoverished people." So hopeless were conditions for the bulk of the population in the two counties, according to Raper, that "the fatalism which accompanies their low plane of living does to their minds what inadequate food, malaria, and hookworm do to their bodies."[60]

The most important examination of southern conditions was the *Report* of President Roosevelt's National Emergency Council. In his letter to the council, Roosevelt stated: "It is my conviction that the South presents right now the Nation's No. 1 economic problem—the Nation's problem, not merely the South's."[61] Although actually written by Clark Foreman and others within the administration and merely endorsed by the council, the *Report on Economic Conditions of the South* was a serious attempt to document the extent of economic devastation in the region. The result made dreary reading. Published in 1938, the *Report* found a ravaged population living on depleted soil and suffering from inadequate diets, poor health, and unacceptable housing. The underpaid work force included too many women and children. Inferior public services, particularly in education and health, were far below national norms.

To account for this disastrous situation, the council pointed to an explanation Tom Watson would have liked: the southern colonial economy. Restricted credit, high interest rates, high tariffs, discriminatory freight rates, and absentee ownership of southern transportation, industry, and other property drained away southern capital and impoverished the South's people. The council also faulted the region's staple crop economy and its landlord-tenant system but identified these with the effects of the South's dependent relationship with the North.

The council's *Report* was a product of its times. It was written by New Dealers sympathetic toward the southern masses and aware that the great reservoir of southern poverty as well as the region's lack of buying power were crucial impediments to national economic recovery. The *Report* was short—just over sixty pages—and it spoke of the majority of southerners, not of the relatively affluent minority. But despite its limitations, the *Report* suggested profoundly important new directions in the relationship between Georgia and the United States, and it accurately recognized the bankruptcy of the old order in the South.

Long ago all that a great many Georgia males wanted "in this creation" was "a pretty little wife and a big plantation." Some got them, and they thereby laid the foundation for a social and economic system that dominated Georgia life for well over a century. Though sometimes modified and occasionally challenged, the system remained intact until the 1930s. During that decade it reached the point that it was no longer able to provide for or to govern its people.

# Chapter Eight

## *The Twilight of the Old Order*

T he breakdown of plantation agriculture, the coming of the New Deal, and the enormous domestic impact of World War II disrupted the social and ideological stability imposed by Progressive reform. With federal farm programs effectively paying farmers not to farm, sharecropping rapidly declined as landlords converted tenants into hired hands or seasonal workers or cast them adrift entirely. Displaced tenants joined the numerous defunct small farmers and the squatters who had endeavored to survive the Depression on uncultivated land in an exodus to Atlanta, Chicago, and Detroit. The mechanization and diversification of agriculture proceeded apace during the 1940s and 1950s, further contributing to the massive migration that depopulated the Georgia countryside. Sizable numbers of Georgians—about one third of the population in 1960—continued to live in nonurban areas. Classified by the census as rural nonfarm, they resided in houses and hamlets along the paved roads and highways that testified to the state's improving road system and commuted to jobs in the towns and cities. Beyond the paved roads and especially those located outside the cities and larger towns, the Georgia hinterlands became increasingly devoid of people. New Deal wage legislation, particularly the Fair Labor Standards Act of 1938, increasingly made mill villages unprofitable enterprises, and during the 1940s workers in the self-contained factory communities, like the tenants on the plantations, moved ever further from the paternal labor relations of an earlier era into a more dynamic system wherein labor was simply a commodity to be bought and sold in the marketplace. The decimation of the agricultural work force, the decline of the mill villages, and the growth of industry and urban services vastly accelerated the process of social modernization and comported with historian Jack T. Kirby's conclusion that "the South was modern and developed by about 1960."[1]

Equally important was the accompanying shift away from community values and folk culture. Civic and legal rights filled the vacuum created by the deterioration of paternal duties and obligations, and formal contractual arrangements expanded as the force of informal personal understandings degenerated. As the postwar era progressed, law gradually usurped religion's role as the ultimate arbitrator of social and ethical behavior. Work became ever further removed from family as men and increasingly women commuted to jobs in factories, chain stores, and office buildings. The importance of family and bloodline declined with the spread of up-town definitions of material success and consumer affluence. Georgia society was becoming, in the words of a conservative critic, "transient and rootless and divorced from nature."[2] Like William Faulkner's Flem Snopes, "who apparently never looked directly or long enough at any face to remember the name which went with it, yet who never made mistakes in any matter pertaining to money,"[3] a great many Georgians learned to participate in an impersonal market economy.

Some Georgians benefited considerably more than others from these upheavals. Those people with experience in the emerging modern world of cash, commerce, and checking accounts faced less traumatic adjustments than did the suppressed sharecroppers in the plantation counties, the isolated small farmers of the Georgia mountains, the hapless and often deeply indebted marginal farmers as well as squatters on the less fertile lands of the hills and wiregrass, and numerous other Georgians insulated from "progress" by the state's low-wage colonial economy and its folk culture. The 320,000 or so Georgians who served in the armed forces during World War II found opportunities to broaden their cultural horizons, and, when mustered out of uniform, received access to the various veterans programs—popularly lumped together as the G.I. Bill of Rights—that offered opportunities for further education, home ownership, and other benefits. While most servicemen were in fact male, the wives of soldiers and sailors received fifty dollars a month in addition to thirty dollars for one child and twenty dollars for each additional child. Fewer than two of every ten Georgians served in the armed forces or was a spouse or offspring thereof. Nonetheless, many citizens found employment in the booming shipyards of Savannah and Brunswick and the munitions factories in Macon and Milledgeville or as civilian employees at the mushrooming military bases that during World War II and afterward made Georgia one of the more heavily occupied political entities in the world. Pete Daniel in his study of southern agriculture was surely correct when he observed that "the armed forces and defense work became the resettlement administration for rural southerners. In this respect the war proved providential."[4] The fortuitous arrival of World War II and other developments fueled the state's long-awaited transformation into an urban, industrial, and diverse society.

Growing numbers of Georgians moved into urban-oriented white-collar occupations, which formed the most rapidly expanding part of the

Georgia labor market. In 1940 about one in five workers held jobs in wholesale and retail trade, finance, insurance, real estate, and white-collar services; by 1960 well over one in three did. These employment categories encompassed a wide range of occupations and included that ten percent of the Georgia population who in 1940 were executives, proprietors, professionals, managers, and the like, positions that suggested an uptown residence. Despite substantial numbers of female teachers and nurses, white males monopolized most of these occupational categories, and nonsouthern immigrants were particularly prominent. In their biting 1941 critique entitled *Sharecroppers All*, Arthur F. Raper and Ira De A. Reid described Atlanta as a "branch-house town," a city that contained "1,500 branches of national businesses" and was largely controlled by "itinerant and overseer executives," most of whom had nonsouthern backgrounds and "non-Southern interests to protect."[5] Two decades later, Atlanta journalist Ralph W. McGill offered a more generous assessment of "the executives, young and old, who poured into the South to direct the new assembly and production plants and the burgeoning retail businesses" that were mostly "organized and managed by outside corporations." According to McGill, this migration enriched Atlanta and other communities and contributed significantly to the state's "progress," especially in light of the fact that many southern business families "had gone to seed, insofar as risk or venture capital was concerned." Many southern businessmen and investors "were willing, often eager, to have the makers of the New South buy out the old family mill or plant, or the long-held, long-unimproved real estate."[6] Academic studies produced by the Committee of the South confirmed the domination of outside corporations, reporting that in 1939 branch plants produced 70 percent of the total value of manufactured products in the southeastern region and that during the 1940s outside expansion into the South accounted for most of the region's industrial growth.[7]

The expanding urban middle class, often supported by ambitious if less affluent white-collar subordinates, invigorated the long-standing uptown desire for new factories and economic progress. In 1952 journalist Samuel Lubell explained: "The fever for new industry probably runs strongest among the rising middle class in the Southern cities. The young lawyer searching for clients, the college graduate seeking a supervisory post in the mills, merchants and salesmen with something to sell, bankers hunting new investment outlets for growing deposits, doctors building their practice, all the numerous property holders who hope the cities they live in will grow out to the land they own and strike them rich—all are building their dream castles upon the growth of industry."[8] By 1960 this white-collar middle class—the executives, bankers, and businessmen, the accountants, clergymen, engineers, and lawyers, and the numerous others who held managerial, professional, and proprietary positions—numbered 225,000 and made up 17 percent of the work force. The growth of the urban-metropolitan middle class correlated closely with Georgia's ever more fervent quest for new factories, office buildings, and enterprises.

Not entirely inaccurately, critics sometimes depicted the southern man in the gray flannel suit as "a rootless nomad whose primary, and sometimes only, loyalty is to business" and whose concept of social policy was determined entirely by the exigencies of the real estate market.[9] But in a real sense it was also true, as Lubell argued, that "this new middle class, the branch plant managers and their college-trained supervisors, merchants, doctors and lawyers, newspaper publishers, and realtors, all seemingly so conservative, . . . are the real political rebels in the South today."[10] Merely as a result of their general commitment to atomistic individualism, consumer materialism, upward mobility, and unfettered economic development, the metropolitan middle class questioned the fundamental tenets of the paternal order. Leonard Reissman described the nature of the conflict: "Land as a source of wealth and power is challenged by money; ascribed status is challenged by status through achievement; and traditionalism is challenged by pragmatism."[11] As rebels, middle-class Georgians earned a reputation mainly for reluctance, but nonetheless they represented a formidable and expanding social group that threatened the power and prerogatives of county seat elites. In 1960 some 46 percent of Georgia's population resided in metropolitan areas, with the Atlanta area containing more than one million people, housing one-fourth of the state's population, and employing more than one-third of the white-collar business and professional middle class. The exploding cities and their uptown leadership placed mounting pressure on Georgia's established county-oriented political structure.

More numerous than the business-professional middle class during the post–World War II years was the white-collar proletariat composed of clerical and sales workers. Raper and Reid in their *Sharecroppers All* suggested that "only a little less dependent and insecure than the South's landless farmers are chain-store clerks, salesmen, [and] insurance agents." Although there were successful sales people and real estate agents who earned substantial incomes, many bank tellers, cashiers, and counter clerks, like typists, telephone operators, and salesgirls, often received "white collar status without white collar pay, and so their white collars are frequently frayed."[12] Such a description would have applied in varying degrees to the one in ten Georgia workers who in 1940 held clerical, sales, and kindred positions. Even if not particularly lucrative, these jobs did generate far more purchasing power than did tenant farming and contributed to the developing consumer economy. Land and community retreated before the lure of six-dollar dresses, seventy-dollar refrigerators, and eight-hundred-dollar automobiles.

White women increasingly filled the ranks of the clerical and sales work force, which by 1960 numbered a quarter of a million people and encompassed almost 20 percent of total employment. In 1940 approximately one-third of these workers were white women; by 1960 a substantial majority of the bookkeepers, secretaries, stenographers, and others who toiled in clerical and sales capacities were white women. Gunnar Myrdal observed in 1944 that women, like black males, monopolized certain occupational categories that "are regularly in the low salary bracket and do not offer much of a career." The place of both Negroes and women, Myrdal wrote, was "originally determined in a paternalistic order of society."[13] Despite the decline of the paternal ideal, the statement remained valid in the postwar years and within the "new" white-collar classes. In 1960 the large majority of white women worked in a predictable range of white-blouse occupational categories and drew salaries that were little more than half those received by white-collar males. Few blacks—well under 10 percent of those employed—found a place in the white-collar market at all.

During most of the twentieth century, blue-collar employees were substantially more numerous than white-collar workers. In 1940 more than four of every ten employed Georgians held manufacturing, construction, transportation, and service jobs that might be broadly termed blue-collar occupations; by 1960 these workers composed more than half of the total labor force. Factory workers were the most numerous and most strategically located. In 1940 almost one in five employed Georgians was an industrial worker; by 1960 more than one-fourth were so employed. As in the past, traditional, low-wage, labor-intensive industries dominated Georgia manufacturing. In the mid-1950s, seven out of ten factory workers labored in textiles, apparel, lumber, furniture, and food processing. Transportation and construction workers, who made up 9 percent of the work force in 1940 and 13 percent in 1960, held positions that were roughly comparable to factory jobs.

Generalizations about manufacturing workers are difficult. In 1939 Solomon Barkin, New York research director for the Congress of Industrial Organizations' Textile Workers Union of America, toured the southern textile belt and delivered his report on "The General Nature of the Problem" of organizing southern workers. The problem, Barkin concluded,

was the southern textile worker. He "is a small-town, suspicious individual, who is extremely provincial, petty, gossip-mongering" and "is
most suspicious of every outsider." As a group, textile workers were clannish people who "prefer to be left alone and isolated." If sufficiently
pressed by stretch-outs or wage cuts, they were willing—too willing, according to Barkin—to strike, even on the massive scale of the 1934 textile
strike, but they lacked the discipline and patience to carry their walkouts
to successful conclusions. In 1942 George Baldanzi, vice president of the
Textile Workers Union, also studied southern workers and reported on
"The Problems of Organization in the South." Baldanzi agreed with Barkin that "Southerners are not a cosmopolitan group," but beyond that the
two men's conclusions were fundamentally different. Among southern
workers, according to Baldanzi, there "is a much greater appreciation of
human values than is found in the North; they are by nature kindly, react
to human tragedy with a sort of calm fatalism, and are strongly religious."
Baldanzi found it refreshing that southern workers were less cynical and
less materialistic than those in the North. To Baldanzi "The Problem of
Organization in the South" had more to do with C.I.O. organizers than
with southern textile workers. Both reports included an element of con-
descension, and both surely contained an element of accuracy. If Georgia
workers around 1940 were clannish—"encapsulated" by the "mill village
culture," as an academic study in the late 1940s phrased it—they also had
a sense of place and community.[14] A mill village, a textile worker explained, "was kind of one big family."[15]

The mill villages along with the lumber towns and other company communities disintegrated during the postwar years. Federal labor legislation
and improved housing standards made the villages an increasing drain on
profits, and companies responded by selling the mill houses, often to the
workers who occupied them. Various studies of the process were in
general agreement that the breakup was not so much a matter of experienced mill workers moving to other neighborhoods and other jobs as it
was the departure of young people who grew up in the villages. For boys
the move away from the village often involved an intermediate stint in the
armed forces; girls were more likely to finish high school and to seek
white-collar employment or to marry into higher status. Most boys and
girls, however, remained in blue-collar occupational categories or married
into them, and many appear to have taken jobs in the textile mills even if
they did not live in company houses as their parents had done. In any
event, the decline of the mill village contributed to the creation of a more
mobile and dynamic labor system. Historians interviewing former mill
village residents discovered a sense of loss and nostalgia. Respondents

tended to view "the unraveling of social relations as a personal loss" and to regret the severance of work from community.[16]

Although wages in the South were generally low relative to those paid elsewhere in the nation, working conditions improved during the 1940s and 1950s. By that time air-conditioning had become normal in southern factories, and during World War II the War Labor Board pushed up regional wages, especially in textiles. As in the past, craftsmen, skilled workers in industry, transportation, and construction, and blue-collar supervisory personnel fared reasonably well in the Georgia economy. By 1960 these workers, most of whom were white men, made up 12 percent of the total state labor force. Electricians, foremen, locomotive engineers, typesetters, toolmakers, and even factory operatives in such high-wage industries as paper products and transportation equipment were well compensated, at least by Georgia standards. Those white males who held craft, skilled, or supervisory jobs made almost as much as white male clerical and sales workers and considerably more than female or black white-collar employees.

The bulk of the blue-collar work force—about four of every ten employed Georgians in 1960—were semiskilled operatives, service workers, and laborers. More than half—some 300,000 people—were operatives, a census term that encompassed a wide range of factory jobs as well as such occupations as meat cutter, sailor, truck driver, and welder. The federal government roughly defined poverty as a family income in 1960 of less than $3,000, which was about $500 less than the median wage of white male operatives and about one-third more than the average pay of the female and black male operatives who made up one-half of the occupational category. Far below the poverty level were the 90,000 or so nonfarm laborers, the large majority of whom were black men; the 80,000 or so private household workers, an occupation dominated by black women whose average yearly income was less than $600; and the more than 100,000 nonhousehold service employees who worked as janitors, hairdressers, cooks, waitresses, and the like. Included among service workers were a few relatively well-paying and predominantly white male occupations such as policemen and firemen, which were virtually the only service jobs that paid above poverty wages.

As these figures suggest, huge numbers of Georgians drew less than poverty-level wages. About half of all employed males and three-quarters of employed females held jobs that in 1960 paid less than three thousand dollars per year. To be sure, part-time workers and youngsters getting started at the bottom of the occupational ladder filled some of these positions, and many were held by married people making a contribution to larger overall family incomes; still, low-wage occupations continued to be a fundamental factor in the Georgia economy. A third of working males and more than two in ten females held jobs that paid somewhat more adequate wages in the three thousand- to six thousand-dollar range. Thus more than eight out of ten employed males and virtually all females received what were essentially working-class incomes or less, regardless of whether they were paid in the form of salaries, commissions, tips, or wages. Almost two in ten males and a few thousand females earned more comfortable incomes of over six thousand dollars a year and most of these workers occupied business-professional, white-collar positions. In the main, however, working-class incomes dominated the Georgia labor market.

During the late 1930s and in the mid-1940s, blue-collar workers threatened to become a force in state power and politics. C.I.O. organizing drives, a government in Washington friendly toward labor unions and toward southern liberalism, and the sheer size of the expanding working class prompted labor organizers and middle-class reformers to dream of "political and industrial democracy" wherein unionized workers with access to the ballot box would not only gain higher wages, better working conditions, and a voice in their own economic affairs but would also replace Georgia's predominantly Bourbon congressional delegation with New Deal liberals. Such was the dream, however briefly held. In practice the obstacles confronting the creation of a self-conscious working class were formidable. Georgia factories were small compared to those above the Ohio River; huge numbers of underemployed rural Georgians were eager to accept almost any job that promised a steady wage; law enforcement and state policy remained under the control of county elites hostile to social change; and, perhaps most of all, the tradition of paternal labor relations influenced the outlook and aspirations of working-class men just as it did those of blacks and women. For a time labor militancy did generate considerable conflict and controversy and represented yet another threat to the traditional order.

White- and blue-collar occupations in Georgia grew at the expense of employment in agriculture. In 1940 farmers and farm laborers were one-third of the state work force. In 1960 they were less than 10 percent. The collapse of agriculture's long dominant position in the Georgia economy produced ambivalent consequences. The material standard of living clearly improved; people ate better, lived longer, and consumed more. Per capita income increased from 57 percent of the national average in 1940 to 73 percent in 1960. Rising incomes and federal mortgage guarantee programs made better housing available to more families. In 1940 home owners resided in 30 percent of occupied housing units, of which 35 percent had indoor plumbing and about half had electricity. By 1960 home owners lived in a clear majority—56 percent—of occupied dwellings, and almost two-thirds of Georgia domiciles had indoor plumbing, eight of ten contained television sets, more than six of ten reported telephones, and 12 percent boasted air conditioning. An increasing number of these residences were located in suburban housing developments, whence people commuted to the city to work, consumed at supermarkets and shopping centers rather than country stores, and sent their children to consolidated and in 1960 still segregated schools.

Georgia's people paid a considerable price for "progress." The traditional Georgia virtues that revolved around family, clan, community, and church found little support in a maturing market society and consumer economy. A leading historian of southern agriculture lamented: "What one could mourn was the passing of the underpinnings of the old culture—the families that were broken and dispersed to the cities, the communities that wilted, the small rural churches that had bonded such communities, and the neighborliness that allowed such deprived people to endure even the vicissitudes of sharecropping."[17] Ben Robertson, who grew up on a large South Carolina farm and who, like so many Georgians, departed to seek his fortune elsewhere, could in 1942 still rest secure in the knowledge that "someone is always keeping the home place. . . . It is a great comfort to a rambling people to know that somewhere there is a permanent home—perhaps it is the most final of comforts they ever really know."[18] But even as Robertson wrote, the day of the "home place" was passing. Houses in Georgia became more comfortable but they also became capital investments rather than home places.

The mechanization and diversification of agriculture and the dispersion of the farming population failed to dissipate the long-standing animosity between city and country. Doubtlessly many planters, farmers, and small town dwellers watched the disintegration of their way of life with mounting horror and hostility. Their children moved away to the cities and many of their towns and communities wilted. Vast and impersonal social and intellectual changes as well as labor union organizers and black civil rights proponents challenged what a perceptive observer referred to in the late 1940s as "values which have been set for three or four generations in the hard concrete of custom."[19] In the early 1960s historian Dewey W. Grantham wrote: "Adverse economic and demographic forces have baffled and frustrated many rural people, exacerbating their fears of social change and their bitter hostility toward the city. Their declining economic and social status has made them more than ever the great conservators of the South's traditions."[20]

The pattern of Georgia's industrial growth also contributed to rural-urban dissension. World War II was primarily an urban economic bonanza, and thereafter industrial growth in the country further diverged from economic expansion in the city. Between 1946 and 1955, almost five hundred new factories employing twenty-five or more workers appeared in Georgia, thereby increasing the number of such plants by 40 percent. About half of these factories were traditional low-wage, labor-intensive enterprises in textiles, apparel, lumber, and food services, and they usually moved into semirural areas to take advantage of the cheap labor being released by agriculture and to swell the rural nonfarm work force. They also were the firms that hired the fewest black workers except for the more exploitive jobs in lumber and sawmill operations. The other half were "new type" enterprises in paper, chemicals, machinery, printing, and the like that normally paid considerably higher wages. These factories overwhelmingly moved into urban-metropolitan communities.[21]

Thus Georgia's industrial growth tended further to concentrate the traditional defenders of a low-wage economic system and a paternal ideology—that is, the textile and lumber mill operators, planters, and county seat elites generally—in the nonurban areas. Many of the larger towns in these counties contained their easily recognizable "uptowns," "milltowns," and "niggertowns." Such orderly arrangements contributed to social stability, divided white from black workers, and ensured a cheap labor force in addition of course to being the natural order of things. In the countryside, planters purchased tractors and other farm machinery, grew more cattle, peanuts, and soybeans and less cotton, and collected their subsidy checks from the federal government, but their agricultural operations still needed substantial labor during planting and harvest. County seat elites in piedmont industrial towns and in plantation-belt farming communities remained wedded to the time-tested colonial virtues of racial segregation, cheap labor, and the southern way of life.*

The dismal economic plight of blacks became a more pressing problem as the living standard of whites improved. In 1950 the per capita family income of white Georgians was $2,189; that of black Georgians was $909.

---

*None of this is to suggest that urban industrialists customarily crusaded on behalf of higher wages for their employees or that metropolitan suburbanites normally complained about racial segregation, but these issues were of less immediate importance in capital-intensive enterprises where wages were a smaller part of the overall budget and in lily-white suburbs where integration seemed a rather remote prospect.

Studies of southern black communities in the 1940s found that eight or nine of every ten people, depending on the criteria employed, were lower class, and Gunnar Myrdal in 1944 reported that in the South "the majority of the Negro population suffers from severe malnutrition."[22] A careful examination of a black community in a neighboring state in the late 1940s found that 90 percent lived "on streets that are unpaved and without sidewalks," that 80 to 90 percent of the houses were "badly in need of major repairs," that more than 90 percent lacked indoor plumbing, and that 90 percent of employed people were unskilled workers and laborers.[23] Conditions in most Georgia "niggertowns" would have been little different. In 1960 the median income of black Georgia families was 27 percent below the national poverty level and was 45 percent of the income received by white Georgia families.

The most obvious explanation for such conditions was of course segregation, which prevented black Georgians from finding places in the expanding economy. A northern journalist who toured Georgia and other southern states in the late 1940s reported: "From his birth, when he's born in a Jim Crow hospital—if he's lucky enough to rate that kind of birth—until the day he dies in a Jim Crow slum, is coffined by a Jim Crow undertaker, [and] is buried in a Jim Crow cemetery," a Negro consistently encounters "the savage oppression and the brutal intolerance" that define the boundaries of "the land of Jim Crow."[24] The tone of the Pittsburgh reporter's comments may have been a bit impassioned—southern conservatives in Georgia and elsewhere denounced the series of articles that appeared in a New York newspaper in the summer of 1948—but the comments were essentially accurate. In response, blacks continued to escape from Georgia in massive numbers. The upheavals during World War II spurred black migration, which had abated during the 1930s. "The Japanese got us out of the South," a black southerner who had moved to California quipped. "Every time you see one, hug 'em."[25] At mid-century 36 percent of Georgia-born blacks lived in other states, and the exodus continued unabated during the 1950s and 1960s. As Negroes left the state and sizable numbers of whites moved into it, the relative number of blacks in the population steadily declined. In 1910 Afro-Americans were 45 percent of the population, in 1940 they were 35 percent, and in 1970 little more than 25 percent.

The disruption of the old order touched off a broad-ranging debate about the future in Georgia and the South. From Atlanta Ralph McGill observed the "excitement" of the Depression–New Deal years that generated "a mighty surge of discussion, debate, self-examination, confession and release." "Few towns," he stated, "were too small to have their study groups."[26] Some Georgians, led by Governor E. D. Rivers, looked to the New Deal for solutions to the state's massive economic problems. Eugene Talmadge headed the forces of reaction that sought to restore the old regime. Ellis G. Arnall and a number of Atlanta uptown spokesmen revived Ben Hill's long forgotten program and promoted a homemade New South based on entrepreneurial capitalism. Other economic growth advocates invigorated and expanded the Henry Grady policy of looking to the North for investment in the South. Liberals, emboldened by the Depression and by New Deal sponsorship, plotted a strategy of political and industrial democracy that visualized mass enfranchisement and the organization of labor. Georgia's tortured political universe of one-party politics, white supremacy policies, truncated electorates, rotten borough legislature, and entrenched county elites circumscribed the options open to those advocating new directions, but the controversies of the 1930s and 1940s did for a time broaden the public agenda. The tides of change had become so powerful by March 1939 that the general assembly ratified the first ten amendments—the Bill of Rights—to the United States Constitution, an act most other states had accomplished one hundred and fifty or so years earlier.

The New Deal was a crucial force in the creation of a "rationalized," "modernized" state governmental structure. In 1936 more than one-third of the state's potential white electorate turned out in a hotly contested white primary to choose Eurith D. Rivers governor in preference to a Talmadge lieutenant, and Rivers launched a "Little New Deal" in Georgia. Rivers was not particularly knowledgeable on the subjects of welfare reform and governmental administration; his objectives were limited to redistributing some of society's resources rather than to restructuring society; and his ambitious program generated monetary outlays that exceeded the state's capacity to fund. The resulting financial crisis led to charges of incompetence and corruption, and Rivers left the governorship in disgrace in 1941. Yet his administration was by Georgia standards exceptionally innovative.

Much of the Rivers program was simply enactment of the legislation and constitutional amendments that permitted Georgia to participate in New Deal programs. In so doing, Rivers created a state planning board to coordinate projects and to plan the state's economic development. Such agencies were by no means unique to Georgia, but the planning board was the first post-Reconstruction effort to provide state leadership for private economic progress. Similarly, Rivers was a leader of the southern opposition to discriminatory freight rates.

Long before, railroad corporations had established freight pricing policies designed to "stabilize" interstate transportation. Southern shippers received low rates for sending raw materials and unfinished or low-grade products to the Northeast but paid extravagant rates to transport finished manufactured goods to northern markets. The rate structure encouraged northern industrialists to ship manufactures to the southern and western provinces and the provinces to return raw materials in exchange.

For decades Georgia elites had accepted the situation because they produced and shipped cotton and other raw materials. But with the decimation of plantation agriculture, rate discrimination loomed as a barrier to economic progress, as indeed it had been all along. Rivers was the foremost spokesman popularizing southern opposition to discriminatory freight rates, expanding the Southeastern Governors' Conference into the Southern Governors' Conference to lead the sectional crusade and forcing the Interstate Commerce Commission to restudy the issue. Ultimately, the position championed by Rivers prevailed.

One of the governor's major accomplishments was the formulation of a scheme whereby the state could borrow money. The constitution of 1877 restricted public borrowing and thereby banned large-scale state public improvement projects. Local communities often won voter approval of constitutional amendments permitting them to borrow beyond constitutional limitations for specific projects, a costly, time-consuming, and uncertain process, but the state remained locked into pay-as-you-go financing. Initially Rivers circumvented the constitution by encouraging New Deal agencies to finance the construction of public projects which the state would then lease and contribute state matching funds in the form of lease payments. In 1939 the Roosevelt administration ended this policy.

The Rivers administration responded by creating an "independent" State Hospital Authority and empowering it to sell bonds. Georgia used the money thus borrowed to match federal construction funds for health facilities and backed the bonds by leasing the finished buildings. Thereafter came a proliferation of authorities for parks, ports, roads, bridges, school buildings, office buildings, and a variety of other enterprises. Although a clumsy arrangement that resulted in high interest payments, this approach permitted Georgia for the first time since the Reconstruction era to finance large projects for public welfare and economic development. Ironically, the state launched its new debt structure under the fiction of independent authorities at virtually the same time that it finally paid off the last of the old debts inherited from the 1870s. Not until 1972 did voters ratify a constitutional amendment that permitted the state to incur debt openly.

The New Deal and the Rivers administration vastly improved public health in Georgia. Despite Eugene Talmadge's contention that "country folks don't believe in germs,"[27] government programs for the first time expanded public health care beyond the larger cities. The Rural Electrification Administration extended electricity and telephone service into the countryside, and federal relief and welfare measures removed the aged, dependent, and poor from sole reliance on county "poorhouses" or meager grants. The Rivers administration centralized law enforcement by creating a Department of Public Safety and a State Highway Patrol and committed the state to support the common schools more adequately by decreeing a state-financed seven-month school term. Rivers even attempted to establish a merit system for state employees, but that was too extreme for patronage-conscious Georgia legislators.

Few of these programs were immediately successful. Governor Rivers chose to encourage voters to approve the Little New Deal constitutional amendments before making an issue of the money the new programs would require. When the legislature refused to vote new taxes, the Rivers administration foundered, drifting from one financial crisis to the next while repeatedly slashing already underfunded social programs. Nonetheless, the Rivers administration and the New Deal launched Georgia in new directions and influenced the formation of the new system being structured on the ruins of plantation agriculture.

By 1940 the Rivers regime was politically bankrupt. The Little New Deal had generated a sufficient number of programs directed from Atlanta or from Washington to alarm locally sensitive county elites. The Georgia Association of County Commissioners predicted in a resolution the approaching "end of counties as governmental units and the ultimate abolition of the county unit rule."[28] Talmadge reiterated his fear that New Deal experiments would destroy state rights and "abolish practically every county in the state of Georgia."[29] After advocating new taxes to finance the programs for which he was being condemned, Rivers came under attack for extravagance and mismanagement. With his administration collapsing, Rivers resorted to martial law and defied a federal court injunction. This act led to the governor's arrest on contempt charges, and later he was indicted though not convicted on separate charges in Atlanta. It was, one newspaper bemoaned, "anything but inspiring to see the governor of Georgia placed under arrest."[30] Rivers became increasingly discouraged; a political friend later recalled that the governor became so disillusioned that "he just didn't give a damn."[31]

His disillusionment was understandable. Rivers was an ambitious politician who seemed to take seriously his common-man, anti-interest rhetoric. Born in Arkansas, Rivers completed college in Georgia. Both he and his wife taught school in south Georgia while Rivers earned a law degree through correspondence courses. A successful lawyer in a small south Georgia county seat, Rivers edited a newspaper, invested in local business enterprises, and became a member of the Lanier County elite. During the 1920s he was a state legislator and an active member of the Ku Klux Klan. Through the Klan and in the course of two unsuccessful gubernatorial campaigns, Rivers made friends over the state who were to be important to his political organization. When Eugene Talmadge swept into power in the early 1930s, Rivers supported the governor's program in the state legislature. After breaking with Talmadge, Rivers won the governorship in 1936 as the champion of President Roosevelt's program in an election that amounted to a referendum on the New Deal. In the end Rivers sponsored just enough reform to antagonize county elites without accomplishing enough to persuade the white "outs" to abandon Talmadge.

The travails of the Rivers administration discredited the anti-Talmadge coalition and opened the way for Talmadge to charge back into the governor's chair. In his 1940 gubernatorial campaign, Talmadge championed conservative but not avowedly anti–New Deal positions. "The 1940 platform," his biographer has observed, "was the strongest and most far-sighted of Talmadge's career."[32] In 1936 Talmadge had launched an all-out frontal assault on Roosevelt and the New Deal when he had attempted to unseat Richard B. Russell, Georgia's junior senator. Russell defended the president and his program and cruised to a solid victory. That election seemed to suggest that it was not the apex of political wisdom directly to oppose the New Deal in Georgia, a lesson that Gene's son Herman took particularly to heart. Herman was campaign manager in Talmadge's unsuccessful effort to retire Senator Walter F. George in 1938 and in his successful 1940 gubernatorial campaign.

But if Gene Talmadge's campaign rhetoric had moderated, his hatred of Roosevelt and the New Deal and his hostility to new ideas and cultural innovations grew ever more rancorous. To Talmadge and his friends, the Rivers administration had established a beachhead in Georgia for the "ultraliberals" who were sponsored by the New Deal and often financed by foundations. A Talmadge lieutenant explained: "Their objectives varied as to purpose. Some were bent upon ending the segregation of the black and white races in the South; others worked for the abolition of the county unit system; and still others agitated for the repeal of the poll tax."[33] One of the developing strongholds for these ultraliberals, it seemed, was the state university system.

Soon after his inauguration, Talmadge launched an attack on "foreign professors trying to destroy the sacred traditions of the South," some of whom were not only educated in "foreign" universities in the Midwest and elsewhere but were identified with the Rosenwald Fund or, as Talmadge phrased it, were receiving "Jew money for niggers."[34] Talmadge, who was an ex officio member of the Board of Regents, led the move to fire the president of the teachers college at Statesboro, the dean of the University of Georgia college of education, and eight other university system employees. At one point Talmadge apparently intended to fire all "foreign" employees in the university system. When he learned the universities employed more than seven hundred educators who were not Georgians, Talmadge concluded that was an impossible goal and dropped the idea. Committees sanctioned by the governor conducted searches for "subversive" publications on the common school textbook list and in university system libraries. In response, the Southern Association of Colleges and Secondary Schools and other accreditation organizations dropped Georgia's ten state-supported colleges for whites.

Talmadge's activities outraged respectable opinion and generated a storm of protest. The Atlanta *Journal* fumed during the 1942 gubernatorial campaign that "his candidacy is an insult to Georgia's intelligence."[35] The uptown white-collar middle class—for the first time emerging in sufficient number to be recognized by the rather apt sobriquet "the better element"—supported Attorney General Ellis G. Arnall, an ally of former governor Rivers. Arnall made academic freedom his central issue and denounced Talmadge as a dictator and a demagogue. Talmadge grumbled: "They talk about education. It ain't never taught a man to plant cotton."[36] Supported by Rivers and a number of other talented political organizers who had fallen out with Talmadge, Arnall won an easy victory.

Arnall proved to be an able and innovative governor. World War II brought prosperity to Georgia and thus freed Arnall from the constant financial debacles that had complicated the problems of the Rivers administration. In the wake of Rivers's monetary improprieties and what Arnall chose to describe as Talmadge's "bigoted efforts to impose his personal prejudices on Georgia's state school system," the new governor managed affairs of state with what V. O. Key termed "a dignity refreshing to many of his fellow citizens."[37] Arnall promoted a series of constitutional amendments and the ratification of a revised constitution that abolished the poll tax, lowered the voting age to eighteen, provided for an independent Board of Regents, strengthened the state's commitment to public education, created a teacher-retirement program, established a merit system for state employees, and eased some of the more stringent restrictions of the constitution of 1877. The new constitution updated but did not basically change Georgia's fundamental law, and Arnall's refusal to seek new taxes limited his administration's accomplishments. At the same time, as one of Talmadge's advisers disgustedly—and correctly—observed, Arnall was "striking at the Constitution of 1877 with its limitations upon taxing and spending and its decentralization of power to local units of government."[38]

Born into a wealthy merchant and textile family in the town of Newnan located southwest of Atlanta, Arnall was a grammar school student when a teacher in a Halloween fortune-telling contest prophesied "Governor you will be."[39] After being awarded his law degree at the University of Georgia, Arnall returned to Newnan to begin a career as an attorney and to fulfill his destiny as a politician. At the age of twenty-five he was elected to the legislature, where he became a friend and ally of E. D. Rivers. Arnall, Rivers, and Augusta legislator Roy V. Harris were the leading organizers of the anti-Talmadge faction that elected Rivers governor in 1936. Three years later Rivers appointed Arnall attorney general, the office from which Arnall assumed leadership of the anti-Talmadge forces and launched his bid for governor. Reared in a business family, selected while in the general assembly as state president of the junior chamber of commerce, and elected governor with the enthusiastic support of the uptown better element, Arnall was an avid proponent of economic growth. The region, said Arnall, "is a great economic frontier, crying for development," and, he added, southerners themselves should do much of the developing.[40]

Arnall's most articulate ally in his crusade for homemade economic progress was George C. Biggers, general manager of the Atlanta *Journal*. A leading member of a council Arnall established to plan the state's postwar development, Biggers apparently was the first to describe the South as "The Nation's No. 1 Economic Opportunity," a term coined in response to Roosevelt's depiction of the region in 1938 as "The Nation's No. 1 Economic Problem." At the Southern Governors' Conference held in New Orleans in December 1945, Biggers attacked those who sit "with our hands folded, complacently waiting for the damn Yankee to come down here and build factories and open new businesses." Such a policy was defeatist; it would ensure that the region remained "a colonial economy indefinitely." Instead, Biggers stated, Dixie "should pay more attention to the development of its own industries; to the investment of its own capital." Rather than "waiting for Northerners to come in here and do it for us," southerners themselves should promote "improved education and technical training" and should launch the enterprises that would take advantage of the expanded home markets and the enlarged skilled and semiskilled work force created by wartime economic growth. In his speech Biggers recognized the need for investments from outside the region and emphasized the importance of a favorable business environment to encourage either "local capital or foreign capital."[41] Clearly the Biggers strategy recognized that the South would need outside assistance in establishing the one great factory but southerners themselves should erect the hundred little workshops.

To accomplish such a goal, Arnall promoted a variety of policies and programs. High on the list was the elimination of the discriminatory freight rate structure, which the governor and many Atlanta businessmen thought to be particularly burdensome on small enterprise. Arnall initiated legal proceedings on the grounds that the railroad rate practices violated national antitrust law, and in 1945 the United States Supreme Court agreed to hear the case. The court never issued a decision because in May 1945 the Interstate Commerce Commission surrendered and issued a uniform rate ruling that was gradually implemented over the next several years. Arnall also faulted the United States government for requiring state matching funds before making grants for social programs. Georgia and the South were too poor, Arnall insisted, to participate adequately and thus did not receive their fair share of New Deal largess. Federal spending, he said, should be based on need. Although Arnall's struggle against discriminatory freight rates produced a great deal of favorable publicity, the battle had largely been won before the governor's Supreme Court appearance, and the decline of the national railroad system in the postwar era made the victory of decreasing consequence. Similarly, changes in national taxing and spending policies had already begun to offer more generous terms to the South well before Arnall chose to air the issue. The last year in which the southern states paid more in federal taxes than they received in federal expenditures was 1940. Thereafter, Georgia and the South fared extremely well; in 1952 the region received $1.50 in federal outlays for each $1.00 it paid in federal taxes.

The demise of discriminatory freight rates and federal subsidization of a consumer economy in Georgia did not spark an indigenous industrial revolution nor did any of the governor's other programs. His most innovative effort was the attempt to create a state Reconstruction Finance Corporation, modeled on the federal agency of the same name. As originally proposed, the "little RFC" would have been authorized to issue up to one hundred million dollars in debentures to provide capital for public and private projects that would contribute to economic development. The little RFC never received legislative approval; instead, the Agricultural and Industrial Development Board created in 1943 to advertise economic opportunities in Georgia and to assist new factories and firms to locate in the state more accurately denoted future directions. Arnall envisioned the board working with the little RFC to encourage local as well as imported enterprises; but following the failure to fund the RFC, the agency devoted its attention during the postwar era to cajoling northern corporations to expand into Georgia. The legislature provided in 1945 for the construction of vocational schools to train workers for employment in manufacturing, but the fifteen such schools that were promptly erected probably trained rather few workers who found employment in Georgia-owned enterprises. Arnall did successfully sponsor a constitutional amendment curtailing tax exemptions for new industries on the grounds that such concessions encouraged low wage firms to move into the state, but in the main the campaign by the governor and his allies to promote entrepreneurial capitalism ended in failure.

Arnall insisted that Georgia's poverty lay at the base of the state's problems. Political demagoguery, racial wrongs, and other ills all rested on the inadequacies of the economy. One approach to the alleviation of economic distress—the one that Arnall most persistently pursued—was rapid economic development. Doubtless because of his frequently expressed antipathy toward monopolies, economic centralization, and "the bureaucracy of big business" and his reiterated admiration for free enterprise and the virtues of "little business," he endeavored to counter the "centralization of industry within an imperial and favored region"—by which he of course meant the Northeast—by encouraging local enterprise in Georgia. To ensure that Georgia workers shared in Georgia's economic growth, Arnall supported the organization of labor. "The South is turning toward unionization," he stated, "and the benefits are apparent." Because the "entire racial problem in the South is economic, at its roots," the solution to the race issue was clearly related to economic growth and union wages. Negroes, Arnall stated, "are not a special, separate problem, any more than they are a special and separate resource."[42] In his insistence that progress in race relations was dependent on expanded economic opportunities for blacks and on the creation of strong biracial unions rather than upon a redefinition of Negro civil rights, Arnall mirrored the strategy of mainstream southern liberals.

From the mid-1930s into the late 1940s the majority of Georgians and other southerners consistently identified themselves to pollsters as "liberals" and endorsed President Roosevelt and his New Deal policies. The South, the polls reported, was the most liberal and New Dealish region in the nation. Self-identified liberals were most numerous among lower income groups, which of course included those Georgians least likely to have access to the ballot box. Thus Georgia continued to be dominated at least on the local and congressional levels by conservative and reactionary politicians. "There is another South composed of the great mass of small farmers, the sharecroppers, the industrial workers white and colored, for the most part disfranchised . . . and without spokesmen either in Congress, in their state legislatures or in the press," Clark Foreman wrote in 1944. "This latter South comprises about 80% of the population." If these people could be organized and enfranchised, "the South can become in a very short time, the most liberal region in the Nation."[43] Reared in an affluent Atlanta family, Foreman was one among the many southern liberals who found no place in the conservative-dominated governments at home and who gained position and influence in New Deal agencies. Foreman was the principal author of the 1938 *Report on Economic Conditions of the South;* after leaving governmental service, he became president of the Southern Conference for Human Welfare, which in the mid-1940s was the region's premier liberal organization.

Like Arnall, Foreman and his Southern Conference associates subordinated black civil rights to the broader search for political and industrial democracy. A leading Southern Conference spokesman was Stetson Kennedy, a Florida journalist and author whom Arnall employed to join and report on the activities of the Georgia Ku Klux Klan. Kennedy insisted that "the southern Negro must be emancipated economically and politically before he can be emancipated socially." Unlike Arnall, the Southern Conference did officially reject segregation in 1946, but its emphasis continued to be focused on "the union card and the ballot." Such a strategy had its practical advantages. Kennedy pointed out that "the case for economic and even political equality can be argued on the street corner— yes, even in a Klan meeting—without necessarily making oneself a candidate for lynching," but white hostility to social equality was too overwhelming to be effectively opposed.[44] In any event, social equality was a secondary issue. As a correspondent summarized the matter in a letter to Foreman, "we are not going to do anything fundamentally in the South without organization of the little people, and that is not going to be accomplished except through a widespread, democratic and UNIVERSAL labor movement that will be strong [enough] to prevail against the red herrings of race, communism, CIO, etc. etc. There flatly isn't any other way than through power."[45]

In the spring of 1946 the Congress of Industrial Organizations launched an organizing drive in the South that the press promptly dubbed "Operation Dixie." Philip F. Murray, president of the six-million-member union, pronounced the project "the most important drive of its kind ever undertaken by any labor organization in the history of this country."[46] The Southern Organizing Committee established headquarters in Atlanta, and the union poured organizers and resources into the campaign. The flight of industry and jobs to the South and the lower wage scales in the region threatened the interests of blue-collar workers and of unions nationally as did the antilabor southern congressional delegations. Operation Dixie placed its greatest emphasis on the southern textile belt stretching from Alabama to Virginia, and the Textile Workers Union, the union most endangered by the shift of employment from the unionized Northeast to the nonunion South, committed all of its organizers and most of its budget to the effort. George Baldanzi, who had earlier expressed favorable views about southern textile workers, was deputy director of the Southern Organizing Committee. Baldanzi insisted that southern organizers be mainly southern natives who could relate to the less-than-cosmopolitan southern workers.

Operation Dixie enjoyed some early success in Georgia and elsewhere. Ironically, most of the new unionists recruited in the drive were branch plant employees of large northern corporations wherein the northern unions could exert pressure on the corporations to accept southern unions. These factories were concentrated in metropolitan areas. Elsewhere union organizers often met ferocious resistance. Lucy Randolph Mason, the offspring of a patrician Virginia family who moved from work with the YWCA to the National Consumers League to become a "community relations representative" for the CIO, frequently ventured from her Atlanta office to apply her charm, toughness, and upper-class southern accent to hostile local officials who employed public authority to harass organizers. In Cuthbert, Georgia, Mason attended the trial of an organizer who had failed to purchase for $1,500 the locally decreed license required of union recruiters. According to Mason's account, she asked the town mayor, who was also the trial judge, whether he believed in the Bill of Rights. "What is the Bill of Rights?" responded the mayor-judge. Mason informed him it was the part of the Constitution that guaranteed such liberties as freedom of assembly. "We don't need any of that in Cuthbert," the mayor replied, adding in true county elite fashion that "the only laws we know are local laws." On another occasion in Tift County, the sheriff and his deputies had constantly followed and harassed CIO organizers and continued the practice when Mason arrived in Tifton. Mason talked with organizers and workers to gather information before confronting the sheriff. Like the mayor-judge in Cuthbert, the sheriff in Tifton responded to Mason's defense of civil rights by insisting that his job was to enforce local laws, and anyway he added: "You been associating with niggers and white trash—you ain't seen no decent people since you got here."[47] In a legal environment so dominated by the force of local custom and personal status, the CIO's organizing problems were understandable.

By late 1946 Operation Dixie had ground virtually to a halt. Mason's experiences exemplified the inveterate opposition of county seat elites. The American Federation of Labor and its Georgia affiliate endeavored to protect skilled workers from the incursions of the mass-based CIO by endlessly denouncing Operation Dixie as a communist effort that, according to the Georgia Federation's *Journal of Labor*, "has openly followed the communist line and is following that line today."[48] Industrialists campaigned vigorously to defend the "freedom" of their employees, and northern branch plant executives solemnly denounced southern organizers as "outside agitators." The uptown press led by editor Ralph McGill and the Atlanta *Constitution* joined in the campaign to link liberalism with subversion. The death of President Roosevelt a year prior to the beginning of Operation Dixie had brought to office a president who demonstrated little interest in the problems of labor unions or southern liberals but who soon became consumed by the menace of communism at home and abroad. Congress reacted to Operation Dixie by enacting in early 1947 the Taft-Hartley law, which threw additional roadblocks in the paths of union organizers and opened the way for Georgia and other southern states to enact right-to-work provisions.

The liberal front soon collapsed. The CIO became increasingly engrossed in its internal struggles between its conservative right wing and the liberal-radical left wing that the conservatives denounced as communist, and similar divisions rent the Southern Conference. The United States Congress officially branded the Southern Conference a "deviously camouflaged Communist-front organization" in June 1947,[49] and in 1948 Foreman and his associates disbanded the organization. Despite what Baldanzi termed its continuing "lack of progress," the CIO doggedly pushed on with Operation Dixie until 1951, when the Textile Workers Unions disastrously lost a major strike involving half its southern membership.[50] The failure of Operation Dixie marked the end of serious efforts to organize the masses of Georgia and southern workers.

During this period most concerned blacks endorsed "the doctrine of labor solidarity," agreeing with white liberals that the race problem was fundamentally economic.[51] Numerous blacks were members of the Southern Conference, and the CIO employed black organizers and vigorously recruited black workers. The failure of the liberal crusade enhanced the position of Negro bourgeois proponents of civil rights, as did the growing success of the National Association for the Advancement of

Colored People in its attack on discrimination in the federal courts. In 1944 the United States Supreme Court declared the white primary to be unconstitutional, and two years later a federal district court decision opened the Georgia primary to black voters. Voter leagues, often sponsored by the NAACP, sprang up in Georgia cities, and by the time of the 1946 gubernatorial primary some one hundred thousand black Georgians had registered to vote and some thirteen thousand were members of the NAACP.

Black voters made their first impact in Georgia politics by helping to elect a white woman. In a 1946 special election, Helen Douglas Mankin solicited support from Atlanta blacks and, in part because of solid black support, became the first woman elected to Congress from Georgia. The daughter of well-educated and affluent parents in Atlanta, Helen Douglas attended a fashionable private high school, took her college degree in Illinois, and earned a law degree from an Atlanta school founded by her father. At the end of World War I she served for a year as an ambulance driver in France, and in 1922 she and her sister made a highly publicized automobile tour of the United States, beginning their trip by driving from Atlanta to Seattle and repairing some sixty-eight blowouts en route. After her marriage, Helen Douglas Mankin moved around with her electrical engineer husband for several years before returning to Atlanta during the Depression. She practiced law and served several terms in the state legislature, where she was an avid proponent of Arnall's uptown policies, before running for Congress in the 1946 special election. She was elected to fill an unexpired term and thus served less than a year. In the regular Democratic primary in 1946, she won a majority of the popular votes but a minority of the crucial county unit ballots.

To Eugene Talmadge the "spectacle of Atlanta negroes sending a Congresswoman to Washington" was yet another gross violation of Georgia's cultural heritage. The election of "that woman from the wicked city of Atlanta,"[52] black voting, the CIO organizing campaign, Arnall's governmental reforms, the growing number of antidiscrimination decisions spewing from the federal courts, and other developments undermined white supremacy and long-honored custom. As Talmadge biographer William Anderson explained, the former governor "was a man who saw the world war as a devastating follow-up to the New Deal in the changes it was wreaking upon conservatism and the traditions of his people."[53] In the 1946 gubernatorial primary, Talmadge once again took to the campaign trail, promising to restore the white primary, to defend white supremacy, and to protect the state from the schemes of "radicals and renegades financed by Rosenwald's thirty pieces of silver and NAACP money."[54]

In the campaign the Talmadge forces made little pretense of appealing to a majority of Georgians or even to a majority of Georgia voters. The 1946 Talmadge campaign was in fact among the most unabashedly antidemocratic efforts in Georgia history. Roy Harris, one of the original organizers of the anti-Talmadge faction, abandoned Arnall and his friends to enlist in the Talmadge crusade, and he and Herman Talmadge, who had returned from serving in the Pacific theater during World War II, directed Ole Gene's last campaign. The strategy was to concentrate time and resources on a sufficient number of small, largely rural counties to win a majority of county unit votes and essentially to ignore the uptown better element and other unfriendly whites. To counter the threat of the emerging black voters, the Talmadge forces sought to purge the new registrants and to intimidate potential voters. The Talmadge headquarters sent tens of thousands of registration challenge forms to supporters and Talmadge clubs and especially to those in the targeted rural counties, and Eugene Talmadge advised that "if the good white people will explain it to the negroes around over the state just right I don't think they will want to vote."[55] Such an antiurban, antiblack strategy contributed to the vitriolic nature of the contest.

Constitutionally ineligible for reelection, Arnall (who was the first governor to serve a four-year term as a result of a recent constitutional amendment) supported James V. Carmichael, an Atlanta-area businessman. While Rivers was governor during the late 1930s, Carmichael had served in the legislature and had frequently clashed with the governor. During World War II, Carmichael had been general manager of the giant Bell bomber plant, located in Marietta—the largest private employer in the state—and had gained a reputation as a competent executive. Carmichael was an attractive candidate. In an election where winning popular votes was important, his campaign would doubtless have been more effective. In Georgia's county unit morass, however, Carmichael and his advisers saw fit to try to counter Talmadge's backwoods appeal by basing much of their campaign on the defense of county unit politics, white supremacy, and rural conventions, even though they generally opposed the policies they advocated. The frustrations inherent in such a hypocritical campaign were further exacerbated by E. D. Rivers's entry into the fray. Another of the original organizers of the anti-Talmadge faction, the mercurial Rivers had supported Arnall in 1942 and expected the governor to return the favor. When Arnall chose instead to support an avowed opponent, Rivers ran for the office anyway, thereby producing a three-contender race and splitting the anti-Talmadge vote. To counter Rivers as well as to remind the electorate that he was running against two former governors who had never displayed observable talents for management, Carmichael promised an honest, efficient administration and pictured himself as the "good government" candidate, leading Talmadge to observe that he had "never heard of anyone advocating bad government."[56]

Yet despite the frustrations of the candidates, the confusion of the campaign, and the intimidation of potential voters, the election provoked virulent animosities and a high turnout at the polls. The uptown press overwhelmingly supported Carmichael and displayed a new level of antagonism toward Talmadge. In a lengthy and prominently displayed editorial, the Atlanta *Journal* depicted Talmadge as "this blatant demagogue, this fomenter of strife, this panderer to the passions of the ignorant and to the fears of the timid, [who should be] exposed for what he is, that is, a blatherskite, a cheap fraud and a menace to the security and the welfare of us all."[57] Some seven hundred thousand voters, one-third of the potential white and black electorate, turned out to give a solid plurality of their votes to Carmichael and a majority of the county unit votes and the election to Talmadge. In the same primary, Mankin won a popular majority in the Atlanta fifth congressional district, and James C. Davis, a reactionary state judge, won the county unit vote and the election. It appeared that the forces of reaction could not attract a majority of voters even within Georgia's truncated electorate, while the forces of "progress" could not achieve a county unit majority.

Katharine Du Pre Lumpkin, a reform-minded Georgian writing her memoirs in 1946, observed: "I saw this come to pass—the old life continuing, yet a rising tide against it."[58] Eurith D. Rivers had sought to improve the lot of ordinary Georgians—or at least the lot of white common men—with a program of "little New Deal" reform, and he left the governorship in disgrace. Eugene Talmadge had endeavored to ignore the mounting social and economic turmoil in the state and to restore the old regime, and in 1943 he left the governorship in disgrace. Ellis G. Arnall had attempted to redirect the course of economic development through the promotion of indigenous entrepreneurial capitalism, and although he departed the governor's office with his administration's prestige intact, his program ended in failure. New Deal liberals had made their bid for political and industrial democracy and had been routed. The 1946 primary election produced sharp conflict but failed to resolve pressing issues. Georgia had been an integral part of the struggle for the future of the South, but the battles had not produced victors.

The situation grew even more confused and confrontational in the aftermath of the primary election. Talmadge was the Democratic nominee, but between the primary and the November 1946 general election it became clear that his health was failing. To be on the safe side, a group of Talmadge supporters quietly organized a write-in campaign on behalf of Eugene's son Herman. Eugene Talmadge won the general election, but he died shortly before his inauguration as governor, touching off a wild scramble for the office.

The Talmadge forces insisted that Herman should inherit the statehouse. The constitution charged the legislature with counting the ballots and declaring the "person" with a majority the winner. If "no person" had a majority, the legislature was to make the selection from the two candidates having the most votes. Pro-Talmadge legislators argued that the elder Talmadge was no longer a "person" in a legal sense, and consequently the legislature should choose the governor from the two candidates with the largest number of write-in votes, of whom young Herman would be a logical choice. Rejecting this solution, Governor Arnall quoted the portion of the constitution that required the outgoing governor to remain in office "until his successor shall be chosen and qualified" and insisted he would surrender the office only to incoming Lieutenant Governor Melvin E. Thompson, whom Arnall felt was the rightful heir and who had served during the World War II years as Arnall's executive secretary.

In the midst of the debate, the legislature met and counted the ballots. Talmadge leaders were stunned at the results: 669 diehard anti-Talmadge voters had written in Carmichael's name; 637 Republicans had written in D. Talmadge Bowers, the nominal Republican candidate; and Talmadge had only 619 votes, apparently eliminating him from consideration. Fortuitously, the Talmadge managers "found" an additional 56 ballots for Talmadge from the family's home county of Telfair that had been misfiled among the votes for lieutenant governor. From a political science perspective, the 56 voters who cast the newly discovered ballots were most interesting: the majority had precisely the same handwriting and some resided in graveyards. An awed journalist stated: "Do you know that they rose from the dead in Telfair County, marched in alphabetical order to the polls, cast their votes for Herman Talmadge, and went back to their last repose?"[59] But from the perspective of county unit politics, Herman Talmadge now had 675 votes and thus was the leader among the write-in candidates. The legislature promptly elected him governor. When Arnall refused to accept this decision, the Talmadge forces physically seized both the governor's office and the executive mansion. Soon afterward Arnall surrendered his governorship in favor of Thompson, who set up a downtown office as governor in exile. Ultimately the state supreme court declared Thompson to be acting governor.

The impasse in Georgia politics and government continued during the two years of the Thompson administration. Thompson became acting governor in March 1947 only days before the legislature adjourned, and he had little opportunity to shape policy. He vetoed a legislative measure that sought to restore the white primary, and he signed an antilabor right-to-work law.* Otherwise he endeavored without much success to continue Arnall's policies. Having become governor by accident, under constant attack by the Talmadge forces, and facing a special election in the summer of 1948, Thompson was never able to control developments. Instead the main beneficiary of the tragicomic struggle for the governorship was Herman Talmadge, who solidified his leadership of his father's faction and established a campaign issue for the 1948 primary. When the state supreme court named Thompson governor in 1947, Talmadge ironically vowed to take his case to "the court of last resort . . . the people of Georgia."[60]

Talmadge and Thompson were the major candidates in the 1948 gubernatorial primary. Talmadge sought vindication for his stand during the gubernatorial succession crisis, and he championed white supremacy. In early 1948 President Harry S. Truman asked Congress for enactment of civil rights legislation, and that summer the Democratic national convention endorsed a plank supporting Truman's position. Talmadge denounced "this oppressive, communistic, anti-South legislation" and like his father before him became the state's leading defender of "the southern way of life."[61] Talmadge won the election carrying the county unit vote and even winning a slight majority of the popular ballots. After less than two rather lackluster years in office, Talmadge ran for reelection in 1950, again narrowly beating Thompson. This time Talmadge carried the county unit vote and won a plurality of the popular vote. These elections proved to be crucial to the evolution of public affairs in Georgia. Despite a hesitant beginning, the Talmadge administration formulated the policies that were to dominate Georgia politics and government for more than a decade.

Herman Talmadge quickly established a reputation as "the South's foremost spokesman" for the defenders of white supremacy.[62] He and other state officials endlessly condemned the communists, the federal courts, the NAACP, and all the other outside meddlers and fellow travelers who were presumably seeking to disrupt Georgia's harmonious race relations and insisted that in Georgia "the races will not be mixed come hell or high

---

*Perhaps symbolically significant was the fact that the Thompson administration purchased Jekyll Island from its "millionaires' club" owners. During World War II, the Roosevelt administration required the evacuation of club members on the grounds that such a concentration of national leadership might tempt the Germans to raid the island. The club never resumed operations, and the island now serves as a public resort.

water."[63] Despite the fulminations emanating from the statehouse, black Georgians did make token progress in civic matters. Voter registration gradually increased; Negro educators won election to the school boards in Augusta and Atlanta during the early 1950s; and blacks achieved some influence in urban affairs. State politics remained the domain of the Talmadge forces, and in the main they successfully maintained white supremacy and racial stability in an age of social and economic change.

While seizing leadership of the resurgence of the old order, Talmadge at the same time demonstrated a sense of urban and industrial progress. The governor's ability to balance economic modernization with racial traditionalism was best exemplified in public education. The federal courts had begun to insist that if schools were separate they must also be equal. Segregationists found common cause with the proponents of school reform. In 1949 the legislature enacted the Minimum Foundation Program, which promised a minimum level of school funding for all Georgia students. But like the seven-month school term law engineered by the Rivers administration, the Minimum Foundation law meant little until adequately funded. Although expenditures increased during the prosperous post–World War II years, Georgia still had a hodgepodge system of common schools that ranged from a relatively adequate education for white youngsters in affluent urban areas to whatever one underpaid educator could accomplish in the rural one-teacher schools, most of which were for black students. In 1951 Talmadge pushed through the legislature a 3 percent sales tax that dramatically increased state income and provided funding for the Minimum Foundation Program. For the first time Georgia established a public school system. It was among the most important of the "modernizing" reforms of the era. Shortly afterward the legislature passed and the voters ratified a constitutional amendment permitting the abandonment of public education in the event of forced desegregation.

Economic prosperity and the sales tax greatly expanded the state's income and provided the resources for extensive highway construction and other public projects as well as public school reform. The increased spending and its accompanying patronage did much to solidify the influence of the Talmadge forces in the rural–small town counties. Whereas Eugene Talmadge had made little effort to cultivate county elites, relying instead on charisma and demagoguery to attract voters, Herman Talmadge developed strong ties with the county courthouses and thereby stabilized and strengthened the Talmadge faction. At the same time the program of expanded state services based on consumer taxes won applause in uptown areas. Unlike his father, Talmadge was perceived as a competent executive rather than as "a menace to the security and welfare of us all." The hostility of the uptown newspapers rapidly waned, and although uptown voters still by and large rejected Talmadge and his friends at the polls in favor of more "respectable" candidates, the sharply polarized conflicts of the mid-1940s dissolved. Unable to compete, the anti-Talmadge faction disintegrated. The Talmadge administration and those that followed during the 1950s propitiated business, opposed organized labor, courted outside investors, and denigrated black people. These policies proved to be enormously effective politically, and the newfound political unity at home was reinforced by the state government's mounting struggle with the judicial branch of the federal government.

The developing conflict between the federal courts and Georgia politicians came to a head when in 1954 the United States Supreme Court in *Brown* v. *Board of Education* ruled that public school segregation denied black students "the equal protection of the law guaranteed by the Fourteenth Amendment."[64] Black citizens in several cities promptly petitioned for the inauguration of a desegregation policy. Georgia politicians responded predictably. All the governors during the 1950s—Talmadge, Marvin Griffin, and Ernest Vandiver—insisted upon "massive resistance" to desegregation and vowed to close the public schools rather than integrate them. The state legislature pronounced the *Brown* decision "null, void and of no force or effect" and enacted scores of laws purporting to protect the Jim Crow system.[65] A number of these laws prohibited any schools from enrolling both white and black students. Georgia, its political leadership insisted, might have public schools, private schools, or no schools, but it would not have desegregated schools. Such a program kept Georgia race relations locked in the practices of the past throughout the decade.

Following the acerbic social and political conflicts of the 1940s, Georgia arrived at something of a South African solution to its economic and social conundrums. State authority supported economic modernization without social change. The liberals and labor organizers who wished to redistribute power and resources, the little New Dealers who promoted common man social reform, the entrepreneurial capitalists who favored internally generated economic growth, the anti-Talmadge forces who offered an alternative at the polls, and even the raw reactionaries no longer found a place in Georgia political equations. The influence of the growing black vote was effectively nullified, at least outside the central cities of metropolitan areas. Disorganized, powerless, and still largely voteless, the masses of black and white Georgians watched from afar.

# Chapter Nine
## *A New Beginning*

Once upon a time, down South," Lillian E. Smith wrote in 1943, "a rich white made a bargain with a poor white": "you boss the nigger, and I'll boss the money." Because of the limited capital available in the South, the rich man explained, high profits required low wages, but "remember you're a sight better off and better than the black man. And remember this too: there's nothing so good for folks as to go to church on Sundays." So long as poor whites did not concern themselves with strikes, voting, and other such incidentals, they "were free to lynch and flog, to burn and threaten and nothing would happen, for they had a bargain." Thus did the poor white become "boss of everything but wages and hours and prices and jobs and credit and the vote—and his own living." In compliance with the bargain, whites "segregated southern money from the poor white and they segregated southern manners from the rich white and they segregated southern churches from Christianity, and they segregated southern minds from honest thinking, and they segregated the Negro from everything." The bargain was a great success; "the South had no Negro problem, it was all settled."

Both the rich white and the poor white had originally been too racist and too guilt-stricken to consider a bargain with the Negro, but now, Smith stated, conditions were changing. Southerners were talking of Christian brotherhood; poor whites were joining poor blacks in labor unions; and new questions were being raised "about money and wages and jobs and hours and things like that." The rich white blamed the unsettled state of affairs "on the damyankee and the New Deal and the communist and Mrs. Roosevelt and the Negro press and the social scientist" and so on and reminded all who would listen that any change in race relations would provoke the wrath of the poor white. The rich white continued to drive "down the road that went nowhere," but the poor black in the back seat and the poor white in the front were becoming increasingly restive and disgruntled. "The bargain was breaking."

Up to this point Smith's "Parable of the Solid South" was generally in keeping with mainstream liberal thinking in the early 1940s. Class issues overrode racial differences, and the rational arrangement would be a bar-

gain in which working-class whites and working class blacks joined hands
in a drive for biracial political and industrial democracy. Clark Foreman
and his associates in the Southern Conference for Human Welfare would
doubtless have agreed, and indeed in 1944 Smith was herself a member of
the Conference. But in the concluding paragraphs of the "Parable," the
focus of the analysis underwent a crucial shift. Let them talk of brotherhood and democracy and unions, whispered Something, but as long as
there is segregation nothing will happen. Segregation rather than low
wages, disorganization, and disfranchisement was the fundamental southern social problem, and, Smith continued, the ultimate explanation for
segregation was personal and individual. The more important bargain, it
turned out, was not the compact between rich white and poor white but
the individual psychological bargain made within the mind of each. Con-
ceit, ambition, hypocrisy, and selfishness—the desire to ride always in
the front seat and the refusal to share it with others—were the ultimate
explanation for the corrupt social bargain between rich white and poor
white.

To be sure the white southern mind was a divided one. An internal
Voice pleaded to be heard: "sometimes it sounded as quiet and simple as
Jesus; and sometimes as plain-written as the Bill of Rights; and sometimes
it sounded like rain after a dry spell; and sometimes like your mother's
step when you call her; and sometimes like a mind that has found itself."
This Voice was not the one to which a southern white listened. The
strange fruit that was a white southerner held to the psychological bargain
upon which segregation rested. Something said: "I'm that which splits a
mind from its reason, a soul from its conscience, a heart from its loving, a
people from humanity. I'm the seed of hate and fear and guilt. You are its
strange fruit which I feed on." The root cause of southern social pathology
was segregation, and the crux of southern reform was not mass organization among out-groups but the Manichaean struggle within the white
southern mind.[1]

The peculiar metamorphosis that transformed Smith's analysis was a
prescient depiction of the general redefinition of human rights in post–
World War II America. Smith identified Georgia's central problem not in
terms of "money and wages and jobs and hours and things like that" but as
racial segregation, and she insisted that segregation would collapse "as
rapidly as each of us can change his own heart."[2] Smith's intensely individualistic approach to social reform received powerful reinforcement
with the publication of Gunnar Myrdal's enormously influential *An American Dilemma*, which appeared in 1944. In his examination of "The Negro
Problem and Modern Democracy," Myrdal concluded that "the present

irrational and illegal caste system" in the South was a "tremendous" social burden on the nation as a whole and that it undermined American prestige abroad. A decaying social institution that had lost intellectual respectability, segregation was a mounting moral quandary within the American conscience. The dilemma a white American faced was "the ever-raging conflict" between the "American Creed of liberty, equality, justice, and fair opportunity" and the American practice of racial discrimination. "The American Negro problem is a problem in the heart of the American," Myrdal wrote. "It is there that the decisive struggle goes on."[3] As Smith stated in 1944, economic and political reform will not solve southern social problems because "man is not an economic or political unit." To Smith, as her biographer observed, segregation and white supremacy could only "be eliminated by an act of individual will."[4]

Born in a county seat town in northern Florida, Lillian Smith was the daughter of an affluent lumber and naval stores dealer. She and her eight brothers and sisters grew up in comfort and security, but Smith found her young life rent with contradictions. She developed a love-hate relationship with her mother. She learned to love a merciful and beneficent God who was wrathful and vengeful and who was worshiped in a segregated church. She was taught that her body was a temple that was white and good and was a "thing of shame" containing segregated areas "that you should touch only when necessary" and that should not be revealed in nakedness. She mastered the southern hospitality and courtesy that was not to be extended to black people. She dealt with the contradictions inherent in "the race-sex-sin spiral" as other children did, she wrote, "by closing door after door until one's mind and heart and conscience are blocked off from each other and from reality." The result was the strange fruit that produced southern white culture; "the killers of the dream are ourselves."[5] According to Smith, there was no "Negro problem," but there was "the problem, for Negroes, of finding some way to live with white people" and "the problem, for whites, of learning to live with themselves."[6]

Smith had just graduated from high school in 1915 when her father's business failed and the family moved to north Georgia and opened Laurel Falls Hotel at the site of the Smith's summer home on Old Screamer Mountain near the town of Clayton. For the next decade, Smith alternated between attending various colleges in Georgia and elsewhere, teaching at country schools around Clayton, and serving three years as an instructor at a missionary school in China. In 1925 she returned to Georgia to assume responsibility for managing Laurel Falls, which had been converted from a hotel to a private camp for girls. During the mid-1930s

Smith and her friend Paula Snelling, a high school teacher in Macon and a camp counselor, began publication of a magazine (originally titled *Pseudopodia*, then *North Georgia Review,* and finally *South Today*), and Smith launched a vigorous writing career that included authorship of a best-selling novel and numerous books and articles dissecting southern culture and race relations. Smith was Georgia's best-known critic of segregation. She insisted on the immediate elimination of racial segregation because it warped "the personality and character of every child, every grown-up, white and colored, in the South today," and she was contemptuous of the southern "moderates" who stressed gradualism or who sought economic progress within a separate but equal social order. Ralph McGill, the centrist editor of the Atlanta *Constitution,* and Ellis Arnall, who according to Smith "simply has better manners than Gene Talmadge, that is about all," were among her favorite targets.[7] Increasingly, she identified good race relations at home with effective cold war policy abroad, insisting that integration in the South would greatly strengthen the nation's ability to defend Asia and Africa from the communist menace. Originally a member of the Southern Conference for Human Welfare, she resigned from the organization in 1945 in part because she disagreed with the Conference strategy for reform and in part because she feared the influence of those members "who follow the Communist line."[8] Smith insisted that racial segregation was the South's number-one problem, that the solution was individual and personal, and that abolition of the problem was good anti-communist strategy. Her argument accurately heralded emerging intellectual trends in America, if not in Georgia, and the growing salience of the moral issue of racial segregation in the South.

The unifying experience of World War II and the Cold War as well as the material prosperity of the postwar era undermined class conflict and helped to focus attention on the sorry state of southern race relations, and the Supreme Court's school desegregation decision in 1954 elevated the issue to the top of the national reform agenda. The federal courts, Afro-Americans, nonsouthern Democrats, the northern intelligentsia, and numerous other groups demanded an end to de jure segregation in the South. Lillian Smith promptly prepared a book entitled *Now Is the Time* that called for immediate desegregation, but she was among the very few white Georgians publicly to support the *Brown* decision. Segregation was part of the traditional order in the state; public opinion polls consistently reported that most whites were segregationists. The Talmadge administration etched the race issue sharply and manned the barricades in defense of white supremacy. Under attack from the forces of Yankee respectability, many Georgia whites and virtually all of the state's nonmetropolitan political leadership joined the Talmadge administration's campaign of "massive resistance" to social change. Yet the apparent white consensus on the virtues of segregation masked fundamental divisions.

To many whites in the plantation counties, closing the public schools was not too high a price to pay for the protection of "the southern way of life." The plantation belt at the time of the Second Reconstruction was not the same as it had been in the days of Henry M. Turner and Emory Bryant. By the 1950s the rapidly declining number of tenants and agricultural laborers and the spread of mechanized, capitalist farming had undermined the commitment to a paternalistic ideology. Yet the economic, social, and ideological forces that had traditionally supported white supremacy in the plantation region had not disappeared. Plantation agriculture, despite the deterioration of its position in the state's overall economy, remained an important part of lowland economic life; blacks continued to provide much of the agricultural and town labor in the region; and white supremacy still defined relations between employers and employed. The mythology of the Lost Cause and rudiments of the old paternalism yet flourished, and the Confederate battle flag was conspicuous at segregationist rallies.

Desegregation also presented formidable practical problems in the plantation counties. In a region with a relatively high number of impoverished, deprived, and undereducated black children, integration seemed certain to lower standards in the formerly white schools. Federal protection of black civil rights was a further invasion of local prerogatives. Black voting would surely threaten the position of county elites. It was not surprising that many plantation-belt whites supported massive resistance to any relaxation of the state's racial code. They agreed with Georgia's attorney general, who insisted: "For segregation to remain an integral part of Georgia's social customs and traditions, it must and will be practiced twenty-four hours a day, seven days a week, and three hundred and sixty-five days a year."[9]

Plantation county elites formed the core of the opposition to desegregation. They found numerous allies among the white "outs" throughout the state. The white working class in Georgia's towns and cities and their wool-hat relatives in the country had long been insulated from mainstream developments, and the failure of Operation Dixie and other liberal organizational efforts ensured that their alienation would remain a continuing factor in Georgia political life. Indeed, by defining the civil rights crusade in terms of individual morality, Smith, Myrdal, and other proponents of racial change offered blue-collar whites little beyond the right to compete with blacks for jobs and opportunities. New Deal liberals had earlier talked of "money and wages and jobs and hours and things like that" for both whites and blacks. Postwar civil rights advocates talked of civic liberties for black southerners. Ordinary Georgia whites, already being deluged by the great economic and demographic upheavals sweeping over the state, often viewed racial desegregation as yet another unwanted change being engineered by outside forces beyond their control.

Nevertheless, the currents of change ran against the defenders of the status quo. Georgia's rapid urbanization augmented the size and influence of the uptown-suburban population. Most white business and professional people were segregationists, but their ideological commitment was to capitalist economic expansion. In Atlanta the commanding position of dominant economic elites was an established tradition. "When you talked about the 'power structure' or the 'establishment' in Atlanta," Mayor Ivan Allen, Jr., explained, "you were really talking about the leaders of the top fifty or so businesses in the city." The generation of leaders that included Allen came to power in the 1950s. Before that, Allen noted, "the older group, which included my father, had guided Atlanta from behind the scenes for nearly four decades."[10] Floyd Hunter's well-known study of the Atlanta "power structure" added scholarly endorsement to Allen's first-hand observations.[11]

The basic ethos of the Atlanta leadership was, of course, economic growth. Ivan Allen, Sr., who was a prominent member of "the older group" and co-chairman of the Forward Atlanta Commission, endeavored to consolidate Atlanta's position as the "distribution City to the South."[12] Ivan Allen, Jr., as president of the city chamber of commerce thirty years later, visualized "Atlanta's future role as a national city rather than merely a regional distribution center."[13] Last-ditch efforts to preserve white supremacy that included closing the public schools hardly contributed to the achievement of the "future role" envisioned by Allen. "Atlanta's public schools must stay open," he insisted, "and the Chamber should provide its share of vigorous leadership in seeing that they do."[14]

Similar tendencies appeared in other cities. In the 1920s the Augusta chamber of commerce, emulating the Forward Atlanta program, had advertised nationally Augusta's economic virtues and opportunities. During the depression years, however, leadership of city government passed to the Cracker party, a ward-based, patronage-and-favor-oriented machine that drew its strongest support from white working-class areas. Just after World War II a business-dominated independent movement overturned Cracker control, and thereafter the Augusta "establishment" molded a political consensus in support of economic growth. The election of Millard Beckum as mayor in 1957 and the formation of the Committee of 100, an organization of community leaders to promote industrial development, consolidated city political leadership behind a program of "energetic boosterism."[15] In some urban areas the growth ethos generated policies designed to do little more than provide additional favors for established industries, but even the most benighted city had its expanding middle class eager to share in Georgia's economic development.

Atlanta was the first Georgia community to be placed under a federal court order requiring desegregation in the schools. Although the courts permitted Atlanta officials to delay the implementation of the *Brown* decision, it seemed obvious that the confrontation between Georgia's massive resistance politicians and the federal judiciary would occur in Atlanta. The city's mayor during the 1950s was William B. Hartsfield. Beginning his political career as a traditional southern segregationist, Hartsfield vigorously promoted economic expansion and soon relegated white supremacy to a secondary position. The mayor and his establishment allies increasingly worried about a closed public school system and popular perceptions of Atlanta's image. "It will do little good to bring about more brick, stone and concrete," Hartsfield asserted, "while a shocked and amazed world looks at a hundred thousand innocent children roaming the streets."[16]

The steadily growing black vote in the cities encouraged urban racial moderation. Faced with a choice between Talmadge-oriented segregationists and upper-class moderates, blacks voted heavily in favor of the latter. Black ballots helped to ensure the success of the independent movement in Augusta and in 1957 saved Hartsfield from defeat when the large majority of whites voted for his opponent. Hartsfield became increasingly outspoken in defense of racial moderation.

So too did uptown groups generally. Organizations such as Help Our Public Education (HOPE) mobilized popular support for open schools in Atlanta and in other Georgia cities. Uptown ministerial alliances, PTAs, professional organizations, educational associations, and women's groups added to the growing urban clamor for an end to massive resistance, and the state's metropolitan newspapers ensured that the uptown position received prominent coverage. By the time Georgia faced its desegregation crisis, open schools had become a part of the economic growth consensus. Atlanta, Hartsfield said, was a city "too busy to hate."[17]

State and county political leaders denounced the open schools campaign. The Georgia Association of County Commissioners resolved opposition to "any race mixing in any Georgia schools anywhere, at any time, under any circumstances."[18] Governor Ernest Vandiver stated: "I have no patience with those who are now coming out in the open and demanding that the races be mixed in the classrooms in the schools of Georgia, contrary to the laws and constitution of this state." Atlanta moderates, Vandiver ranted, were running up "the flag of surrender over our capital city" and displaying "a defeatest spirit."[19] Other state leaders echoed similar sentiments, but it became increasingly obvious that Governor Vandiver, Senator Herman Talmadge, and many of the others had themselves been influenced by uptown ideology and by the knowledge that the locus of economic power and population had passed to the metropolitan areas. The perils of purblind resistance became evident when in April 1959 Ellis Arnall, like a modern Rip Van Winkle, arose from a long political slumber to demand that the schools be kept open. Should they be closed, Arnall announced, "I will be candidate for governor in 1962, and I will be elected."[20] The threat of Arnall's reentry into Georgia politics further encouraged Talmadge-oriented elites to reevaluate their policies.

The massive resistance front gradually disintegrated. James S. Peters, chairman of the State Board of Education and the reigning patriarch in the Talmadge camp, counseled a strategic retreat. "Some form of integration is inevitable," Peters stated, "and the only question left unanswered today is whether this integration will be under the control of the friends of segregation or the proponents of integration." Public sentiment is changing, Peters wrote, and "we are heading towards defeat and the loss of our power and influence in the government of this state." If "Herman Talmadge and his friends" were to be inundated in the backwash of a schools crisis, "the integrationists" might well entrench themselves in government "for decades to come."[21] Such a dire development would permit integration to be undertaken by people who wanted integration to succeed. By compromising, "the friends of segregation" could dominate the coming of desegregation, thereby ensuring that social change would be as limited and as difficult as possible. To the moralistic Lillian Smith, integration offered whites the opportunity to redeem their souls; to the practical James Peters, desegregation was an unwanted disruption to be contained within the existing political culture.

Governor Vandiver continued publicly to shout defiance but privately hinted that desegregation was inevitable. In 1960 Vandiver and the legislature created a committee on schools to hold hearings throughout the state and to make recommendations. The chairman of the committee was John A. Sibley, lawyer, businessman, banker, and a leading member of the Atlanta establishment. The Sibley committee recommended a policy of local option that would permit local communities to respond to desegregation in whatever manner they chose. The plantation counties held enormous power in the malapportioned legislature, however, and the issue remained in doubt until the actual desegregation of a Georgia school forced a decision. Although observers assumed that the crisis would come in Atlanta, a federal judge ordered the University of Georgia to accept two qualified black students in January 1961. Their enrollment required the legislature to close the university or to alter state policy. Soon afterward the legislature adopted the Sibley committee recommendations and thereby accepted public school desegregation, at least on a token level.

The urban victory over rural areas in the school desegregation controversy symbolized the transfer of power in Georgia from county-seat elites to uptown metropolitan elites. Federal court decisions promptly ratified the new balance of forces. In 1962 the federal judiciary ruled the county unit system unconstitutional and required the state legislature to reapportion on the basis of population rather than counties. The decisions obliterated two of the basic institutional supports for the old regime. Yet the shift of power in Georgia was of such epic proportions that it required a further decade of strife to consolidate. During the 1960s both the black civil rights movement and the white reaction to rapid social changes kept the state in turmoil.

During the 1950s the established black leadership in the cities maintained generally effective control of the emerging black protest. In Atlanta a black establishment composed of business and professional people paralleled that of the white community. Bourgeois blacks counseled gradualism, worked for "better race relations," and allied with bourgeois whites in support of racial moderation and economic growth. They also insisted that black neighborhoods receive improved public services, fairer law enforcement, and the like; but, as Ivan Allen, Jr., later observed, an "established black community and a pragmatic white business 'power structure'" normally managed to compromise differences.[22] Similar patterns appeared in Augusta and other urban communities. In Savannah a traditional black leadership that "had achieved economic and social status within the existing system" was, in the words of one study, "in no hurry to change the status quo."[23] Savannah's conservative black elites placed few pressures on a white leadership that was deeply committed to social traditionalism.

The slow progress of school desegregation—half a dozen years after the *Brown* decision not a single white child attended a school with a black child enrolled—encouraged less patient blacks to demand a change in strategy. By the late 1950s Georgia membership in the National Association for the Advancement of Colored People, heretofore the acknowledged leader of the civil rights movement, was declining, and new and more militant organizations were emerging to challenge its court-oriented, gradualist methods. The Southern Christian Leadership Conference, formed by Dr. Martin Luther King, Jr., after he had successfully led the Montgomery, Alabama, bus boycott, held its first nonviolent institute at Spelman College in 1959, and in early 1960 King returned to his home town of Atlanta, accepting co-pastorship with his father at the Ebenezer Baptist Church.

The direct action movement arrived in Georgia in March 1960. Inspired by the sit-ins that began in North Carolina earlier in the year, Atlanta University students published in the city's daily papers "An Appeal for Human Rights," announcing their intention "to use every legal and nonviolent means at our disposal to secure full citizenship rights as members of this great democracy of ours." One week later some two hundred black collegians staged the state's first sit-in. Thereafter the movement spread rapidly to other cities and ultimately to the towns and counties. "We do not," the students stated in their Atlanta manifesto, "intend to wait placidly for those rights which are already legally and morally ours to be meted out to us."[24]

The protest campaign sparked sharp controversy among black urban elites. Many older, conservative members of the black establishment denounced a movement that threatened to disrupt long-standing alliances and to produce dreaded "racial tensions." Only a few weeks after moving to Atlanta, King observed: "The sit-in movement is a revolt against those Negroes in the middle class who have indulged themselves in big cars and ranch style homes, rather than joining in the movement for freedom."[25] The momentum of the movement tended to mute or at least to temper public opposition from conservative blacks, as did the fact that the leadership of the sit-in demonstrations was middle class and, if militant, conservatively so. During the early 1960s the movement relied heavily on the support of black high school and college students. It spoke primarily for young, educated, aspiring blacks who had cast aside paternalistic bonds and who demanded entry into the white marketplace.

A member of the older black establishment in Atlanta was Martin Luther King, Sr. Born in a rural county southeast of Atlanta, King grew up as one of nine children in a sharecropper's cabin. His mother was deeply religious, and King absorbed "this tradition of rural Baptist worship, respecting and loving it." He became a licensed minister at the age of fifteen, established "a reputation as a pretty good country preacher," and decided to move to Atlanta, where he had earlier lived briefly after running away from home following an altercation with his father, who had increasingly sought to drown his frustrations in alcohol. King quickly learned that being "a pretty good country preacher" in Henry County did not guarantee success in Atlanta. He worked at odd jobs, attempted to establish himself in the ministry, and concluded that he needed a high school education to succeed in an urban world. When he applied for admission and took the entrance examinations at a private high school, he was informed that he could be admitted to the fifth grade. King was almost twenty-one, had completed the eighth grade in a one-teacher country school, and "could scarcely read books intended for a ten-year-old child."[26]

Swallowing his pride, King earned a high school diploma by attending night school, drove a delivery truck by day, and preached at a small church on Sundays. In 1926 he enrolled at Morehouse to work toward a college degree. The same year he married Alberta Williams, daughter of the pastor of Ebenezer Baptist Church. Just after King completed college the Reverend Williams died, and King became pastor at one of the city's largest black churches in 1931.

As a successful minister King was soon a part of the black establishment. King was not docile; he promoted voter registration drives, was a leader in the struggle to win equal pay for black public school teachers in the city, and engaged in various other black improvement projects. But King also held membership in a black bourgeoisie that during the post–World War II years had achieved sufficient power to force white leaders to compromise and to be able to deliver favors for the black community. For people who could remember a sharecropper's life on a plantation and who had struggled against the solidly entrenched white supremacy of the 1930s, race relations were not so bad as some youngsters might think.

Martin Luther King, Jr., was born only a year before his father assumed his ministerial duties at Ebenezer. He grew up in a comfortably affluent middle-class household with proud parents who protected him from most of the indignities that taught blacks their place in a segregated society. His most memorable experience with Jim Crow practices occurred when he was a fourteen-year-old high school student. Accompanied by one of his teachers, King participated in an oratorical contest sponsored by the Negro Elks in Dublin, Georgia. Interestingly, King's topic was "The Negro and the Constitution." After the contest, King and his chaperon took the night bus back to Atlanta. As King later recalled, "at a small town along the way, some white passengers boarded the bus, and the white driver ordered us to get up and give the whites our seats. We didn't move quickly enough to suit him, so he began cursing us, calling us 'black sons of bitches.'" For the next ninety miles, the two Negro travelers stood in the aisle of the bus. "That night," King stated in 1965, "will never leave my memory."[27] It was perhaps fitting that soon after beginning his ministerial career in Montgomery, events catapulted the young parson into leadership of the Montgomery bus boycott, a position that he filled with distinction.

Unlike his father, King was an excellent student; before finishing high school he enrolled at Morehouse and from there went on to study at Crozer Theological Seminary and Boston University. Both as a student and as a protest leader, King pondered the nature of segregation and the philosophy of nonviolence. At Boston University, King was introduced to and was strongly influenced by the philosophy of personalism, a theological doctrine encompassing the proposition that "the meaning of ultimate reality is found in personality." Segregation warped the personalities of both blacks and whites; it denied blacks self-respect, opportunity, and the sense of "somebodiness," and it scarred the souls of whites with guilt, fear, and "a false sense of superiority." To obliterate a social system that produced such disastrous human consequences, King called upon blacks to confront the white conscience and "thereby bring about a transformation and change of heart." King avowed to white southerners that "in winning our freedom we will so appeal to your heart and conscience that we will win you in the process." Much as Myrdal had posited in an "American dilemma," King pointed to the nation's "schizophrenic personality" on racial matters. America "has been torn between selves—a self in which she has proudly professed democracy and a self in which she has sadly practiced the antithesis of democracy." Nonviolent direct action promised to force a confrontation between these two selves and to convert the white oppressor to justice. The object, King stated, was not "to defeat or humiliate the opponent, but to win his friendship and understanding."

Back in Atlanta, King supported the demonstrators. To him, "when these disinherited children of God sat down at lunch counters, they were in reality standing up for what is best in the American dream and for the sacred values in our Judeo-Christian heritage." King and his Southern Christian Leadership Conference promoted nonviolent civil disobedience on the theory that moral law took precedence over secular law. "In the final analysis the problem of race is not a political but a moral issue," and as King explained in a memorable "Letter from Birmingham Jail," "one has a moral responsibility to disobey unjust laws." While branding segregation "morally wrong and sinful," King did not seriously question the broader structure of American society or the nature of the American economic system. Self-development was an important part of King's program, and blacks, he wrote, must "vigorously seek to improve our personal standards" and "must work assiduously to aspire to excellence."[28] Individual hard work, thrift, and self-help were key ingredients for economic success, and the goal of the movement was the integration of blacks into the existing order. King demanded justice from whites and self-improvement from blacks; together upward-striving blacks and converted whites would build an integrated social order. King and the "disinherited children of God" expressed and expanded autonomous individualism as blacks broke out of their "place" in Georgia society and compelled whites to confront the changed relationship.

The civil rights movement spread through Georgia as it did through the rest of the South. In the spring of 1960 student leaders organized the Student Nonviolent Coordinating Committee, which established headquarters in Atlanta. In the beginning SNCC was a loosely knit group of part-time volunteers who endeavored to provide coordination and administrative support for the student movement. It rapidly evolved into a cadre of full-time community organizers who served as the vanguard of the movement. Charles Sherrod, a twenty-two-year-old black graduate of Virginia Union University, was SNCC's first paid field secretary, and in the fall of 1961 he and eighteen-year-old Cordell Reagon arrived in Albany to launch what became the Albany Movement and the Southwest Georgia Project. A growing number of SNCC members drifted into the counties around Albany to promote voter registration, civil rights protest, and community organization. "We feel that we are engaged in a psychological battle for the minds of the enslaved," Sherrod explained. "Our criterion for success is not how many people we register, but how many people we can get to begin initiating decisions solely on the basis of their personal opinion."[29]

Displaying the élan, courage, and self-sacrifice that made them the model for American student activists generally, SNCC field workers, as Sherrod reported from Terrell County, survived "on the three C's of health, well, at least our health—crackers, cucumbers, and collards." The comradeship, the sense of mission, and the constant presence of danger sustained morale, but the intransigence of white segregationists and the cautious conservatism of many blacks placed great pressure on field workers. "People have been shot, Mass Meetings have been raided, churches blown up, and SNCC headquarters shot into many, many times and ultimately blown up," a SNCC member reported from a southwestern Georgia county. "I have been arrested three times recently," another wrote, "on trumped up charges after taking people down to register."[30] In the county-seat town of Americus, four civil rights workers were arrested and charged with "inciting an insurrection," which carried the death penalty. The charge was eventually overturned. By promoting confrontation, SNCC members and local volunteers placed established black elites in a

difficult middle position between white segregationists and black militants, and often the older leadership chose circumspection rather than
valor. Sherrod angrily denounced a group of middle-class black administrative employees in Albany as people "who refuse to think further than
a new car, a bulging refrigerator, and an insatiable lust for more than
enough of everything we call leisure."[31] Yet after a black woman informed
a SNCC canvasser, "I didn't know that colored people could vote," the
field worker could only observe: "And people ask why we are down
here."[32]

The largest and most widely publicized confrontations in Georgia occurred in the cities. In November 1961, several members of SNCC and
representatives of local groups created the Albany Movement, which
adopted as its objectives the desegregation of public facilities, equal employment opportunities, and fair law enforcement. During the following
month the Albany Movement initiated large-scale demonstrations, and
King and SCLC staffers arrived to support the protest campaign. So massive were the demonstrations and so energetic were the local police that
ultimately one of every twenty black people in the city served time in jail.
Despite the size and vigor of the campaign, however, it failed to record
significant tangible accomplishments. "Albany was successful," sniffed the
regional NAACP director, "only if the goal was to go to jail."[33] In Savannah the Chatham County Crusade for Voters, led by Hosea Williams,
organized what one civil rights scholar has described as "some of the
largest and most assertive street protests ever seen in the South during
the summer of 1963.[34] The Southeastern Georgia Crusade for Voters, also
headed by Williams, carried the movement into the southeastern part of
the state much as SNCC did in southwestern Georgia.

White elites in Atlanta demonstrated a greater willingness to negotiate
and to compromise than did the leadership in other Georgia cities, but
even in Atlanta black gains were limited. "While boasting of its civic virtue," King observed in 1963, "Atlanta has allowed itself to fall behind
almost every major southern city in progress toward desegregation."[35] In
December 1963, SNCC launched a substantial direct-action campaign in
the capital city. Nevertheless, Atlanta retained its reputation as a city "too
busy to hate." Not only were SCLC, SNCC, and other civil rights organizations headquartered there but Atlanta, in the words of a SNCC field
worker, was also "behind the lines, a place where the organizers could
unwind for two or three days before returning to the front."[36]

Tens of thousands of black people and some whites participated in the
sit-in movement, which reached its highest level of activity in Georgia
during 1963. The demonstrations in Georgia and elsewhere in the South

accomplished relatively little desegregation, at least in a direct sense, but they did ultimately force the federal government to respond with the enactment of the 1964 and 1965 civil rights laws. The 1964 law accomplished what the demonstrations had largely failed to do and thereby changed the character of the movement. Not only did the ubiquitous "White" and "Colored" signs that had staked out the boundaries of a segregated society rapidly disappear from the southern scene but also the law's equal economic opportunity provisions vastly broadened opportunities for the black middle class. Having accomplished their goals, many of the original protesters began to drop out of the movement to take advantage of the opportunities. Yet in 1965, "the movement," as one student of the period has observed, "was just beginning to reach the smaller, out of the way towns" and the depths of Georgia's inner city ghettos.[37]

The surging black protest infuriated massive resistance politicians, but it also helped to convince them that Jim Crow segregation could no longer be defended. Even while berating United States Supreme Court justices for "high crimes and misdemeanors," Georgia's political leadership grew ever more dedicated to the economic growth ethos. Governor Ernest Vandiver vigorously defended segregation and denounced black demonstrators, but he was also largely responsible for expanding the state's vocational-technical training program and for the enactment of a law permitting local governments to market revenue bonds for the construction of factory buildings which would be turned over to private companies through lease-purchase agreements. Thus, to woo a corporate client, Georgia might construct the factory, train the work force, and provide other assistance. Northern industrialists sometimes learned more about these advantages during a visit from the state's chief executive. "If you send an industrial representative to these places," Vandiver explained, "he talks to his counterpart in the business, but a governor—any governor—gets to the president and chairman of the board where the final decisions are made."[38] Vandiver's remark was an interesting commentary on the relationship between business and government; the trick was not for corporation lobbyists to arrange to talk with the governor but for the governor to be able to see top corporate executives. Increasingly the promotion and protection of Georgia interests came to mean the advancement of corporate capitalist interests.

During the 1960s the most articulate exponent of the growth ideology was Governor Carl E. Sanders. Born into a prominent Richmond County family, Sanders was a high school football hero, lettered in three separate sports at the University of Georgia, and served as a bomber pilot during World War II. He studied law at the state university, married Georgia's first maid of cotton, and by age twenty-seven headed his own highly successful law firm in Augusta. After serving in both houses of the state legislature, Sanders ran for governor in 1962. In his campaign platform he called for a "new Georgia" and stated: "It shall be my purpose to unify our people for economic growth and progress—not to divide them in stagnation."[39]

Former Governor Marvin Griffin was Sanders's chief opponent in the 1962 Democratic primary election. During the 1950s, Griffin had eulogized "Georgia's two greatest traditions—segregation and the county unit system," and he had vowed that segregation would be continued "come hell or high water." A good-old-boy spoils politician and a lax administrator, Governor Griffin had devoted much of his energy to the defense of white supremacy, and his administration earned a well-deserved reputation for corruption and ineptness. An Atlanta journalist referred to "the 'if-you-ain't-for-stealing-you-ain't-for-segregation' modus operandi of Griffin's administration" and Governor Vandiver, Griffin's successor, wailed: "The state of Georgia was buying rowboats that would not float. Some were wisely sent to parks without lakes." During the 1962 campaign, Griffin promised to "put Martin Luther King so far back in the jail that you have to pump air to him."[40] In style and substance Griffin stood for the old days. Sanders was young, successful, and progressive, and his well-financed campaign bore a tailored-for-television flavor that was new to the Georgia hustings. The election was something of a referendum on the "New Georgia," and for the first time since the early twentieth century a gubernatorial primary was decided by popular rather than county unit votes.

Sanders massively swept the urban and suburban counties to win the election. In his inaugural address Sanders announced: "This is a new Georgia. This is a new day. This is a new era. A Georgia on the threshold of new greatness."[41] Sanders claimed to be a racial moderate. "In my case," he explained to a reporter, "'moderate' means that I am a segregationist but not a damned fool." Georgians, Sanders stated, "are going to obey the laws; we are not going to close any schools." Instead, he continued, "I am determined that during my Administration this state will move ahead—fast."[42] As governor Sanders vigorously pursued industrial development and economic growth. The director of the Southern Regional Council, an Atlanta reformist group, might have had Sanders in mind when he mused: "Southern governors have become the de facto executive directors of the state chambers of commerce, and spend their time competing with each other as supplicants for new plants. We have talked of state socialism and state capitalism, but what do we call governments whose chief affair it is to entice and propitiate business?"[43]

During these years the Georgia economy made gigantic strides. The state's real gross product doubled between 1950 and 1964, and by 1979 it had doubled once again. Per capita income, which in 1940 was 57 percent of the national average, neared 70 percent by 1950 and reached 85 percent in 1970. This economic boom resulted from the proliferation of new enterprises, not from the expansion of traditional textile and lumber manufacturing. Textiles and lumber products remained important industries, but their relative contributions declined as a diverse economy emerged from the wreckage of the old system. Georgia's cheap labor, low taxes, and antiunion, pro-business outlook contributed to the state's attractiveness as a haven for business enterprise, but of greater importance was the evolution of a less static social system, a more flexible labor force, and a home market capable of supporting business and service industries. In this regard federal government spending seems to have been of crucial significance. Federal farm price supports, social welfare projects, and especially military expenditures during World War II and the postwar era all contributed to a steady flow of consumer demand. Among the military bases scattered over the state, nine were adjacent to the state's nine largest cities. Military personnel and civilian employees at military installations and in defense industries, when combined with substantial numbers of military retirees, reservists, and national guardsmen, buttressed the economy and incidentally ensured popular support for imperialist adventures abroad and jingoism at home.

Rising per capita income also reflected the fact that the breakdown of plantation agriculture drove large numbers of poor people out of the state. In 1950 approximately three of every ten Georgia-born citizens lived elsewhere. Between 1950 and 1960 the state had a net migration loss of 204,000 blacks and 9,000 whites. After 1960 more people moved into Georgia than fled from it, but the new arrivals tended to be skilled whites seeking places in the expanding economy while those departing included the people displaced from the Georgia countryside. In 1940 Georgia contained 1,364,000 rural-farm people, which was 44 percent of the population; in 1960 the rural-farm population was 407,000, hardly 10 percent of all Georgians. The national urban crisis, so much discussed in the 1960s and so largely ignored thereafter, had its roots in the country counties of Georgia and the rest of the South.

The Atlanta metropolitan area dominated the state's economic development. By 1970 the five-county region contained approximately one-third of Georgia's people, 38 percent of its jobs, and 42 percent of its personal income. In 1973 the census bureau recognized this growth by expanding the metropolitan area to encompass ten additional counties. Ivan Allen,

Jr., first as president of the Atlanta chamber of commerce and then during eight years as mayor in the 1960s, presided over what he termed the transformation of Atlanta from "a somewhat sluggish regional distribution center to a position as one of the dozen or so truly 'national cities' in the United States."[44] Allen launched a new "Forward Atlanta" program that included urban renewal developments, more expressways, promotional advertising, and other measures. During these years Peachtree Center, Colony Square, the Omni complex, the World Congress Center, and other projects changed the face and the skyline of the city.

At least in a material sense, huge numbers of Georgians benefited from the state's economic metamorphosis. Not since the early nineteenth century had opportunities for social advancement been so abundant. Despite the often tragic population upheavals in the country, those who successfully made the transition had much for which to be thankful. Those who did not might have agreed with the country song that lamented life in "De-troit city" and plaintively stated "I wanna go home." Even for those who did not necessarily "wanna go home," economic opportunity often demanded profound attitudinal adjustments. As a critical observer commented, "in the almost touching lust of its chambers of commerce for new chemical plants, glassy-mazed office parks, and instant subdivisions, the South is becoming etherized in all those ways a people are subtly rendered pastless, memoryless, blank of identity, by assimilation into chrome and asphalt and plastic."[45]

But even if Georgia was attempting—in the words of the same observer—"to re-create itself into a tinfoil-twinkling simulation of Southern California," the process raised difficult and ambiguous questions. In spite of imaginative performances by home-grown entrepreneurs, Georgia imported its industrial revolution. "And like a dependent nation," one study has observed, "much of the Sunbelt's industry and a significant portion of its finances remain under the control of outside economic actors."[46] In 1981 a journalist raised the question: "Who Owns Atlanta?" After interviewing knowledgeable people, the writer reported: "Atlanta has become a city owned by absentee landlords." He found that "most of the prime properties in town are controlled by interests head-quartered elsewhere: New York, Dallas, Boston, Toronto, Hamburg, Amsterdam, Al Kuwait."[47] Georgia rejoined the nation during the apparent transition from national to international corporate capitalism, and Atlanta provided Georgia's best example of the trend. "The nascent attractiveness of downtown Atlanta to national and international business activities and the movement away from activities related to the local population," in the words of another study, "has created a city core whose vitality is becoming less dependent on the state and region and more on national and global business."[48] Georgians enjoyed higher standards of living, but they may have exchanged one form of colonial dependency for another.

Certainly it was true that Atlanta was becoming divorced from its surrounding suburbs. Mayor Allen's Forward Atlanta program produced impressive office buildings, convention centers, and hotels, but the bulk of the jobs and economic growth went to the suburban office parks, shopping centers, and industrial parks. During the 1960s the Atlanta metropolitan area outside the city's limits more than doubled in population, and employment increased by 120 percent. Atlanta declined in population, and employment increased by only 17 percent. Between 1963 and 1972 Atlanta retail sales increased by 78 percent; in the metropolitan area outside the city they grew by 286 percent. In 1963 Atlanta had 4,276 retail firms, compared to 3,870 in the remainder of the metropolitan area. In 1972 Atlanta had 4,605 retail firms, while the number outside the city had increased to 7,948. "Of all the major sunbelt cities," a study of southern urban development has reported, "Atlanta stands at the greatest social and economic disadvantage in relationship to its suburban ring."[49] While the prospering and increasingly self-sufficient suburbs became more economically independent of Atlanta, the city became a great administration center oriented toward the world of multinational corporations.

The city's people—two-thirds of them by 1980—were black. Although the Atlanta area contained a vigorous black middle class, the majority of blacks were far removed from the flourishing suburbs that surrounded them and the corporate offices and board rooms in the buildings that rose above them. The civil rights crusade filtered into the lower strata of black society, but there its middle-class aims were often irrelevant. Equal opportunity meant little to untrained, undereducated, and psychologically unprepared people starting the race for capitalist accumulation far behind many of the whites with whom they were to compete, because, of course, Georgia urbanized and industrialized before it desegregated. The economic growth that promised to benefit both the white middle class and the newly liberated black middle class threatened to leave many other people as far behind as ever. Indeed, urban economic growth often included expressways, urban renewal, and other programs of progress that cynics termed "Negro removal" and that disrupted urban black slum life more than ever. Atlanta during the growth years from 1957 to 1967 destroyed twenty-one thousand housing units and displaced some sixty-seven thousand residents. In 1966 there were racial disturbances in Atlanta, and in 1970 blacks in Augusta exploded into frustrated rioting.

The Student Nonviolent Coordinating Committee responded to the problems of inner-city ghettos with a demand for "black power for black people." SNCC workers had long sought to develop indigenous community organizations and to encourage the emergence of local black civil rights leaders. "It's not radical if SNCC people get political offices, or if M. L. King becomes President, if decisions are still made from the top down," Stokely Carmichael stated. "If decisions get made from the bottom up, then that's radical."[50] After the enactment of the 1964 civil rights law and the 1965 Voting Rights Act, SNCC became more urban-oriented and less content with a nonviolent integrationist strategy. "Political and economic power is what black people have to have," Carmichael said; "integration is irrelevant."[51] In 1966 the SNCC staff rejected nonviolence, endorsed black power, and elected Carmichael chairman.

An effective and articulate organizer, Carmichael popularized the rhetoric of black power in the South. He was born in the West Indies, reared in New York, and became involved in the civil rights movement while a student at Howard University. Active in numerous SNCC projects, he experimented with black power tactics in a rural county in Alabama and thereafter increasingly imbued his faith in local decision making with racial chauvinism. Integration, according to Carmichael, was "based on the assumption that there was nothing of value in the Negro community" and therefore served only "to siphon off the 'acceptable' Negroes into the surrounding middle-class white community."[52] Under the black power banner, SNCC members endeavored to organize black ghettos, to free them from white control, and to make them culturally, politically, and, as far as possible, economically autonomous. As Carmichael and other radical SNCC spokesmen became more revolutionary in their public pronouncements, they antagonized whites and many blacks and soon found themselves isolated and ineffective.

A crucial factor in at least the timing of SNCC's shift from rural–small town organizing campaigns such as the Southwest Georgia Project to a metropolitan ghetto strategy based on black power was Julian Bond's election to and ejection from the Georgia General Assembly. In 1965 Bond, an Atlanta resident who had dropped out of Morehouse to work full-time with SNCC, won election to the legislature from an Atlanta district. Shortly before the General Assembly convened in 1966, SNCC adopted a statement denouncing the American invasion of Vietnam, and Bond expressed agreement with the SNCC position. The Georgia House of Representatives, which had assiduously defied federal policy on desegregation for a decade, refused to seat Bond because of his opposition to federal policy regarding Vietnam. Bond's electoral success in the wake of court-ordered reapportionment encouraged SNCC staffers to begin organizing drives in urban ghettos, and Bond's banishment led to the formation of the Atlanta Project, which was created to rally support for the ousted legislator-elect but quickly became a center of black-power agitation.

Black power failed as a strategy, but it had important repercussions as a slogan and as a psychological affirmation of black self-worth. Although designed for organizing poor blacks, black power had significant impact on middle-class and upward-striving blacks. White supremacy taught subservience and self-doubt; black power taught individualism and the belief that "black is beautiful." As SNCC grew more disreputable, black power became fashionable. In 1968 a black militant grumbled that the term had been "diluted and prostituted to the point where even the most conservative negroes are now for Black Power."[53]

Martin Luther King, Jr., rejected the separatism inherent in SNCC's version of black power, and he remained true to the philosophy of non-violence. King also recognized the value of black power as "a psychological call to manhood."[54] Insofar as it supported black pride, group identity, and self-development, black power had its virtues, but, according to King, solution of the massive economic problems of the black ghettos demanded an equally massive national effort. King called for an "Economic Bill of Rights for the disadvantaged" and organized a poor people's campaign to pressure Congress for the enactment of such a program. The campaign collapsed after King was assassinated in the spring of 1968. Before that, in 1964, King had become the only Georgian ever to have been awarded the Nobel Prize for Peace.

These developments undermined the urban coalition of uptown and ghetto and widened the gap between city and suburb. Blacks, according to their spokesmen, supplied too many of their neighborhoods for developments that mainly benefited whites, and whites took too much of the political preferment and patronage. An increasing number of blacks campaigned for political offices, particularly in urban areas, and during the 1960s blacks once again appeared in the Georgia legislature. In 1973 Maynard Jackson, the lawyer son of a prominent Baptist minister, became the first black mayor of Atlanta. In both style and program, Jackson threatened the long-standing dominance of the white Atlanta establishment. White visitors to the mayor's office were often taken aback, according to a white journalist, by the "rich, earthy African motif featuring jungle prints and hide-bound chairs that seemed ready to spring on passing small prey."[55] More significantly Jackson insisted on expanding opportunities for minority businesses, ensuring neighborhoods a larger role in city planning and development, and restructuring city agencies, especially the police department. A student of Atlanta politics and government explained:

"Instead of asking downtown leaders for advice, he told them his views—that they should open up high-level professional and managerial jobs to women and minorities and integrate their corporate boards."[56] Jackson ultimately reached an accommodation with the white Atlanta establishment that balanced black political power with white economic power, and his successor, former congressman and former United Nations ambassador Andrew Young, solidified the arrangement. The expanded and integrated Atlanta "power structure" offered black business and professional elites a far greater voice in affairs, but the "power structure" itself remained about as insulated from the masses of people as ever. Black officials increasingly appeared in other Georgia cities. For these and additional reasons, uptown and suburban white voters demonstrated a growing affinity for the Republican party.

The 1964 Civil Rights Act and the spread of the movement into the smaller towns of the state brought black advancement into the daily lives of ordinary whites. Since the days of Tom Watson, huge numbers of common white folk had been alienated from the mainstream of Georgia development. Despite expanding economic opportunities, they remained far removed from uptown and suburbia and hostile to a federal government that through its "war on poverty," its civil rights laws, and its other "Great Society" programs seemed to lavish aid on blacks while ignoring the problems of common whites. In 1964 angry whites voted for Barry Goldwater, the anti–civil rights Republican candidate. Goldwater became the first Republican presidential contender to carry the state.

The growing militance of blue-collar whites coincided with the rapid decline in the political authority of long dominant county-seat elites. Decisively defeated on the issue of school desegregation, the county-seat governing class was the social group that benefited least from the economic and demographic transformation of the state and that suffered most politically from such reforms as legislative reapportionment, black suffrage, the abolition of the county unit system, and the disruption of one-party politics. The expanding Georgia electorate—in the 1960 presidential election 30 percent of voting-age Georgians cast ballots, in 1964 the turnout increased to 45 percent, and in 1968 it reached 48 percent—included large numbers of lower-status whites, and their ballots had a drastic impact on electoral competition. After the old guard conservatives proved unable to turn back the desegregationist tide, rural and working-class whites promoted their own spokesmen and thereby demonstrated that Governor Sanders had been premature in announcing the arrival of a "new era" or at least the arrival of the "new era" he had in mind.

In the gubernatorial wars of 1966, Lester G. Maddox, an outspoken defender of segregation, was the candidate promoted by rural–small town, less affluent whites. Mayor Ivan Allen depicted Maddox precisely: "Although Maddox was an Atlantan in fact, he was not an Atlantan in spirit. His heart was in the small Southern Baptist churches out in the flat stretches of segregated south Georgia rather than in the board rooms of Atlanta corporations."[57] The candidate of the board rooms in the general election was Howard H. Callaway, the first Republican to compete seriously for the statehouse since Rufus Bullock. In the election Maddox piled up enormous majorities in the rural and small town counties while Callaway swept the metropolitan areas. The contest was so close that a write-in campaign on behalf of former Governor Arnall prevented either major party candidate from winning a majority, and the legislature once again selected the winner from the two people receiving the most votes. The predominantly Democratic legislature chose Maddox as governor. Despite being elected by the General Assembly, Maddox was clearly the anti-establishment candidate. There was an element of truth in his observation that winning the governorship wasn't too difficult: "All that was necessary was to defeat the Democrats, the Republicans—on the state and national level—159 courthouses, more than 400 city halls, the railroads, the utility companies, major banks and major industry, and all the daily newspapers and TV stations in Georgia."[58]

As the Democratic party's governor of Georgia, Maddox vigorously opposed the Democratic party's presidential nominee in the 1968 election and supported American Independent party candidate George C. Wallace. After being elected governor of Alabama, Wallace had in 1964 avowed: "I draw the line in the dust and toss the gauntlet before the feet of tyranny. And I say, Segregation now! Segregation tomorrow! Segregation forever!" In his 1968 presidential campaign, Wallace voiced the frustrations of lower-status white southerners. He insisted that there was no real difference between Democrats and Republicans and that both major parties and their "pointy-headed bureaucrats" and their kept "intellectuals" all "look down their noses at you." The Democratic party, Wallace allowed in his final campaign speech delivered on the state capitol grounds in Atlanta, "used to be the party of the working man, now it's the party that wants to take money away from the working man and give it to those that don't want to work."[59] Maddox made numerous speeches in support of the Wallace campaign, soliciting the support of those "patriotic Americans who are working for a living and who are willing to fight for their liberty," and he denounced "the Democratic-Republican Establishment Party" for "following the blood-and-tear-stained path charted by socialists, communists, anarchists, draft card burners, traitors, flag desecrators, looters, rioters, punks, pinks, and polished politicians."[60] In the election, Wallace carried Georgia's electoral votes by winning a plurality of the popular ballots.

The revolt of the common white folk was short-lived. Governor Maddox proved to be unable and even to a degree unwilling to roll back civil rights progress, and Wallace's national appeal proved to be largely confined to the southern countryside and to working-class urban districts. Maddox and Wallace offered their common white following little in the way of practical programs. The Maddox administration was memorable primarily because the feisty governor was not nearly so bad a chief executive as he had promised to be, as well as because of his ability to dismiss such problems as prison reform with the observation that Georgia would never have a decent prison system until it attracted a higher class of criminal. The Wallace crusade was in decline well before a would-be assassin grievously wounded the Alabama governor at a Maryland campaign rally in 1972. Gradually, as Georgia whites experienced desegregation, they accepted it. In 1970 the voters elected Jimmy Carter, whose gubernatorial campaign was more socially conservative than that of his Democratic run-off opponent but who in any case was a considerable change from Lester Maddox.

Carter's tenure as governor confirmed the triumph of a metropolitan ideology that stressed economic expansion, businesslike administration, and free market individualism. His administration endeavored to replace political "pork barrel" bargaining with centralized and expert decision making, to promote continued industrial expansion, and to find a new social stability in the wake of the civil rights movement. Carter was usually conservative on fiscal issues, often innovative on other matters, and virtually always attentive to administrative procedure. Reorganization and other governmental reforms generally made state decision making more centralized and efficient. Compared to previous Georgia governors, Carter displayed an active interest in environmental matters and emphasized long-range state planning.

Carter restructured the debate over racial equality. He stated in his inaugural address: "I say to you quite frankly that the time for racial discrimination is over. Our people have already made this major and difficult decision, but we cannot underestimate the challenge of hundreds of minor decisions yet to be made. . . . No poor, rural, weak, or black person should ever have to bear the additional burden of being deprived of the opportunity of an education, a job, or simple justice."[61] Not since Rufus Bullock had a Georgia governor openly endorsed equality before the law. Lester Maddox, by condemning all forms of integration, had kept alive the controversy over desegregation; Carter, by accepting the demise of segregation, helped to guide public debate toward the "hundreds of minor decisions yet to be made" within a desegregated society.

The acceptance of desegregation—at least on a token level—by whites in Georgia and elsewhere in the South noticeably enhanced the region's national standing. The southern massive resistance to desegregation, the region's virulent and often violent reaction to the black civil rights movement, and the antics of Maddox, Wallace, and other segregationist spokesmen made the region appear once again a benighted land of violence, intolerance, and ignorance. "The majority of movies" set in the region during these years, a study of "the celluloid South" has reported, "presented a [post-Civil War] South populated by pitifully poor farmers, unrepentant bigots, sadistic rednecks, sex objects, and greedy, ambitious members of a corrupt upper class."[62] What had once been the nation's number-one economic problem and had strived to become the nation's number-one economic opportunity became the nation's number-one moral problem, a wicked region in an otherwise virtuous republic. Although Atlanta elites had largely succeeded in maintaining a reputation as a city "too busy to hate," the rest of the state was not so fortunate. The inauguration of Jimmy Carter and other progressive southern governors, the white accommodation to desegregation, the decline of the civil rights movement, and other developments contributed to a decidedly improved national image. At the same time, the North emerged from the 1960s with its virtue severely tarnished. The great ghetto riots in the northern cities during the middle and late 1960s, the tragic consequences of the ill-fated war in Vietnam, and the ultimately serious economic problems in the part of the nation that for a time came to be termed the Snowbelt, the Rustbelt, and less favorable appellations undermined northern moral righteousness. By the mid-1970s the wicked South no longer appeared so wicked, and the virtuous North no longer appeared so virtuous.

In 1975 Kirkpatrick Sale's *Power Shift: The Rise of the Southern Rim and Its Challenge to the Eastern Establishment* appeared in book form, and in early 1976 the New York *Times* ran a six-part series on the emergence of the Sunbelt. Sale was critical of the "cowboy culture" he found along the southern rim, but these publications did popularize the Sunbelt concept, and thereafter the word became a part of the national vocabulary.[63] The "southern way of life," the phrase so ardently defended by southern segregationists and so laden with overtones of racism and provincialism, became the "southern style of life," the phrase so ardently ballyhooed by southern industrial promoters and so pregnant with promises of year-round golf games and barbecue cookouts. The election of Jimmy Carter as president in 1976 solidified the Sunbelt image.

Georgia's popular promotion from the backwater to the Sunbelt recognized the state's impressive economic and demographic growth, but as knowledgeable observers often noted, the state contained far more serious social problems than the Sunbelt image and its metropolitan promoters admitted. Nevertheless for a decade Georgia basked in the sunlight of generally favorable publicity. The bubble was eventually punctured in 1985 when Charles F. Floyd, a University of Georgia economist, published an article documenting the existence of "two Georgias." More than half of all the state's personal income, Floyd pointed out, went to fourteen metropolitan counties, most of them in the Atlanta metropolitan area. The other 145 Georgia counties lagged far behind.[64] One of Floyd's colleagues summarized his findings: "Without Atlanta Georgia is poorer than Mississippi."[65] The "two Georgias" problem touched off a vigorous public controversy. Black leaders insisted that the metropolitan ghettos were at least as economically deprived as rural counties. State and community officials attempted to ignore or sometimes to deny the existence of the problem. Generally, however, the Sunbelt image receded before the growing awareness of what an Atlanta journalist described as "a lush suburban North Georgia, an economic wasteland in South Georgia, and a catch-basin in the City of Atlanta for the impoverished refugees from south of the fall line."[66] The recognition of Georgia's uneven development coincided with the recovery of the northern economy, which made the Sunbelt's "progress" appear less impressive. The "two Georgias" controversy provoked a more realistic appraisal of the state's economy, although by focusing on distinctions between metropolitan and nonmetropolitan counties and between north Georgia and south Georgia, the debate sometimes simplified complex issues.

Rather than "two Georgias," the political configuration of the state's social structure seemed to point to three Georgias. This tripartite division received its clearest expression in the presidential election of 1968. George Wallace carried the state with 43 percent of the votes; Republican Richard M. Nixon finished second with 30 percent; and Democrat Hubert H. Humphrey demonstrated the deteriorating position of the once unassailable Democratic party by running last with 27 percent. In that election, Wallace's blend of anti-establishment rhetoric and social reaction had a powerful appeal to working-class white voters. Nixon's economic conservatism and law-and-order defense of social stability paralleled the attitudes of the metropolitan bourgeois, and he carried the uptown-suburban whites. Humphrey's welfare economics and racial liberalism appealed mainly to black voters and to the declining number of loyalist white Democrats. Thereafter Georgia's white voters supported Republicans in presidential elections, except for the two campaigns in which native son Jimmy Carter was a candidate, while the maturing consensus on the virtues of economic growth and the complacency prompted by Sunbelt hoopla discouraged sharp conflict over clearly defined issues in state politics. Democrats remained generally dominant in state elections, although it was difficult to determine what issues and outlooks distinguished a Georgia Democrat from a Georgia Republican, except for the fact that the latter was often of higher social status than the former. After Georgians ratified a constitutional amendment permitting governors to serve two terms, the Democratic chief executives who succeeded Carter during the 1970s and 1980s routinely served their eight years. Georgia politics displayed a blissful if perhaps beguiling harmony.

Yet the electoral division delineated in the 1968 election remained the social base of Georgia politics. Approximately one-quarter of employed Georgians in 1980 held managerial, proprietary, and professional positions, and they formed the backbone of the uptown-suburban middle class. Because the better educated, more affluent suburbanites were more likely than other Georgians to vote, especially in general elections, they and their allies represented more than one-third of the state electorate. Uptown-suburban whites voted Republican in presidential elections and frequently in state and local contests. They were the foremost proponents of the growth ethos, and they were the ones who benefited most from it.

Approximately three in ten of Georgia's people were minorities. Black Georgians, who made up 27 percent of the population in 1980, composed most of this group, of course, although it included Hispanics, Asians, and other self-conscious minorities. Negroes possessed a wider range of civic rights and opportunities in the post–civil rights era than in the past; every metropolitan area contained a substantial black bourgeoisie. Nevertheless, huge numbers of blacks were largely bypassed by progress. Significantly, blacks were 27 percent of the population; yet they held only 19 percent of the full-time, year-round employment, a statistic that suggested the extent of unemployment, underemployment, underground economics, and public welfare in black communities. Blacks were the most economically deprived of all Georgians, and one needed only to study census tracts or to drive through an Atlanta or Savannah ghetto or to visit a town in the old plantation belt to confirm such an observation. In both state and national politics, black voters remained staunchly loyal to the Democratic party.

The white working class made up well over a third of Georgia's population. As sociologist John Shelton Reed has observed, the vicious, black-hating redneck of the 1960s became the honest, fun-loving good old boy of the 1970s and 1980s.[67] Despite these gains in social respectability—and real gains in economic opportunity—the bulk of the good old boys and girls have benefited only marginally from the state's dedication to economic expansion. In the white working-class districts of the cities, the declining towns and counties that "two Georgias" analysts referred to as "the other Georgia," the fringe districts of metropolitan areas, and the other places occupied by rural-nonfarm workers, large numbers of blue-collar and white-blouse whites—like the masses of blacks—were substantially alienated from the course of Georgia progress. In the mid-1970s pollsters reported that "lower-middle-income and blue collar" southern whites were "the most disenchanted" and politically alienated group in the nation. They felt "left out of the mainstream of American life and taken advantage of by people with power."[68] Their acceptance of the ideology of economic growth was acquiescence rather than commitment. Politically, this group normally voted Republican in national politics and Democratic in state elections.

Such a crude typology of sociopolitical groups is more suggestive than precise, and the fact that a full 50 percent of Georgia's citizens failed to participate in the voting process further complicated political analysis. It was clear, however, that massive numbers of Georgians had or felt they had rather little stake in the shaping of governmental policy. Students of southern politics offered various explanations. One observation that seemed to apply aptly to the partisan electoral process in Georgia was that the southern "one-and-a-half, no-party system has made electoral participation less and less meaningful." The functioning of state government had also changed vastly since the days of Eugene Talmadge. A political scientist has explained: "Precisely at the point when the civil rights movement began the enfranchisement of blacks, effective political and governmental power began shifting from the elected officials in the South to the new professional bureaucratic elites. As a result, the recent liberalization of the suffrage in the South is, to some degree, rendered symbolic."[69] Poll taxes, white primaries, and literacy and understanding clauses no longer barred access to the polling booths, but the new political system was yet to be sharply tested. Whatever the validity of the criticisms that could be and were directed at the electoral and governmental process, Georgia's economic growth consensus rested on rather narrow foundations.

Despite the existence of "two Georgias" and three voting blocs, social modernization continued to modify Georgia society. The 1964 civil rights laws had legislated equality of economic opportunity for women as well as for racial minorities. The black civil rights movement had raised the expectations and altered the behavior of blacks, and although the General Assembly failed to ratify the Equal Rights Amendment, the women's rights movement changed the perspectives and practices of Georgia females. These developments extended free market individualism throughout Georgia society and essentially completed the commodification of the Georgia labor market. The rising expectations of blacks and women combined with the continued expansion of the consumer economy to enlarge the Georgia work force. In 1960 approximately one in three of Georgia's almost four million people were a part of the experienced labor force; in 1980 well over four in ten of the state's five and a half million people held steady employment. To be sure, white males continued to be treated most favorably in the labor market. Even though white men in Georgia were hardly overpaid in comparison to national standards, the paychecks of full-time, year-round black male employees in 1980 averaged 65 percent of white male wages; white women made on the average 60 percent as much as white men; and black women received incomes that were 50 percent of those received by white males. Women and minorities insisted on the implementation of equality in the marketplace, and Georgia responded to the rising expectations and mounting demands generated by equal rights individualism by championing the merits of economic expansion.

Georgia's leadership held to the assumption that economic growth would ameliorate social problems in the state. Since the 1940s Georgia state agencies had cooperated with private organizations in efforts to lure new industry, and increasingly the state courted high-technology firms. The drive became a crusade during the 1970s. Governor Carter invigorated the search for new business, and George Busbee, his successor in office, pursued it with almost single-minded determination. During the 1970s Georgia, not content with a variety of public-private programs to encourage northern corporations to expand into the state, established offices to court foreign industry in Brussels, São Paulo, Tokyo, and Toronto. The symbiotic relationship between private corporate groups and state agencies that uptown had long desired was clearly a reality. The political question that remained was whether state governmental policies that favored public aid for industrialists, that opposed mass labor organization, that supported relatively low taxes and services, and that tailored social policies to the needs of private corporations would benefit Georgia's people as a whole and alleviate racial and other social problems.

In the early nineteenth century, white Georgians structured a society based on plantations, cotton, and slavery. During its formative years that society expanded opportunities for whites, and they in turn lauded its virtues. That dream was betrayed. In the mid-twentieth century, Georgians—this time not all of them white—built a different society. It, too, in its formative stages offered wide-ranging opportunities to many of its citizens. The future of that society is as yet unknown.

# Notes

## PREFACE

1. Kenneth Coleman, Numan V. Bartley, F. N. Boney, William F. Holmes, Phinizy Spalding, and Charles Wynes, *A History of Georgia*, 2d ed. (Athens: University of Georgia Press, 1990).

## CHAPTER ONE
### *"That Paradise with All Her Virgin Beauties"*

1. "Some Account of the Designs of the Trustees for Establishing the Colony of Georgia in America," in Trevor R. Reese, ed., *The Most Delightful Country of the Universe: Promotional Literature of the Colony of Georgia, 1717–1734* (Savannah: Beehive Press, 1972), 69.

2. Quoted in Paul S. Taylor, *Georgia Plan, 1732–1752* (Berkeley: University of California Institute of Business and Economic Research, 1972), 14.

3. "Some Account of the Designs of the Trustees," 71–72.

4. "A New and Accurate Account of the Provinces of South Carolina and Georgia," in Reese, ed., *The Most Delightful Country*, 123, 124.

5. "Reasons for Establishing the Colony of Georgia with Regard to the Trade of Great Britain," ibid., 170.

6. "The Most Delightful Country in the Universe," ibid., 15.

7. Quoted in Taylor, *Georgia Plan*, iii.

8. Phinizy Spalding, *Oglethorpe in America* (Chicago: University of Chicago Press, 1977), 161.

9. Harold E. Davis, *The Fledgling Province: Social and Cultural Life in*

*Colonial Georgia, 1733–1776* (Chapel Hill: University of North Carolina Press, 1976), 98.

10. Milton Sydney Heath, *Constructive Liberalism: The Role of the State in Economic Development in Georgia to 1860* (Cambridge, Mass.: Harvard University Press, 1954), 65.

11. James Habersham to James Wright, August 20, 1772, in Ulrich B. Phillips, ed., *Plantation and Frontier Documents, 1649–1863* (Cleveland: Arthur H. Clark, 1909), 239.

12. Harvey H. Jackson, *Lachlan McIntosh and the Politics of Revolutionary Georgia* (Athens: University of Georgia Press, 1979), 21.

13. George R. Gilmer, *Sketches of Some of the First Settlers of Upper Georgia . . .* (1855; reprint, Baltimore: Genealogical Publishing Company, 1965), 143.

14. Heath, *Constructive Liberalism*, 84.

15. Augusta *Chronicle*, March 28, 1795, quoted in Albert Berry Saye, *A Constitutional History of Georgia, 1732–1968*, rev. ed. (Athens: University of Georgia Press, 1970), 151.

16. Resolution, November 23, 1807, in Spencer B. King, ed., *Georgia Voices: A Documentary History to 1872* (Athens: University of Georgia Press, 1966), 86.

17. Act of the General Assembly, December 18, 1817, ibid., 206.

18. George McHenry, *The Cotton Trade* (London: Saunders, Otley, and Company, 1863), 12.

19. Quoted in James L. Roark, *Masters without Slaves: Southern Planters in the Civil War and Reconstruction* (New York: W. W. Norton, 1977), 150.

## CHAPTER TWO
### *The Cotton Kingdom*

1. James Sterling, *Letters from the Slave States* (London: J. W. Parker and Son, 1857), 204.

2. Quoted in Ulrich Bonnell Phillips, *The Life of Robert Toombs* (New York: Macmillan, 1913), 157.

3. Macon *Georgia Telegraph*, January 25, 1859, quoted in Ralph Betts Flanders, *Plantation Slavery in Georgia* (Chapel Hill: University of North Carolina Press, 1933), 87.

4. John B. Lamar to Mrs. Howell Cobb, December 2, 1845, in Ulrich B. Phillips, ed., *Plantation and Frontier Documents, 1649–1863* (Cleveland: Arthur H. Clark, 1909), 173.

5. Quoted in Ulrich Bonnell Phillips, *American Negro Slavery* (Baton Rouge: Louisiana State University Press, 1918), 290.

6. Flanders, *Plantation Slavery in Georgia*, 137.

7. Charles Colcock to Mary Ruth Colcock, May 11, 1888, in Robert Manson Myers, ed., *The Children of Pride: A True Story of Georgia and the Civil War* (New Haven: Yale University Press, 1972), 19.

8. Charles C. Jones to Charles C. Jones, Jr., June 7, 1854, ibid., 39.

9. John B. Lamar to Howell Cobb, January 10, 1847, in Phillips, ed., *Plantation and Frontier Documents*, 177.

10. Charles C. Jones to Charles C. Jones, Jr., June 7, 1859, in Myers, ed., *Children of Pride*, 487.

11. George Featherstonhaugh, *Excursions through the Slave States . . .* (London: John Murray, 1844), 153.

12. Frederick Law Olmsted, *The Cotton Kingdom: A Traveller's Observations on Cotton and Slavery in the American Slave States* (New York: Alfred A. Knopf, 1953), 213.

13. Featherstonhaugh, *Excursions*, 153.

14. James C. Bonner, "Profile of a Late Antebellum Community," in Elinor Miller and Eugene D. Genovese, eds., *Plantation, Town, and County: Essays on the Local History of American Slave Society* (Urbana: University of Illinois Press, 1974), 40.

15. Gavin Wright, *The Political Economy of the Cotton South: Households, Markets, and Wealth in the Nineteenth Century* (New York: W. W. Norton, 1978), 24–29.

16. Lee Soltow, *Men and Wealth in the United States, 1850–1870* (New Haven: Yale University Press, 1975), 92–101. See also Joseph Karl Menn, "The Large Slaveholders of the Deep South, 1860," 2 vols. (Ph.D. dissertation, University of Texas, 1964).

17. W. J. Cash, *The Mind of the South* (New York: Vintage Books, 1941), 24.

18. Frances Anne Kemble, *Journal of a Residence on a Georgia Plantation in 1838–1839*, ed. John A. Scott (1863; reprint, New York: Alfred A. Knopf, 1961), 182.

19. Quoted in James Leggette Owens, "The Negro in Georgia during Reconstruction, 1864–1872: A Social History" (Ph.D. dissertation, University of Georgia, 1975), 12.

20. Eugene D. Genovese, *Roll, Jordan, Roll: The World the Slaves Made* (New York: Pantheon Books, 1974), 5; Genovese, *The World the Slaveholders Made: Two Essays in Interpretation* (New York: Vintage Books, 1971), 96. The discussion of John Brown is based on F. N. Boney, ed., *Slave Life in Georgia: A Narrative of the Life, Sufferings, and Escape of John Brown, A Fugitive Slave* (1855; reprint, Savannah: Beehive Press, 1972).

21. Atlanta *Daily Intelligencer*, January 9, 1860, in Spencer B. King, Jr., ed., *Georgia Voices: A Documentary History to 1872* (Athens: University of Georgia Press, 1966), 202.

22. William G. Moffat, "The River Road Settlement of Jones County, Georgia: A Social and Economic History" (M.A. thesis, Georgia College, 1979), 32.

23. Olmsted, *Cotton Kingdom*, 21.

24. Margaret Mitchell, *Gone With the Wind* (New York: Macmillan, 1936), 111.

25. Kemble, *Journal*, 63.

26. Resolution passed by Athens Merchants, quoted in King, ed., *Georgia Voices*, 144.

27. Phillips, *American Negro Slavery*, 337.

28. Dorothy Orr, *A History of Education in Georgia* (Chapel Hill: University of North Carolina Press, 1950), 50.

29. Wright, *Political Economy of the Cotton South*, 4.

30. Genovese, *World the Slaveholders Made*, 125.

31. Gunnar Myrdal, *An American Dilemma: The Negro Problem and Modern Democracy*, 2 vols. (1944; reprint, New York: Pantheon Books, 1962), 1: 442.

32. Charles C. Jones, Jr., to the Rev. C. C. Jones, January 28, 1861, in Myers, ed., *Children of Pride*, 648.

33. Joseph E. Brown, "Special Message," November 7, 1860, in Allen D. Candler, comp., *The Confederate Records of the State of Georgia*, 5 vols. (Atlanta: State Printer, 1910), 1: 56.

34. Raimondo Luraghi, *The Rise and Fall of the Plantation South* (New York: New Viewpoints, 1978), 84. See also Emory M. Thomas, *The Confederate Nation, 1861–1865* (New York: Harper Colophon Books, 1979), 190–214.

35. Willard Range, *A Century of Georgia Agriculture, 1850–1950* (Athens: University of Georgia Press, 1954), 107.

36. Joseph E. Brown (and others) to the Rev. Henry Ward Beecher, January 1867, Hargrett Collection, University of Georgia, Athens.

37. R. Toombs to Genl. J. C. Breckinridge, April 30, 1867, Toombs Collection, University of Georgia.

38. Sam B. Sweat to W. H. Garland, October 12, 1867, William Harris Garland Papers, Southern Historical Collection, University of North Carolina, Chapel Hill.

39. Roger L. Ransom and Richard Sutch, *One Kind of Freedom: The Economic Consequences of Emancipation* (New York: Cambridge University Press, 1977), 9–10.

40. Robert Toombs to Alexander H. Stephens, January 30, 1879, in Ulrich Bonnell Phillips, ed., *The Correspondence of Robert Toombs, Alexander H. Stephens, and Howell Cobb* (1913; reprint, New York: Da Capo Press, 1970), 735.

41. Daniel R. Goodloe, "Resources and Industrial Conditions of the Southern States," *Report of the Commissioner of Agriculture, 1865* (Washington, D.C.: U.S. Government Printing Office, 1866), 119.

42. Charles Stearns, *The Black Man of the South and the Rebels* (New York: American News Company, 1872), 99.

43. Howell Cobb to his wife, December 1866, J. D. Collins to John A.

Cobb, July 31, 1865, in Phillips, ed., *Correspondence*, 684, 665. See Lee W. Formwault, "Antebellum Planter Persistence: Southwest Georgia—A Case Study," *Plantation Society in the Americas* 1 (October 1981): 410–29.

44. *Acts of the General Assembly of the State of Georgia, Annual Session, 1866* (Macon: J. W. Burke, 1867), 141.

45. *Acts of the General Assembly of the State of Georgia, Annual Session, 1865–66* (Milledgeville: Barnes and Moore, 1866), 234–35; *Georgia Acts, 1866,* 141.

46. *Georgia Acts, 1866,* 153–54.

47. *Georgia Acts, 1865–66,* 232; *Georgia Acts, 1866,* 26, 151–52.

48. *Testimony Taken by the Joint Select Committee to Inquire into the Condition of Affairs in the Late Insurrectionary States,* 7 vols. (Washington, D.C.: U.S. Government Printing Office, 1872), 6: 308.

49. Pete Daniel, "The Metamorphosis of Slavery, 1865–1900," *Journal of American History* 66 (June 1979): 89.

50. William Faulkner, *The Hamlet: A Novel of the Snopes Family* (New York: Vintage Books, 1931), 5.

51. *Oglethorpe Echo* (Lexington), May 8, 1891, quoted in E. Merton Coulter, *James Monroe Smith: Georgia Planter before Death and After* (Athens: University of Georgia Press, 1961), 39.

52. Department of Commerce, Bureau of the Census, "Plantations in the South," in *Thirteenth Census . . . : Agriculture, 1909 and 1910* (Washington, D.C.: U.S. Government Printing Office, 1912), 877–89.

53. Georgia Department of Agriculture, *Georgia Historical and Industrial* (Atlanta: George W. Harrison, 1901), 352.

54. Charles Lenean Flynn, Jr., "White Land, Black Labor: Property, Ideology, and the Political Economy of Late Nineteenth-Century Georgia" (Ph.D. dissertation, Duke University, 1980), 20.

55. Carolina Lewis Gordon, "Plantation Life with General John B. Gordon," *Georgia Review* 14 (Spring 1960): 22.

56. Quoted in Ray Stannard Baker, *Following the Color Line: American Negro Citizenship in the Progressive Era,* ed. Dewey W. Grantham, Jr. (1908; reprint, New York: Harper Torchbooks, 1964), 77.

57. Erskine Caldwell, "The End of Christy Tucker," in *Jackpot: The Short Stories of Erskine Caldwell* (New York: Duell, Sloan and Pearce, 1931), 229–36.

58. Jane Macguire, comp., *On Shares: Ed Brown's Story* (New York: W. W. Norton, 1975), 76.

59. C. Vann Woodward, *Tom Watson: Agrarian Rebel* (1938; reprint, New York: Oxford University Press, 1978), 129.

60. Quoted in Thomas D. Clark, *Pills, Petticoats and Plows: The Southern Country Store* (Norman: University of Oklahoma Press, 1964), 271.

61. Quoted in J. Wayne Flynt, *Dixie's Forgotten People: The South's Poor Whites* (Bloomington: Indiana University Press, 1979), 61.

62. *Acts and Resolutions of the General Assembly of the State of Georgia,*

*Regular Session, 1873* (Atlanta: W. A. Hemphill, 1873), 42–47; ibid., *Regular Session, 1874* (Savannah: J. H. Estill, 1874), 18; ibid., *Regular Session, 1875* (Savannah: J. H. Estill, 1875), 20.

63. Quoted in Steven Howard Hahn, "The Roots of Southern Populism: Yeomen Farmers and the Transformation of Georgia's Upper Piedmont, 1850–1890" (Ph.D. dissertation, Yale University, 1979), 280.

64. Ransom and Sutch, *One Kind of Freedom*, 143.

65. Stephen J. De Canio, *Agriculture in the Postbellum South: The Economics of Production and Supply* (Cambridge, Mass.: Massachusetts Institute of Technology Press, 1974), 176–80; Julius Rubin, "The Limits of Agricultural Progress in the Nineteenth-Century South," *Agricultural History* 49 (April 1975): 362–73.

66. W. E. Burghardt DuBois, ed., *The Negro American Family* (Atlanta: Atlanta University Press, 1908), 128.

67. Floyd C. Watkins and Charles Hubert Watkins, *Yesterday in the Hills* (Athens: University of Georgia Press, 1973), xi.

68. Macguire, comp., *On Shares*, 43.

69. Albert Colbey Smith, "Down Freedom's Road: The Contours of Race, Class, and Property Crime in Black-Belt Georgia, 1866–1910" (Ph.D. dissertation, University of Georgia, 1982), chapter 6.

70. Augusta *Chronicle*, November 3, 1907.

71. John Dittmer, *Black Georgia in the Progressive Era, 1900–1920* (Urbana: University of Illinois Press, 1977), 25.

## CHAPTER THREE
### *Reconstruction: A Revolution That Failed*

1. Quoted in I. W. Avery, *The History of the State of Georgia from 1850 to 1881* (New York: Brown and Derby, 1881), 338.

2. John T. Trowbridge, *The South: A Tour of its Battlefields and Ruined Cities . . .* (Hartford: L. Stebbins, 1866), 485.

3. Frances B. Leigh, *Ten Years on a Georgia Plantation since the War* (1883; reprint, New York: Negro Universities Press, 1969), 110.

4. Charles J. Jenkins to the People of Georgia, April 10, 1867, in Allen D. Candler, comp., *The Confederate Records of the State of Georgia*, 5 vols. (Atlanta: State Printer, 1910), 4: 74.

5. Quoted in Bell Irvin Wiley, *The Life of Johnny Reb: The Common Soldier of the Confederacy* (Baton Rouge: Louisiana State University Press, 1978), 144.

6. Speech manuscript, August 19, 1868, Hargrett Collection, University of Georgia, Athens.

7. *Journal of the Proceedings of the Constitutional Convention of the People*

*of Georgia Held in the City of Atlanta in the Months of December, 1867, and January, February and March, 1868* (Augusta: E. H. Pughe, 1868), 49.

8. Joseph E. Brown to Ira R. Foster and others, February 23, 1867, Hargrett Collection.

9. John E. Bryant, *The Southern Advance Association* (Philadelphia: Craig, Finley and Co., 1883), 2.

10. *Testimony Taken by the Joint Select Committee to Inquire into the Condition of Affairs in the Late Insurrectionary States*, 7 vols. (Washington, D.C.: U.S. Government Printing Office, 1872), 7: 1034.

11. Special Field Order No. 15, January 16, 1865, in Walter L. Fleming, ed., *Documentary History of Reconstruction* (Cleveland: Arthur H. Clark, 1906), 350.

12. Quoted in E. Merton Coulter, *Negro Legislators in Georgia during the Reconstruction Period* (Athens: Georgia Historical Quarterly, 1968), 48.

13. Testimony of Edward C. Anderson, *Testimony into the Condition of Affairs in the Late Insurrectionary States*, 6: 176.

14. New York *Herald*, December 13, 1867, quoted in Joseph H. Parks, *Joseph E. Brown of Georgia* (Baton Rouge: Louisiana State University Press, 1977), 394.

15. Charles Jenkins to Andrew Johnson, November 23, 1867, Governor's Letterbook, 257, Georgia State Archives, Atlanta.

16. Rome *Weekly Courier*, February 28, 1868, quoted in Alan Conway, *The Reconstruction of Georgia* (Minneapolis: University of Minnesota Press, 1966), 153.

17. Bullock to Senators and Representatives, July 24, 1868, Executive Minutes, 144, Georgia State Archives, Atlanta.

18. Ibid., 154.

19. *Testimony into the Condition of Affairs in the Late Insurrectionary States*, 7: 1041.

20. Quoted in C. Mildred Thompson, *Reconstruction in Georgia: Economic, Social, Political, 1865–1872* (1915; reprint, Freeport, N.Y.: Books for Libraries Press, 1971), 204.

21. Quoted in William Y. Thompson, *Robert Toombs of Georgia* (Baton Rouge: Louisiana State University Press, 1966), 225.

22. Henry W. Grady, dateline July 1, 1879, Philadelphia *Times*, in Thomas E. Watson Papers, Box 26, Southern Historical Collection, University of North Carolina, Chapel Hill.

23. Robert Toombs to Alexander H. Stephens, October 30, 1876, in Ulrich Bonnell Phillips, ed., *The Correspondence of Robert Toombs, Alexander Stephens and Howell Cobb* (1913; reprint, New York: Da Capo Press, 1970), 722.

24. Quoted in Ulrich Bonnell Phillips, *The Life of Robert Toombs* (New York: Macmillan, 1913), 273.

25. Speech manuscript, August 19, 1868, Hargrett Collection.

26. R. Toombs to Genl. J. C. Breckinridge, April 30, 1867, Toombs Collection, University of Georgia, Athens.

27. Quoted in Haywood J. Pearce, *Benjamin H. Hill: Secession and Reconstruction* (1928; reprint, New York: Negro University Press, 1969), 166, and Charles G. Bloom, "The Georgia Election of April, 1868: A Re-Examination of the Politics of Georgia Reconstruction" (M.A. thesis, University of Chicago, 1963), 39.

28. Pressed by a congressional committee to name other leaders of the "brotherhood" that he headed, John B. Gordon mentioned Alfred H. Colquitt, Ambrose R. Wright of Augusta, G. T. Anderson of Atlanta, and A. R. Lawton of Savannah (*Testimony into the Condition of Affairs in the Late Insurrectionary States*, 6: 324). With the addition of Toombs and perhaps one or two others, this list would accurately summarize the Georgia Democratic hierarchy.

29. Lewis N. Wynne, "Planter Politics in Georgia, 1860–1890" (Ph.D. dissertation, University of Georgia, 1980), 177–80; Elizabeth Studley Nathans, *Losing the Peace: Georgia Republicans and Reconstruction, 1865–1871* (Baton Rouge: Louisiana State University Press, 1968), Appendix. Quotation from Rufus B. Bullock, "Reconstruction in Georgia," *Independent* 55 (March 9, 1903): 673.

30. Joseph E. Brown to Genl. U. S. Grant, May 5, 1868, Hargrett Collection.

31. Bullock to Senators and Representatives, July 24, 1868, Executive Minutes, 153–54; January 13, 1869, ibid., 262.

32. Robert Toombs to Alexander H. Stephens, August 9, 1868, in Phillips, ed., *Correspondence*, 703.

33. Donald B. Johnson and Kirk H. Porter, comps., *National Party Platforms, 1840–1972* (Urbana: University of Illinois Press, 1973), 38.

34. Charles Stearns, *The Black Man of the South and the Rebels* (New York: American News Company, 1872), 294.

35. *Testimony into the Condition of Affairs in the Late Insurrectionary States*, 6: 323.

36. Quoted in Thompson, *Reconstruction in Georgia*, 380.

37. R. Toombs to Genl. J. C. Breckinridge, April 30, 1867, Toombs Collection, University of Georgia.

38. Joseph E. Brown to R. B. Bullock, December 3, 1868, Hargrett Collection.

39. *Congressional Globe*, 40th Cong., 3d sess., pt. 1, December 7, 1868, 3.

40. Avery, *History*, 384.

41. Rome *Tri-Weekly Courier*, September 7, 1869, Henry W. Grady Papers, Scrapbook 1, Emory University, Atlanta.

42. "Governor Bullock's Trial," dateline January 2, 1878, New York *Tribune*, ibid., Scrapbook 4.

43. Ruth Currie McDaniel, "Georgia Carpetbagger: John Emory Bryant and the Ambiguity of Reform during Reconstruction" (Ph.D. dissertation, Duke University, 1973), 9.

44. Joseph E. Brown to R. B. Bullock, December 3, 1868, Hargrett Collection.

45. Atlanta *Daily New Era*, November 17, 1866, quoted in Conway, *Reconstruction of Georgia*, 104.

46. Quoted in Allen W. Trelease, *White Terror: The Ku Klux Klan Conspiracy and Southern Reconstruction* (New York: Harper & Row, 1971), 323.

47. Amos T. Akerman to Benjamin Conley, December 28, 1871, Conley Papers, University of Georgia, Athens.

48. Quoted in Avery, *History*, 462.

49. *Address of Rufus B. Bullock to the People of Georgia, October, 1872*, 46, Rare Books Collection, University of Georgia, Athens.

50. Robert Toombs to Alexander H. Stephens, January 24, 1870, in Phillips, ed., *Correspondence*, 708.

51. Rufus B. Bullock to Atlanta *Constitution*, November 6, 1898, Daniel L. Russell Papers, Southern Historical Collection, University of North Carolina, Chapel Hill.

52. Quoted in Thompson, *Reconstruction in Georgia*, 218.

53. McDaniel, "Georgia Carpetbagger," 216.

54. Rufus B. Bullock to J. E. Brown, November 5, 1872, Hargrett Collection.

55. Atlanta *Constitution*, January 23, 1878, quoted in Richard Lee Zuber, "The Role of Rufus Brown Bullock in Georgia Politics" (M.A. thesis, Emory University, 1967), 104.

## CHAPTER FOUR
### The Challenge to Bourbon Democracy

1. Joseph E. Brown to R. B. Bullock, December 3, 1868, Hargrett Collection, University of Georgia, Athens.

2. Benjamin H. Hill, Jr., comp., *Senator Benjamin H. Hill of Georgia: His Life, Speeches and Writings* (Atlanta: T.H.P. Bloodworth, 1893), 305.

3. "Address to the People of Georgia," December 8, 1870, ibid., 58.

4. Hill, comp., *Senator Benjamin H. Hill*, 63.

5. Ibid., 313, 318.

6. Quotations from "Speech Delivered before the Alumni Society . . . " (July 31, 1871), ibid., 334–49.

7. Benjamin H. Hill to Editor, Atlanta *Constitution*, August 3, 1871, ibid., 334.

8. Augusta *Chronicle and Sentinel*, August 24, 1871, quoted in Haywood J. Pearce, *Benjamin H. Hill: Secession and Reconstruction* (1928; reprint, New York: Negro Universities Press, 1969), 243.

9. Robert Toombs to Alexander H. Stephens, December 30, 1874, March 10, 1875, in Ulrich Bonnell Phillips, ed., *The Correspondence of Robert Toombs, Alexander H. Stephens, and Howell Cobb* (1913; reprint, New York: Da Capo Press, 1970), 712, 721.

10. Robert Toombs to L. N. Trammell, April 26, 1877, ibid., 728.

11. Quoted in William P. Brandon, "Calling the Georgia Constitutional Convention of 1877," *Georgia Historical Quarterly* 17 (September 1933): 198.

12. Atlanta *Constitution*, July 24, 1877, quoted in Albert Berry Saye, *A Constitutional History of Georgia, 1732–1968*, revised ed. (Athens: University of Georgia Press, 1970), 282.

13. Charles Jenkins to Gen. G. Meade, January 10, 1868, Governor's Letterbook, 279, Georgia State Archives, Atlanta.

14. Rufus B. Bullock to Atlanta *Constitution*, November 6, 1898, Daniel L. Russell Papers, Document 645, Southern Historical Collection, University of North Carolina, Chapel Hill.

15. Samuel W. Small, *A Stenographic Report of the Proceedings of the Constitutional Convention Held in Atlanta, Georgia, 1877* (Atlanta: Constitution Publishing Company, 1877), 274, 115, 247, 299, 407.

16. Ibid., 299.

17. Ibid., 304.

18. *Acts and Resolutions of the General Assembly of the State of Georgia*, July–August Session, 1872 (Atlanta: W. A. Hemphill, 1872), 69.

19. Small, *Stenographic Report*, 224.

20. Ibid., 217.

21. Hill quotations from "Speech Delivered before the Alumni Society," in Hill, comp., *Senator Benjamin H. Hill*, 343, 349.

22. John Temple Graves, in Atlanta *Constitution*, August 27, 1896, quoted in Alex Mathews Arnett, *The Populist Movement in Georgia: A View of the "Agrarian Crusade" in the Light of Solid-South Politics* (1922; reprint, New York: AMS Press, 1967), 206.

23. H. W. Grady to Joseph E. Brown, May 15, 1880, Hargrett Collection.

24. Quoted in Thomas E. Watson, *Sketches: Historical, Literary, Biographical, Economic, Etc.* (Thomson, Ga.: Jefferson Publishing Company, 1916), 289.

25. Henry W. Grady, "The Atheistic Tide Sweeping over the Continent," in Joel Chandler Harris, ed., *Henry W. Grady: Writings and Speeches* (New York: Cassell Publishing Company, 1890), 234; Henry W. Grady Papers, Scrapbooks 1 and 2, Emory University, Atlanta; Raymond B. Nixon, *Henry W. Grady: Spokesman of the New South* (1943; reprint, New York: Russell and Russell, 1969), 19–20, 271.

26. "The South and Her Problem," in Harris, ed., *Grady*, 115, 110.

27. "Cotton and Its Kingdom," ibid., 272.

28. "A Matter of Millions," dateline October 19, 1882, Atlanta *Constitution*, Grady Papers, Scrapbook 9.

29. Specials to Atlanta *Constitution*, datelines April 14, 21, 1882, ibid.

30. Undated clipping, Atlanta *Constitution*, ibid., Scrapbook 6.

31. Quoted in Nixon, *Grady*, 165.

32. "The New South," in Harris, ed., *Grady*, 88.

33. "The South and Her Problem," ibid., 111–12.

34. "Cotton and Its Kingdom," ibid., 266, 270.

35. "The Solid South," ibid., 130.

36. Henry W. Grady, "In Plain Black and White," *Century Magazine*, n.s., 39 (April 1885): 911.

37. "The South and Her Problem," in Harris, ed., *Grady*, 101, 99.

38. "The Solid South," ibid., 125.

39. Augusta *Chronicle*, July 18, 1888, quoted in Randolph Dennis Werner, "Hegemony and Conflict: The Political Economy of a Southern Region, Augusta, Georgia, 1865–1895" (Ph.D. dissertation, University of Virginia, 1977), 252.

40. Andre Gunder Frank, *Dependent Accumulation and Underdevelopment* (New York: Monthly Review Press, 1979), 98.

41. "Against Centralization," in Harris, ed., *Grady*, 152.

42. "New South Articles from the New York *Ledger*, November–December, 1889," in Mills Lane, comp., *The New South: Writings and Speeches of Henry Grady* (Savannah: Beehive Press, 1971), 107.

43. "Commencement Address" (June 1888), in Thomas E. Watson, *The Life and Speeches of Thomas E. Watson* (Nashville: Privately printed, 1908), 71–72.

44. Watson, *Life and Speeches*, 9.

45. Ibid., 12.

46. "Commencement Address," ibid., 71. The italics are Watson's.

47. "An Address to the People of Georgia," *People's Party Paper*, March 17, 1892, Thomas E. Watson Papers, Box 28, Southern Historical Collection, University of North Carolina, Chapel Hill.

48. Text of Watson Speech at Thomson, 1890, ibid.

49. Reprint of Watson's Speech in Atlanta, May 19, 1894, Hoke Smith Papers, Scrapbook 50, University of Georgia, Athens.

50. Notes for South Georgia speech (1893), Watson Papers, Box 29.

51. Watson, *Life and Speeches*, 114; C. Vann Woodward, *Tom Watson: Agrarian Rebel* (1938; reprint, New York: Oxford University Press, 1978), 248.

52. Watson, *Life and Speeches*, 112, 113.

53. Quoted in Woodward, *Tom Watson*, 350.

54. Notes for speech in Athens, July 25, 1893, Watson Papers, Box 29.

55. Watson, *Life and Speeches*, 265.

56. Notes for speech in Athens, July 25, 1893, notes for South Georgia campaign speech (1893), Watson Papers, Box 29; Reprint of Watson speech in Atlanta, May 19, 1894, Smith Papers, Scrapbook 50.

57. Thomas E. Watson, "The Negro Question in the South," *Arena* 35 (October 1892): 548.

58. Reprint of Watson's speech, *The Cotton Plant* (Orangeburg), October 31, 1891, Watson Papers, Box 1.

59. Quoted in Atlanta *Constitution*, May 17, 1894, ibid., Box 26.

60. Reprint of Watson speech in Atlanta, May 19, 1894, Smith Papers, Scrapbook 50.

61. Notes for speech in Athens, July 25, 1893, Watson Papers, Box 29.

62. Reprint of Watson speech, *The Cotton Plant*, October 31, 1891, ibid., Box 1.

63. "The South and Her Problem," in Harris, ed., *Grady*, 99.

64. Mrs. William H. Felton, *My Memoirs of Georgia Politics* (Atlanta: Index Printing Company, 1911), 644.

65. Robert C. McMath, Jr., *Populist Vanguard: A History of the Southern Farmers' Alliance* (Chapel Hill: University of North Carolina Press, 1975), 62; Steven Howard Hahn, "The Roots of Southern Populism: Yeomen Farmers and the Transformation of Georgia's Upper Piedmont, 1850–1890" (Ph.D. dissertation, Yale University, 1979); Lawrence Goodwyn, *Democratic Promise: The Populist Movement in America* (New York: Oxford University Press, 1976).

66. "The Farmer and the Cities," in Harris, *Grady*, 158.

67. Quoted in McMath, *Populist Vanguard*, 131; Barton C. Shaw, "The Wool-Hat Boys: A History of the Populist Party in Georgia, 1892 to 1910" (Ph.D. dissertation, Emory University, 1979).

68. Atlanta *Constitution*, August 29, 1892, quoted in John Michael Matthews, "Studies in Race Relations in Georgia, 1890–1930" (Ph.D. dissertation, Duke University, 1970), 58.

69. Quoted in Woodward, *Tom Watson*, 228.

70. Chairman, Democratic Executive Committee, to the Democratic Farmers & Employers of Labor of Wilkes Co., September 8, 1892, Watson Papers, Box 1.

71. Howard H. Rabinowitz, *Race Relations in the Urban South, 1865–1890* (New York: Oxford University Press, 1978), 258.

72. William J. Northen to Grover Cleveland, September 15, 1893, quoted in Woodward, *Tom Watson*, 254–55.

73. "The Young Wife's Song," Watson Papers, Box 25.

74. Reprint of Watson speech in Atlanta, May 19, 1894, Smith Papers, Scrapbook 50.

75. Text of Atkinson's opening campaign speech, reprinted in Atlanta *Constitution*, September 7, 1894, Watson Papers, Box 29.

76. Augusta *Chronicle*, September 4, 1892, quoted in Werner, "Hegemony and Conflict," 385.

77. Shaw, "The Wool-Hat Boys," 262–70.

## CHAPTER FIVE
### Myth, Reality, and Social Stability
### in Uptown and County Seat

1. Sam Jones to Atlanta *Journal*, January 5, 1901, Sam Jones Collection, Scrapbook 2, Emory University, Atlanta.

2. Ray Stannard Baker, *Following the Color Line: American Negro Citizenship in the Progressive Era*, ed. Dewey W. Grantham, Jr. (1908; reprint, New York: Harper Torchbooks, 1964), 69.

3. Harper Lee, *To Kill a Mockingbird* (New York: Popular Library, 1960), 133.

4. Jasper Berry Shannon, *Toward a New Politics in the South* (Knoxville: University of Tennessee Press, 1949), 41.

5. *People's Party Paper*, October 18, 1895, quoted in Robert Miller Saunders, "The Ideology of Southern Populists, 1892–1895" (Ph.D. dissertation, University of Virginia, 1967), 156.

6. Charles Reagan Wilson, *Baptized in Blood: The Religion of the Lost Cause, 1865–1920* (Athens: University of Georgia Press, 1980), 1; Lloyd Arthur Hunter, "The Sacred South: Postwar Confederates and Sacralization of Southern Culture" (Ph.D. dissertation, St. Louis University, 1978), 42; Rollin G. Osterweis, *The Myth of the Lost Cause, 1865–1900* (Hamden, Conn.: Archon Book, 1973), 29.

7. Mrs. William Tate, in Athens *Daily News*, July 16, 1968.

8. Undated clipping, Mildred Lewis Rutherford to Athens *Banner-Herald*, Mildred Lewis Rutherford Papers, Box 4, University of Georgia, Athens; "Stone Mountain: What It Means to America and Georgia," speech manuscript, ibid., Box 3; Mildred Lewis Rutherford, *Four Addresses* (Birmingham: Mildred Rutherford Historical Circle, 1916), 51, 4, 14.

9. Quoted in Hunter, "The Sacred South," 70.

10. John B. Gordon, *The Old South: Address Delivered before the Confederate Survivors Association* (Augusta: Chronicle Publishing Company, 1887), 8, 13.

11. Wilson, *Baptized in Blood*, 11.

12. Undated clipping, Atlanta *Constitution*, Henry W. Grady Collection, Scrapbook 10, Emory University, Atlanta; Grady quoted in Raymond B. Nixon, *Henry W. Grady: Spokesman of the New South* (1943; reprint, New York: Russell and Russell, 1969), 230.

13. "Notes for Memorial Day Address," April 1902, Thomas E. Watson Papers, Scrapbook 34, Southern Historical Collection, University of North Carolina, Chapel Hill.

14. Henry W. Grady, "The New South," dateline July 24, 1881, New York *Tribune*, Grady Papers, Scrapbook 5.

15. Richard A. Easterlin, "State Income Estimates," in Simon Kuznets and

Dorothy Swaine Thomas, eds., *Population Redistribution and Economic Growth: United States, 1870–1950* (Philadelphia: American Philosophical Society, 1957), 729–37. The information on mill ownership is from [Georgia] Department of Agriculture, *Georgia: Historical and Industrial* (Atlanta: George W. Harrison, 1901), 337–42.

16. Joseph Persky, "Regional Colonialism and the Southern Economy," *Review of Radical Political Economics* 4 (Fall 1972): 73.

17. Richard A. Easterlin, "Regional Growth of Income: Long Term Tendencies," in Simon Kuznets, Ann Ratner Miller, and Richard A. Easterlin, eds., *Population Redistribution and Economic Growth: United States, 1870–1950* (Philadelphia: American Philosophical Society, 1960), 185.

18. Milledgeville *Federal Union*, February 12, 1867, quoted in C. Mildred Thompson, *Reconstruction in Georgia: Economic, Social, Political, 1865–1872* (1915; reprint, Freeport, N.Y.: Books for Libraries Press, 1971), 310. The term "uptown" is employed in the following pages not because it is uniquely descriptive but because it seemed as effective as any other and it was the word used in Liston Pope, *Millhands and Preachers: A Study of Gastonia* (New Haven: Yale University Press, 1942), a work that has influenced my interpretation of events in Georgia.

19. James Michael Russell, "Leadership and Economic Growth in Nineteenth Century Atlanta," paper presented at the Symposium on Urbanization in the South, University of Georgia, April 30, 1981, 9.

20. Henry W. Grady, "Across the Chasm," dateline March 17, 1876, Augusta *Constitutionalist*, Grady Papers, Scrapbook 2.

21. Ivan Allen, *Atlanta from the Ashes* (Atlanta: Ruralist Press, 1928), 74–81.

22. Broadus Mitchell and George Sinclair Mitchell, *The Industrial Revolution in the South* (Baltimore: Johns Hopkins University Press, 1930), 37.

23. Richard H. L. German, "The Queen City of the Savannah: Augusta, Georgia, during the Urban Progressive Era, 1890–1917" (Ph.D. dissertation, University of Florida, 1971), 35.

24. "The Atlanta Zoning Plan," *Survey* 48 (April 22, 1922): 114; Robert H. Whitten, "Atlanta Adopts Zoning," *American City* 26 (June 1922): 542. This ordinance was later declared unconstitutional.

25. German, "Queen City of the Savannah," 35.

26. Eurith D. Rivers, quoted in Howard L. Preston, *Automobile Age Atlanta: The Making of a Southern Metropolis, 1900–1935* (Athens: University of Georgia Press, 1979), 75.

27. Edmund De S. Brunner, *Church Life in the Rural South: A Study of the Opportunity of Protestantism Based upon Data from Seventy Counties* (New York: George H. Doran, 1923), 35.

28. Victor I. Masters, *Country Church in the South* (Atlanta: Home Missions Board, 1917), 88.

29. Spencer B. King, Jr., ed., *Georgia Voices: A Documentary History to 1872* (Athens: University of Georgia Press, 1966), 173–74.

30. William G. McLoughlin, *Revivals, Awakenings, and Reform: An Essay on Religion and Social Change in America, 1607–1977* (Chicago: University of Chicago Press, 1978), 137.

31. Samuel S. Hill, Jr., *Southern Churches in Crisis* (New York: Holt, Rinehart and Winston, 1967), 12.

32. "Grace and Salvation," in Samuel Porter Jones, *Sermons by Rev. Sam P. Jones* (Philadelphia: Scammell and Company, 1887), 58.

33. Sam Jones to Atlanta *Journal*, undated, Jones Collection, Scrapbook 2; "Grace and Salvation," Jones, *Sermons*, 49.

34. "Drunken Father and Husband," in Sam P. Jones, *Thunderbolts* (Nashville: Jones and Haynes, 1896), 397.

35. Mrs. Sam P. Jones, ed., *The Life and Sayings of Sam P. Jones* (Atlanta: Franklin-Turner Company, 1907), 63, 435, 443; Jones, *Sermons*, 113.

36. Quoted in Jones, ed., *Life and Sayings*, 78–79.

37. Quoted in Raymond Charles Rensi, "Sam Jones: Southern Evangelist" (Ph.D. dissertation, University of Georgia, 1971), 155.

38. W. M. Leftwich, ed., *Hot Shots; or Sermons and Sayings by Rev. Sam P. Jones* (Stanberry, Mo.: Southwestern Publishing House, 1897), 157; "True Repentance," in Jones, *Sermons*, 299; Sam Jones to Atlanta *Journal*, dateline April 26, 1901, Jones Collection, Scrapbook 1.

39. "Let Your Light So Shine," in Jones, *Sermons*, 24.

40. Quoted in Rensi, "Sam Jones," 312.

41. "Grace and Salvation," in Jones, *Sermons*, 51.

42. "Government and Whiskey Traffic," in Jones, *Thunderbolts*, 415.

43. "Grace and Salvation," in Jones, *Sermons*, 53.

44. William G. McLoughlin, Jr., *Modern Revivalism: Charles Grandison Finney to Billy Graham* (New York: Ronald Press, 1959), 289.

45. Rufus B. Spain, *At Ease in Zion: Social History of Southern Baptists, 1865–1900* (Nashville: Vanderbilt University Press, 1961), 175.

46. Anne Firor Scott, *The Southern Lady: From Pedestal to Politics, 1830–1930* (Chicago: University of Chicago Press, 1970), 90.

47. J. B. Gordon to Dear Madam, October 24, 1874, Rebecca Latimer Felton Papers, Box 1, University of Georgia, Athens; John E. Talmadge, *Rebecca Latimer Felton: Nine Stormy Decades* (Athens: University of Georgia Press, 1960), 55; Mrs. William H. Felton, *My Memoirs of Georgia Politics* (Atlanta: Index Printing Company, 1911), 478; "The Georgia Campaign," in New York *Herald*, March 17, 1876, Grady Papers, Scrapbook 2.

48. "Woman's Relations to Temperance," speech manuscript, Felton Papers, Box 19.

49. Untitled speech manuscript, ibid., Box 20; untitled WCTU speech manuscript, ibid., Box 19.

50. "The Duty and Obligation That Lies on Southern Women," speech manuscript, ibid., Box 20; "To the Georgia Senate—Assembled in Atlanta," speech manuscript, ibid.

51. "The South in History," speech manuscript, Rutherford Papers, Box 3; untitled suffrage speech manuscript, Felton Papers, Box 20.

52. "The Duty and Obligation That Lies on Southern Women."

53. Untitled prohibition speech, Felton Papers, Box 19.

54. Statement to the press, November 15, 1898, ibid., Box 5. Felton expressed her views on lynching and race relations in the Macon *Telegraph*, August 18, 1897, and in the Atlanta *Constitution*, December 19, 1898.

55. Rebecca Latimer Felton, *Country Life in Georgia in the Days of My Youth* (1919; reprint, New York: Arno Press, 1980), 73–74.

56. Rebecca Latimer Felton, *The Subjection of Women and the Enfranchisement of Women* (Privately printed, 1915), 13.

57. Darlene Rebecca Roth, "Matronage: Patterns in Women's Organizations, Atlanta, Georgia, 1890–1940" (Ph.D. dissertation, George Washington University, 1978), 56.

58. "The Duty and Obligation That Lies on Southern Women."

59. Roth, "Matronage," 145, 147–48.

60. Undated clipping, *Weekly Jeffersonian* (1915), Nellie Peters Black Papers, Box 11, University of Georgia, Athens.

61. Nellie Peters Black to Atlanta *Constitution*, November 29, 1914, ibid.

62. Edward Atkinson, "The South and Its Development," *Tradesman Annual* (1915), Hoke Smith Papers, Scrapbook 47, University of Georgia, Athens.

# CHAPTER SIX
## Myth, Reality, and Social Stability in Plain Black and White

1. Willie V. Humphries to Thomas E. Watson, October 17, 1921, Thomas E. Watson Papers, Box 13, Southern Historical Collection, University of North Carolina, Chapel Hill.

2. J. Wayne Flynt, *Dixie's Forgotten People: The South's Poor Whites* (Bloomington: Indiana University Press, 1979), 29–136.

3. Corra Harris, *A Circuit Rider's Wife* (Philadelphia: Henry Altemus Company, 1910), 200, 162.

4. Quoted in Asa H. Gordon, *The Georgia Negro: A History* (Ann Arbor: Edwards Brothers, 1937), 87.

5. John Michael Matthews, "Studies in Race Relations in Georgia, 1890–1930" (Ph.D. dissertation, Duke University, 1970), 261.

6. Samuel S. Hill, Jr., *The South and the North in American Religion* (Athens: University of Georgia Press, 1980), 101.

7. Rev. W. H. Holloway, "A Black Belt County, Georgia," in W. E. Burghardt DuBois, ed., *The Negro Church* (Atlanta: Atlanta University Press, 1903), 58.

8. W. J. Cash, *The Mind of the South* (New York: Vintage Books, 1941), 205.

9. Ben Robertson, *Red Hills and Cotton: An Upcountry Memory* (1942; reprint, Columbia: University of South Carolina Press, 1960), 274.

10. Quoted in Henry Groff Lefever, "Ghetto Religion: A Study of the Religious Structures and Styles of a Poor White Community in Atlanta, Georgia" (Ph.D. dissertation, Emory University, 1971), 55.

11. Glenn Gilman, *Human Relations in the Industrial Southeast* (Chapel Hill: University of North Carolina Press, 1956), 154.

12. Clare de Graffenreid, "The Georgia Cracker in the Cotton Mills," *Century Magazine* 41 (February 1891): 486.

13. Liston Pope, *Millhands and Preachers: A Study of Gastonia* (New Haven: Yale University Press, 1942), 68.

14. Tom E. Terrill and Jerrald Hirsch, eds., *Such as Us: Southern Voices in the Thirties* (New York: W. W. Norton, 1979), 147–49.

15. Mrs. W. H. Felton to Atlanta *Constitution*, undated (1891), Rebecca Latimer Felton Papers, Box 27, University of Georgia, Athens.

16. Richard H. L. German, "The Queen City of the Savannah: Augusta, Georgia, during the Urban Progressive Era, 1890–1917" (Ph.D. dissertation, University of Florida, 1971), 36.

17. Atlanta *Constitution*, June 6, 1914.

18. James Michael Russell, "Atlanta: Gate City of the South, 1847 to 1885" (Ph.D. dissertation, Princeton University, 1972), 265.

19. De Graffenreid, "The Georgia Cracker in the Cotton Mills," 483.

20. Quoted in Flynt, *Dixie's Forgotten People*, 61.

21. See the discussions in Herbert J. Lahne, *The Cotton Mill Worker* (New York: Farrar and Rinehart, 1944), 169, and Broadus Mitchell and George Sinclair Mitchell, *The Industrial Revolution in the South* (Baltimore: Johns Hopkins University Press, 1930), 14–15.

22. Richard J. Hopkins, "Patterns of Persistence and Occupational Mobility in a Southern City: Atlanta, 1870–1920" (Ph.D. dissertation, Emory University, 1965).

23. German, "Queen City of the Savannah," 37; W. E. Burghardt Dubois, ed., *The Negro American Family* (Atlanta: Atlanta University Press, 1908), 58; W. E. Burghardt DuBois, *The Souls of Black Folk: Essays and Sketches* (1903; reprint, Greenwich, Conn.: Fawcett Publications, 1961), 20.

24. Blaine A. Brownell, *The Urban Ethos in the South, 1920–1930* (Baton Rouge: Louisiana State University Press, 1975), 57–58; August Meier, *Negro Thought in America, 1880–1915: Racial Ideologies in the Age of Booker T. Washington* (Ann Arbor: University of Michigan Press, 1963); August Meier and David Lewis, "History of the Negro Upper Class in Atlanta, Georgia, 1890–1958," *Journal of Negro Education* 28 (Spring 1959): 128–39.

25. Carter G. Woodson, *The History of the Negro Church* (Washington, D.C.: Associated Publishers, 1921), 246.

26. Michael Leroy Porter, "Black Atlanta: An Interdisciplinary Study of

Blacks on the East Side of Atlanta, 1890–1930" (Ph.D. dissertation, Emory University, 1974), 257.

27. Quoted in Dominique-René de Lerma, *Reflections on Afro-American Music* (Kent: Kent State University Press, 1973), 190.

28. Quoted in George Robinson Ricks, "Some Aspects of the Religious Music of the United States Negro: An Ethnomusicological Study with Special Emphasis on the Gospel Tradition" (Ph.D. dissertation, Northwestern University, 1960), 134.

29. Ibid., 133; Lawrence W. Levine, *Black Culture and Black Consciousness: Afro-American Folk Thought from Slavery to Freedom* (Oxford: Oxford University Press, 1977), 181.

30. Quoted in Tony Heilburt, *The Gospel Sound: Good News and Bad Times* (New York: Simon and Schuster, 1971), 66, 67.

31. John Dollard, *Caste and Class in a Southern Town* (1937; 3d ed., Garden City: Doubleday and Company, 1949), 392–93.

32. Levine, *Black Culture and Black Consciousness*, 233, 279.

33. Quoted in ibid., 278.

34. Rebecca Latimer Felton, *The Romantic Story of Georgia's Women* (Atlanta: Atlanta *Georgian and Sunday American*, 1930), 46.

35. W. J. Northen, *Christianity and the Negro Problem in Georgia*, delivered before the Evangelical Ministers' Association of Atlanta, September 4, 1911 (privately printed), 16.

36. John C. Reed, *The Brothers' War* (Boston: Little, Brown, and Company, 1906), 382, 410.

37. E. B. Holley to Thomas E. Watson, November 14, 1906, Watson Papers, Box 6.

38. Quoted in Ray Stannard Baker, *Following the Color Line: American Negro Citizenship in the Progressive Era*, ed. Dewey W. Grantham, Jr. (1908; reprint, New York: Harper Torchbooks, 1964), 84–85.

39. Pierre L. van den Berghe, *Race and Racism: A Comparative Perspective* (New York: John Wiley and Sons, 1967), 32, 87.

40. Mrs. W. H. Felton to Editor, Macon *Telegraph*, August 18, 1897.

41. Quoted in C. Vann Woodward, *Tom Watson: Agrarian Rebel* (1938; reprint, New York: Oxford University Press, 1938), 432.

42. *A Statement from Governor Hugh M. Dorsey as to the Negro in Georgia* (N.p., 1921), n.p.

43. Jacquelyn Dowd Hall, *Revolt against Chivalry: Jessie Daniel Ames and the Women's Campaign against Lynching* (New York: Columbia University Press, 1979), 153.

44. Unidentified clipping, Felton Papers, Box 5.

45. Margaret Anne Barnes, *Murder in Coweta County* (New York: Pocket Books, 1977).

46. Quoted in Matthews, "Studies in Race Relations," 235, 233, 119.

47. Benjamin J. Davis, *Communist Councilman from Harlem: Autobio-*

*graphical Notes Written in a Federal Penitentiary* (New York: International Publishers, 1969), 21.

48. DuBois, *The Souls of Black Folk*, 48, 49, 43, 54; W. E. B. DuBois to Kelly Miller, February 25, 1903, in Herbert Aptheker, ed., *The Correspondence of W. E. B. DuBois*, 2 vols. (Amherst: University of Massachusetts Press, 1973), 1: 53.

49. W. E. Burghardt DuBois, "Constructive Work," *Horizon* 5 (December 1909): 2; W. E. B. DuBois to John Hope, January 22, 1910, in Aptheker, ed., *Correspondence of DuBois*, 167.

50. Quoted in Matthews, "Studies in Race Relations," 237.

51. William Steuart, "Labor Disturbances in the South," *Tradesman Annual* (1895), Hoke Smith Papers, Scrapbook 47, University of Georgia, Athens. Labor union activity in Georgia and the South are surveyed in Melton Alonza McLaurin, *The Knights of Labor in the South* (Westport, Conn.: Greenwood Press, 1978); McLaurin, *Paternalism and Protest: Southern Cotton Mill Workers and Organized Labor, 1875–1905* (Westport, Conn.: Greenwood, 1971); and Mercer Griffin Evans, "The History of the Organized Labor Movement in Georgia" (Ph.D. dissertation, University of Chicago, 1929).

52. *Journal of Labor*, September 25, 1908.

53. Ibid., June 6, 1913.

# CHAPTER SEVEN
## Progressivism and the End of an Era

1. John Dittmer, *Black Georgia in the Progressive Era, 1900–1920* (Urbana: University of Illinois Press, 1977), 214.

2. Speech manuscript, summer 1890, Thomas E. Watson Papers, Box 28, Southern Historical Collection, University of North Carolina, Chapel Hill.

3. Quoted in Dittmer, *Black Georgia*, 21.

4. Governor Allen D. Candler quoted in John Michael Matthews, "Studies in Race Relations in Georgia, 1890–1930" (Ph.D. dissertation, Duke University, 1970), 288.

5. Quoted in Ray Stannard Baker, *Following the Color Line: American Negro Citizenship in the Progressive Era*, ed. Dewey W. Grantham, Jr. (1908; reprint, New York: Harper Torchbooks, 1964), 249.

6. Quoted in Atlanta *Journal*, October 10, 1906, Hoke Smith Papers, Scrapbook 65, University of Georgia, Athens.

7. Augusta *Chronicle*, April 18, 1899, quoted in Richard H. L. German, "The Queen City of the Savannah: Augusta, Georgia, during the Urban Progressive Era, 1890–1917" (Ph.D. dissertation, University of Florida, 1971), 137.

8. Rufus B. Bullock to Atlanta *Constitution*, October 18, 1898, Daniel L. Russell Papers, Document 645, Southern Historical Collection, University of North Carolina, Chapel Hill.

9. Atlanta *Constitution*, April 18, 1888.

10. Hoke Smith to W. L. Peek, in Atlanta *Journal*, September 15, 1890.

11. Smith quoted in New York *Tribune*, August 8, 1895, Smith Papers, Scrapbook 47; Atlanta *Journal*, July 23, 1895, Watson Papers, Box 29; ibid., June 21, 1894, Smith Papers, Scrapbook 47.

12. Atlanta *Journal*, May 4, 1905.

13. Quoted in Brunswick *Journal*, May 22, 1905, Smith Papers, Scrapbook 57; and Matthews, "Studies in Race Relations," 294.

14. Speech typescript, November 19, 1904, Watson Papers, Box 4.

15. William L. Peek to T. E. Watson, July 2, 1906, ibid., Box 5.

16. Campaign circular, Thomas E. Watson to the People of Georgia, October 22, 1904, ibid., Box 4.

17. Hoke Smith to Thomas E. Watson, September 16, 1905, ibid., Box 5.

18. Alexander J. McKelway, "State Prohibition in Georgia and the South," *Outlook* 86 (August 24, 1907): 947; untitled prohibition speech manuscript, Rebecca Latimer Felton Papers, Box 20, University of Georgia, Athens.

19. Dorothy Orr, *A History of Education in Georgia* (Chapel Hill: University of North Carolina Press, 1950), 315.

20. Nancy Telfair, *A History of Columbus, Georgia, 1828–1928* (Columbus: Historical Publishing Company, 1929), 202.

21. Terrell was a member of the "conservative" faction of the Democratic party, as opposed to the "Progressive" Smith faction. Actually, the differences between the two were small. Alton DuMar Jones, the historian of Georgia Progressivism, has argued—convincingly, in my opinion—that Terrell is most accurately viewed as a Progressive governor (Jones, "The Administration of Joseph M. Terrell Viewed in the Light of the Progressive Movement," *Georgia Historical Quarterly* 48 [September 1964]: 271–90).

22. Alton DuMar Jones, "Progressivism in Georgia, 1898–1918" (Ph.D. dissertation, Emory University, 1963), 162.

23. T. W. Hardwick to Thomas E. Watson, October 11, 1907, Watson Papers, Box 7.

24. State Democratic Platform, reprinted in Atlanta *Journal*, September 5, 1906.

25. Clark Howell to Thos. Watson, May 14, 1908, Watson Papers, Box 9.

26. C. Vann Woodward, *Tom Watson: Agrarian Rebel* (1938; reprint, New York: Oxford University Press, 1938), 386. The best account of the Glover case is Alfred H. Hicks, "Tom Watson and the Arthur Glover Case in Georgia Politics," *Georgia Historical Quarterly* 53 (September 1969): 265–86.

27. A. P. Glover to Mr. Watson, May 12, 1907, Watson Papers, Box 6; Hoke Smith to Thomas E. Watson, January 28, 1908, ibid., Box 8.

28. Glover to Watson, May 12, 1907.

29. William M. Gabard, "Joseph Mackey Brown: A Study in Conservatism" (Ph.D. dissertation, Tulane University, 1963), 69.

30. Joseph M. Brown to People of Georgia, Atlanta *Constitution*, January 5, 1908.

31. Quoted in Dewey W. Grantham, Jr., *Hoke Smith and the Politics of the New South* (1958; reprint, Baton Rouge: Louisiana State University Press, 1967), 190.

32. Robert W. Haynie (of Bogart) to Thomas E. Watson, May 1, 1908, Watson Papers, Box 9; T. W. Hardwick to Thomas E. Watson, April 13, 1908, ibid.

33. Quoted in Atlanta *Constitution*, May 14, 1910, July 26, 1914.

34. Thom. E. Watson to Harry Tracy, July 1, 1913 (copy), Watson papers, Box 11.

35. Woodward, *Tom Watson*, 419.

36. Notes on Augusta speech, August 6, 1908, Watson Papers, Box 10.

37. Quoted in Grantham, *Hoke Smith*, 354.

38. Quoted in Leonard Dinnerstein, *The Leo Frank Case* (New York: Columbia University Press, 1968), 98, 202, note 20.

39. Ibid., viii–ix.

40. Steven Hertzberg, *Strangers within the Gate City: The Jews of Atlanta, 1845–1915* (Philadelphia: Jewish Publications Society, 1978), 203.

41. *Jones County News*, October 23, 1919, quoted in William G. Moffat, "The River Road Settlement of Jones County, Georgia: A Social and Economic History" (M.A. thesis, Georgia College, 1979), 84; C. G. Peebles (of Hubert) to Julia Peebles, June 22, July 8, 1923, Southall and Bowen Papers, Folder 54, Southern Historical Collection, University of North Carolina, Chapel Hill.

42. Ben Robertson, *Red Hills and Cotton: An Upcountry Memory* (1942; reprint, Columbia: University of South Carolina, 1960), 278.

43. Atlanta *Constitution*, September 20, 1925, quoting the manager of a leading Atlanta bank real estate department.

44. Ralph McGill, *The South and the Southerner* (Boston: Little, Brown and Company, 1964), 131.

45. Recommendations from the Jefferson Davis Klan (Vicksburg), October 7, 1921, Watson Papers, Box 13.

46. Quoted in Maynard Shipley, *The War on Modern Science: A Short History of the Fundamentalist Attacks on Evolution and Modernism* (New York: Alfred A. Knopf, 1927), 130.

47. David R. Goldfield, "The Urban South: A Regional Framework," *American Historical Review* 86 (December 1981): 1030.

48. C. G. Peebles to Julia Peebles, September 9, 1931, Southall and Bowen Papers, Folder 54.

49. Erskine Caldwell, *Call It Experience: The Years of Learning How to Write* (New York: New American Library, 1956), 81.

50. Erskine Caldwell, *Tobacco Road* (New York: Duell, Sloan and Pearce, 1932), 24.

51. Quoted in Roy Edward Fossett, "The Impact of the New Deal on Georgia Politics, 1933–1941" (Ph.D. dissertation, University of Florida, 1960), 107, note 128.

52. Quoted in Atlanta *Constitution*, August 5, 1934.

53. Quoted in Atlanta *Constitution*, May 7, 1935.

54. Ibid., July 4, 5, 1935, and Atlanta *Journal*, April 21, 1937.

55. Quoted in Fossett, "Impact of the New Deal," 110; and John E. Allen, "Eugene Talmadge and the Great Textile Strike in Georgia, September 1934," in Gary M. Fink and Merl E. Reed, eds., *Essays in Southern Labor History: Selected Papers, Southern Labor History Conference, 1976* (Westport, Conn.: Greenwood Press, 1977), 237.

56. Quoted in William Anderson, *The Wild Man from Sugar Creek: The Political Career of Eugene Talmadge* (Baton Rouge: Louisiana State University Press, 1975), 103.

57. Quoted in Paul E. Mertz, *New Deal Policy and Southern Rural Poverty* (Baton Rouge: Louisiana State University Press, 1978), 234.

58. Quoted in George Brown Tindall, *Emergence of the New South, 1913–1945* (Baton Rouge: Louisiana State University Press, 1967), 208.

59. Charles Angoff and H. L. Mencken, "The Worst American State," *American Mercury* 24 (September 1931): 1–16; (October 1931): 175–88; (November 1931): 355–71.

60. Arthur F. Raper, *Preface to Peasantry: A Tale of Two Black Belt Counties* (Chapel Hill: University of North Carolina Press, 1936), viii, 3, 405.

61. National Emergency Council, *Report on Economic Conditions of the South* (Washington, D.C.: U.S. Government Printing Office, 1938), 1.

## CHAPTER EIGHT
### The Twilight of the Old Order

1. Jack Temple Kirby, *Rural Worlds Lost: The American South, 1920–1960* (Baton Rouge: Louisiana State University Press, 1987), 117.

2. Herman E. Talmadge with Mark Royden Winchell, *Talmadge: A Political Legacy, a Politician's Life* (Atlanta: Peachtree Publishers, 1987), 223.

3. William Faulkner, *The Hamlet* (New York: Random House, 1940), 56.

4. Pete Daniel, *Breaking the Land: The Transformation of Cotton, Tobacco, and Rice Cultures Since 1880* (Urbana: University of Illinois Press, 1985), 243.

5. Arthur F. Raper and Ira De A. Reid, *Sharecroppers All* (Chapel Hill: University of North Carolina Press, 1941), 203–4.

6. Ralph McGill, *The South and the Southerner* (Boston: Little, Brown and Company, 1963), 208–9.

7. Glenn E. McLaughlin and Stefan Robock, *Why Industry Moves South: A*

*Study of Factors Influencing the Recent Location of Manufacturing Plants in the South* (National Planning Association, Kingsport: Kingsport Press, 1949), 3–20, 129–30; Calvin B. Hoover and B. U. Ratchford, *Economic Resources and Policies of the South* (National Planning Association, New York: Macmillan, 1951), 161–94.

8. Samuel Lubell, *The Future of American Politics*, 2d ed., rev. (Garden City: Doubleday Anchor Books, 1956 [1952]), 119.

9. Robert J. Steamer, "Southern Disaffection with the National Democratic Party," in Allan P. Sindler, ed., *Change in the Contemporary South* (Durham: Duke University Press, 1963), 153.

10. Lubell, *The Future of American Politics*, 119.

11. Leonard Reissman, "Social Development and the American South," *Journal of Social Issues* 22 (January 1966): 106.

12. Raper and Reid, *Sharecroppers All*, v, 189.

13. Gunnar Myrdal, *An American Dilemma: The Negro Problem and Modern Democracy*, 2 vols. (1944; reprint, New York: Pantheon Books, 1962), 2:1077–1078.

14. Solomon Barkin to Emil Rieve re My Trip South, October 25, 1939; George Baldanzi to Emil Rieve and others, memorandum, April 8, 1942, Textile Workers Union of America Papers, Series A, File 1A, Box 11, Archives Division, State Historical Society of Wisconsin, Madison, Wisconsin; John Kenneth Morland, *Millways of Kent* (Chapel Hill: University of North Carolina Press, 1958), ix.

15. Quoted in Jacquelyn Dowd Hall et al., *Like A Family: The Making of a Southern Cotton Mill World* (Chapel Hill: University of North Carolina Press, 1987), xi.

16. Jacquelyn Dowd Hall, Robert Korstad, and James Leloudis, "Cotton Mill People: Work, Community, and Protest in the Textile South, 1880–1940," *American Historical Review* 91 (April 1986): 285. Important studies include Morland, *Millways of Kent*; Morland, "Kent Revisited: Blue-Collar Aspirations and Achievements," in Arthur B. Shostak and William Gomberg, eds., *Blue Collar World: Studies of the American Worker* (Englewood Cliffs: Prentice-Hall, 1964), 134–43; Hall et al., *Like a Family*; Herbert J. Lahne, *The Cotton Mill Worker* (New York: Farrar & Rinehart, 1944); and Harriet L. Herring, *Passing of the Mill Village: Revolution in a Southern Institution* (Chapel Hill: University of North Carolina Press, 1949).

17. Pete Daniel, *Standing at the Crossroads: Southern Life Since 1900* (New York: Hill and Wang, 1986), 123.

18. Ben Robertson, *Red Hills and Cotton: An Upcountry Memory* (Columbia: University of South Carolina Press, 1942), 20.

19. Jasper Berry Shannon, *Toward a New Politics in the South* (Knoxville: University of Tennessee Press, 1949), 51.

20. Dewey W. Grantham, Jr., *The Democratic South* (Athens: University of Georgia Press, 1963), 88.

21. These generalizations are based on Hammer and Company, *Post War Industrial Development in the South* (Atlanta: Harper and Company and the Southern Regional Council, 1956), and U.S. Congress, Senate, *Selected Materials on*

the Economy of the South: Report of the Committee on Banking and Currency, 84th Cong., 2d sess. (Washington: Government Printing Office, 1956).

22. Myrdal, *An American Dilemma*, 1:375.

23. Hylan Lewis, *Blackways of Kent* (Chapel Hill: University of North Carolina Press, 1955), 33–35.

24. Ray Sprigle, *In the Land of Jim Crow* (New York: Simon and Schuster, 1949), 7–8.

25. Quoted in Bryon R. Skinner, "The Double 'V': The Impact of World War II on Black America" (Ph.D. dissertation, University of California-Berkeley, 1978), 105.

26. McGill, *The South and the Southerner*, 159.

27. Quoted in William Anderson, *The Wild Man from Sugar Creek: The Political Career of Eugene Talmadge* (Baton Rouge: Louisiana State University Press, 1975), 104.

28. Quoted in Jane Walker Herndon, "Eurith Dickinson Rivers: A Political Biography" (Ph.D. dissertation, University of Georgia, 1974), 213.

29. Quoted in Atlanta *Journal*, April 21, 1937.

30. Rome *News-Tribune*, reprinted in Atlanta *Journal*, March 19, 1940.

31. Roy V. Harris quoted in Herndon, "Rivers," 343.

32. Anderson, *The Wild Man from Sugar Creek*, 191.

33. Allen Lumpkin Henson, *Red Galluses: A Story of Georgia Politics* (Boston: House of Edinboro, 1945), 222.

34. Quoted in James F. Cook, Jr., "Politics and Education in the Talmadge Era: The Controversy over the University System of Georgia, 1941–42" (Ph.D. dissertation, University of Georgia, 1972), 187, 118.

35. Atlanta *Journal*, July 25, 1942.

36. Quoted in Anderson, *The Wild Man from Sugar Creek*, 209.

37. Ellis Arnall, "Revolution Down South," *Collier's*, July 28, 1945: 17; V. O. Key, Jr., *Southern Politics in State and Nation* (New York: Alfred A. Knopf, 1949), 128.

38. Henson, *Red Galluses*, 250.

39. Ellis G. Arnall, "Governor You Will Be," in Harold P. Henderson and Gary L. Roberts, eds., *Georgia Governors in an Age of Change: From Ellis Arnall to George Busbee* (Athens: University of Georgia Press, 1988), 40.

40. Quoted in *Black Dispatch* (Oklahoma City), August 18, 1945.

41. Quoted in Atlanta *Journal*, December 9, 1945.

42. Ellis Gibbs Arnall, *The Shore Dimly Seen* (New York: J. B. Lippincott, 1946), 108, 116; Arnall, *What the People Want* (New York: J. B. Lippincott, 1948), 29, 270; Arnall, "Revolution Down South," 72.

43. Clark Foreman and James Dombrowski, "Memo for the CIO Executive Board," November 13, 1944, Records of the Southern Conference for Human Welfare, Box 43, Tuskegee Institute Archives.

44. Stetson Kennedy, *Southern Exposure* (Garden City: Doubleday, 1946), 349, 357; Kennedy, "Total Equality and How to Get It," *Common Ground* (Winter 1946), 63.

45. Tarleton Collier to Clark Foreman, June 12, 1942, Southern Conference for Human Welfare Collection, Foreman File, Box 35, Trevor Arnett Library, Atlanta University.

46. Quoted in New York *Times,* April 11, 1946.

47. Lucy Randolph Mason, *To Win These Rights: A Personal Story of the CIO in the South* (New York: Harper and Brothers, 1952), 84, 116.

48. *Journal of Labor,* May 17, 1946.

49. House Committee on Un-American Activities, *Report on Southern Conference for Human Welfare,* 80th Cong., 1st sess. (Washington: Government Printing Office, 1947), 17.

50. George Baldanzi to Emil Rieve, October 1, 1949, Textile Workers Union of America Papers, Series A, File 1A, Box 1, Archives Division, State Historical Society of Wisconsin, Madison, Wisconsin; "Report on Southern Strike," June 26, 1951, ibid., File 5A, Box 1.

51. Myrdal, *An American Dilemma,* 2:788–90.

52. Quoted in Lorraine Nelson Spritzer, *The Belle of Ashby Street: A Political Biography of Helen Douglas Mankin* (Athens: University of Georgia Press, 1982), 100, 85.

53. Anderson, *The Wild Man from Sugar Creek,* 213.

54. Quoted in Savannah *Morning News,* July 9, 1946.

55. *The Statesman,* March 14, 1946.

56. Quoted in Atlanta *Journal,* June 14, 1946.

57. Atlanta *Journal,* June 9, 1946.

58. Katharine Du Pre Lumpkin, *The Making of a Southerner* (New York: Alfred A. Knopf, 1947), 235.

59. Quoted in Talmadge, *Talmadge,* 92.

60. Quoted in Harold P. Henderson, "M. E. Thompson and the Politics of Succession," in Henderson and Roberts, eds., *Georgia Governors in an Age of Change,* 61.

61. Ibid., 64.

62. John N. Popham in New York *Times,* September 9, 1954.

63. New York *Times,* May 18, 1954, quoting Lieutenant Governor Marvin Griffin.

64. *Brown* v. *Board of Education,* in *Race Relations Law Reporter* 1 (February 1956):5.

65. House Resolution No. 185, ibid. 1 (April 1956):440.

# CHAPTER NINE
## A New Beginning

1. Lillian E. Smith, "Two Men and a Bargain: A Parable of the Solid South," *South Today* 7 (Spring 1943): 5–15.

2. Lillian E. Smith, "Addressed to White Liberals," *New Republic* 111 (September 18, 1944): 332.

3. Gunnar Myrdal, *An American Dilemma: The Negro Problem and Modern Democracy*, 2 vols. (1944; reprint, New York: Pantheon Books, 1962), 1:lxix–lxx, 2:1009.

4. Smith "Addressed to White Liberals," 332; Anne C. Loveland, *Lillian Smith: A Southerner Confronting the South, A Biography* (Baton Rouge: Louisiana State University Press, 1986), 82.

5. Lillian E. Smith, *Killers of the Dream* (New York: Norton, 1949), 18–20, 81; "A Skeleton Chronology . . . of the very private things . . . ," Lillian Smith Papers, University of Georgia, Series 1, Box 1.

6. Lillian E. Smith, "Humans in Bondage," *Social Action*, February 15, 1944, reprinted in Michelle Cliff, ed., *The Winner Names the Age: A Collection of Writings by Lillian Smith* (New York: Norton, 1978), 38.

7. Smith, "Addressed to White Liberals," 333.

8. Lillian Smith to James Dombrowski, May 7, 1945; Smith to Clark Foreman, May 9, 1945, Southern Conference for Human Welfare Collection, Foreman File, Box 40, Atlanta University.

9. "Opinion of the Attorney General," in *Race Relations Law Reporter* 2 (February 1957): 267.

10. Ivan Allen, Jr., with Paul Hemphill, *Mayor: Notes on the Sixties* (New York: Simon and Schuster, 1971), 31, 29.

11. Floyd Hunter, *Community Power Structure: A Study of Decision Makers* (Chapel Hill: University of North Carolina Press, 1953), and Hunter, *Community Power Succession: Atlanta's Policy-Makers Revisited* (Chapel Hill: University of North Carolina Press, 1980).

12. Ivan Allen, Sr., *Atlanta from the Ashes* (Atlanta: Ruralist Press, 1928), 5.

13. Allen, *Mayor*, 52.

14. Quoted in Atlanta *Constitution*, November 29, 1960.

15. James C. Cobb, "Politics in a New South City: Augusta, Georgia, 1946–1971" (Ph.D. dissertation, University of Georgia, 1975), 87.

16. Quoted in Harold H. Martin, *William Berry Hartsfield: Mayor of Atlanta* (Athens: University of Georgia Press, 1978), 144.

17. Quoted in Atlanta *Constitution*, October 13, 1959.

18. Ibid., March 30, 1960.

19. Quoted in Atlanta *Journal*, December 15, 1958, and in Atlanta *Constitution*, February 9, 1960.

20. Quoted in Atlanta *Journal*, April 19, 1959.

21. James S. Peters to Roy V. Harris, December 30, 1959, in Atlanta *Journal and Constitution*, January 17, 1960.

22. Allen, *Mayor*, 91–92.

23. Karen L. Kolmar, "Southern Black Elites and the New Deal: A Case Study of Savannah," *Georgia Historical Quarterly* 65 (Winter 1981): 343.

24. Atlanta *Constitution*, March 9, 1960.

25. Quoted in Jack Newfield, *A Prophetic Minority* (New York: New American Library, 1966), 61.

26. Martin Luther King, Sr., with Clayton Riley, *Daddy King: An Autobiography* (New York: William Morrow, 1980), 27, 15, 19.

27. "Interview," *Playboy* 12 (January 1965): 66.

28. Quotations from Martin Luther King, Jr., *Stride Toward Freedom: The Montgomery Story* (New York: Harper, 1958), and *Why We Can't Wait* (New York: Harper and Row, 1964), the latter of which reprints "Letter from Birmingham Jail."

29. Quoted in Pat Watters and Reese Cleghorn, *Climbing Jacob's Ladder: The Arrival of Negroes in Southern Politics* (New York: Harcourt, Brace and World, 1967), 6.

30. Don Harris, "Field Report," March 27, 1964, and Willie Ricks, "Field Report," March 15, 1964, Voter Education Project Papers, Box 18, Atlanta University.

31. Quoted in Howard Zinn, *SNCC: The New Abolitionists* (Boston: Beacon Press, 1964), 126.

32. Penny Patch to Wiley Branton, December 11, 1962, Voter Education Project Papers, Box 6.

33. Quoted in Eugene P. Walker, "A History of the Southern Christian Leadership Conference, 1955–1965: The Evolution of a Strategy for Social Change" (Ph.D. dissertation, Duke University, 1978), 130.

34. Adam Fairclough, *To Redeem the Soul of America: The Southern Christian Leadership Conference and Martin Luther King, Jr.* (Athens: University of Georgia Press, 1987), 143.

35. Martin Luther King, Jr., "Pilgrimage for Democracy," Speech Manuscript, December 15, 1963, Southern Christian Leadership Conference Papers, Series 2, Box 27, Martin Luther King, Jr., Center for Social Change, Atlanta.

36. Cleveland Sellers with Robert Terrell, *The River of No Return: The Autobiography of a Black Militant and the Life and Death of SNCC* (New York: William Morrow, 1973), 52.

37. Paul Douglas Bolster, "Civil Rights Movement in Twentieth Century Georgia" (Ph.D. dissertation, University of Georgia, 1972), 224.

38. Quoted in James C. Cobb, *The Selling of the South: The Southern Crusade for Industrial Development, 1936–1980* (Baton Rouge: Louisiana State University Press, 1982), 75.

39. Campaign Platform, Carl E. Sanders Papers, Box 6, University of Georgia, Athens.

40. Griffin quoted in Joseph L. Bernd, "Georgia: Static and Dynamic," in William C. Harvard, ed., *The Changing Politics of the South* (Baton Rouge: Louisiana State University Press, 1972), 328, and in New York *Times*, September 3, 1962; Charles Pou and Vandiver quoted in Robert Sherrill, *Gothic Politics in the Deep South: Stars of the New Confederacy* (New York: Grossman, 1968), 90.

41. Inaugural Address, Sanders Papers, Box 7.

42. Quoted in Ben Hibbs, "Progress Goes Marching through Georgia," *Saturday Evening Post*, February 16, 1963, 70.

43. Leslie W. Dunbar, "The Changing Mind of the South: The Exposed Nerve," *Journal of Politics* 26 (February 1964): 20.

44. Allen, *Mayor*, 145.

45. Marshall Frady, *Southerners: A Journalist's Odyssey* (New York: New American Library, 1980), 281.

46. Robert B. Cohen, "Multinational Corporations, International Finance, and the Sunbelt," in David C. Perry and Alfred J. Watkins, eds., *The Rise of the Sunbelt Cities* (Beverly Hills: Sage Publications, 1977), 225.

47. Neil Shister, "Who Owns Atlanta?," *Atlanta* 20 (January 1981): 51.

48. Truman A. Hartshorn, *Metropolis in Georgia: Atlanta's Rise as a Major Transaction Center* (Cambridge, Mass.: Ballinger Publishing Company, 1976), 14.

49. Carl Abbott, *The New Urban America: Growth and Politics in Sunbelt Cities* (Chapel Hill: University of North Carolina Press, 1981), 229.

50. Quoted in Clayborne Carson, *In Struggle: SNCC and the Black Awakening of the 1960s* (Cambridge, Mass.: Harvard University Press, 1981), 154.

51. Quoted in New York *Times*, May 24, 1966.

52. "Stokely Carmichael Speaks to the Howard University School of Law," May 24, 1966, Howard Zinn Papers, Box 2, State Historical Society of Wisconsin, Madison.

53. Hubert (Rap) Brown quoted in Carson, *In Struggle*, 289.

54. Martin Luther King, Jr., *Where Do We Go from Here: Chaos or Community?* (New York: Harper and Row, 1967), 38.

55. Phil Garner, "Maynard Jackson," Atlanta *Journal and Constitution Magazine*, November 11, 1979, 26.

56. Clarence N. Stone in Atlanta *Journal and Constitution*, October 8, 1989.

57. Allen, *Mayor*, 140–41.

58. Quoted in Bradley R. Rice, "Lester Maddox and the Politics of Populism," in Harold P. Henderson and Gary L. Roberts, eds., *Georgia Governors in an Age of Change: From Ellis Arnall to George Busbee* (Athens: University of Georgia Press, 1988), 200.

59. Quoted in Marshall Frady, *Wallace* (New York: World, 1968), 142; in Dewey W. Grantham, *The Life and Death of the Solid South: A Political History* (Lexington: University Press of Kentucky, 1988), 174; and in Margaret Shannon, "The Next President's Georgia Campaign," Atlanta *Journal and Constitution Magazine*, November 3, 1968, 9.

60. Quoted in Rice, "Lester Maddox and the Politics of Populism," 205, and in Shannon, "The Next President's Georgia Campaign," 9.

61. Quoted in Jimmy Carter, *Why Not the Best?* (New York: Bantam, 1976), 120.

62. Edward D. C. Campbell, Jr., *The Celluloid South: Hollywood and the Southern Myth* (Knoxville: University of Tennessee Press, 1981), 143.

63. Kirkpatrick Sale, *Power Shift: The Rise of the Southern Rim and Its Chal-

*lenge to the Eastern Establishment* (New York: Random House, 1975); New York *Times*, February 8–13, 1976.

64. Charles F. Floyd, "The 'Two Georgias' Problem," *Georgia Business and Economic Conditions* 45 (March–April 1985): 3–13; Floyd, "The Two Georgias Revisited," ibid. 46 (May–June 1986): 1–6.

65. Albert W. Niemi quoted in Atlanta *Journal and Constitution*, August 3, 1985.

66. Bill Shipp in ibid., December 7, 1985.

67. John Shelton Reed, *Southern Folk, Plain and Fancy: Native White Social Types* (Athens: University of Georgia Press, 1986), 34–61.

68. Louis Harris in Atlanta *Constitution*, September 20, 1976.

69. John Van Wingen and David Valentine, "Partisan Politics: A One-and-a-Half, No-Party System," in James F. Lea, ed., *Contemporary Southern Politics* (Baton Rouge: Louisiana State University Press, 1988), 147, and Edward M. Wheat, "The Bureaucratization of the South: From Traditional Fragmentation to Administrative Incoherence," ibid., 281.

# Index